STUDIES IN BIBLICAL THEOLOGY No. 23

Promise and Fulfilment

The Eschatological Message of Jesus

W. G. Kümmel

SCM PRESS

About the Author

WERNER GEORG KÜMMEL was born in Heidelberg in 1905. He was educated in Heidelberg, where he graduated in 1928, in Berlin and in Marburg. From 1930 he taught in Marburg for some years before being appointed to a Chair in Zürich in 1946. In 1951 he became a professor at Mainz. Since 1952 he has been Professor of New Testament at the University of Marburg. He is also a Doctor of Theology. His publications include: *Röm. 7 und die Bekehrung des Paulus*, 1929; *Das Bild des Menschen im Neuen Testament*, 1948; a revised edition of Lietzmann's commentary on I and II Corinthians; completion of Dibelius' *Paulus* 1950 (Eng. tr. 1953).

Studies in Biblical Theology

A SERIES OF MONOGRAPHS designed to provide clergy and laymen with the best work in Biblical scholarship both in this country and abroad.

The Advisory Editors for this series are:

C. F. D. Moule, M.A., *Lady Margaret Professor of Divinity in the University of Cambridge*, J. Barr, M.A., B.D., *Professor of Old Testament Literature and Theology, Princeton Theological Seminary*, Floyd V. Filson, Th.D., D.D., *Professor of New Testament Literature and History, McCormick Theological Seminary, Chicago*, G. Ernest Wright, Ph.D., D.D., *Professor of Old Testament History and Theology at Harvard University.*

PROMISE AND
FULFILMENT

STUDIES IN BIBLICAL THEOLOGY

PROMISE AND FULFILMENT

*The Eschatological Message
of Jesus*

WERNER GEORG KÜMMEL

*Doctor of Theology
Professor at the University of Marburg*

SCM PRESS LTD
56 BLOOMSBURY STREET
LONDON

Translated by Dorothea M. Barton, M.A., from the German
VERHEISSUNG UND ERFÜLLUNG
Zwingli-Verlag, Zürich
Third and completely revised edition

First published in English 1957
Second English edition 1961

Printed in Great Britain
by W. & J. Mackay & Co. Ltd, Chatham

CONTENTS

TRANSLATOR'S NOTE

I welcome this opportunity of expressing my very warm thanks to Professor W. G. Kümmel for his great kindness in devoting his wide command of English and his meticulous care to the revision of this translation which he has approved. But of course I remain responsible for any blunders.

When I was asked some time ago by the publisher whether I would agree to a new edition of this book, I did not doubt for a moment that only a comprehensive revision could be considered. For when I finished the work on the first edition in the last year of the second World War, I had had no access even in Switzerland to any of the English and American publications published since 1940 which, as it happens, were particularly relevant to the subject dealt with here. Besides, critical discussion as well as my own work had shown me that the book contained gaps which it was imperative to fill.

This complete revision has not altered my view of the problems as a whole. But I have incorporated all the literature which has appeared or has become accessible to me in the interval; in several places I have also inserted extensive sections which strengthen the course of the argument and are in particular intended to give fuller consideration to the tradition relating to Jesus' actions. My chief concern from beginning to end has been to interrogate the sources judiciously and critically, and by means of exegesis to show that both the 'konsequent' as well as the 'realized' eschatology are untenable as an interpretation of Jesus' message. It is my firm conviction that the strictly exegetical examination will lead also to a better understanding of Jesus' preaching with our own message in view.

Without the well-furnished bookstocks in the Central Library in Zürich it would hardly have been possible to make use of foreign publications to so large an extent. I should like to express here my sincere thanks to the Director of the Central Library, Professor L. Forrer, for his permission to go on using in Germany a few works which were indispensable for completing my task.

Marburg/Lahn   WERNER GEORG KÜMMEL
12 January 1953

7

Preface to the Third German Edition

Since the second edition of this work was exhausted after a short time, the publisher approached me to ask whether I would agree to a new edition being reprinted without any alterations. In spite of some hesitation I felt I could not refuse this request. Of course research has not stood still during the last three years and several books and essays have appeared which it would be necessary and profitable to discuss. Yet I cannot persuade myself that the objections raised to my interpretation of Jesus' message or the fresh general accounts of Jesus which have been published have thrown any serious doubts upon the correctness of the historical picture presented here; a discussion of these works could therefore serve only to prove more fully particular points in my interpretation and to forestall possible misintrepretations. So it seems to be sufficient for me to add to this preface a list of the most important works which have dealt with the problems here discussed since the second edition of this book appeared, without examining the literature in detail.

Marburg/Lahn
28 March 1956

Werner Georg Kümmel

LIST OF ABBREVIATIONS

ACKERMANN, *Jesus*	H. Ackermann, *Jesus. Seine Botschaft und deren Aufnahme im Abendland*, 1952.
BAUER, *Wörterbuch*	W. Bauer, *Griechisch-deutsches Wörterbuch zu den Schriften des Neuen Testaments und der übrigen urchristlichen Literatur*, [4]1952.
BARRETT, *Spirit*	C. K. Barrett, *The Holy Spirit and the Gospel Tradition*, 1947.
M. BARTH, *Augenzeuge*	M. Barth, *Der Augenzeuge. Eine Untersuchung über die Wahrnehmung des Menschensohnes durch die Apostel*, 1946.
BL.-DEBR.	F. Blass, *Grammatik des neutestamentlichen Griechisch*, bearbeitet von. A. Debrunner, [7]1943.
BOWMAN, *Intention*	J. W. Bowman, *The Intention of Jesus*, 1943.
BOWMAN, *Maturity*	J. W. Bowman, *The Religion of Maturity*, 1948.
BRANSCOMB, *Mark*	B. H. Branscomb, *The Gospel of Mark*, 1937 (= [5]1948).
BULTMANN, *Jesus*	R. Bultmann, *Jesus*, 1926.
BULTMANN, *Tradition*	R. Bultmann, *Die Geschichte der synoptischen Tradition*, [2]1931.
BULTMANN, *Urchristentum*	R. Bultmann, *Das Urchristentum im Rahmen der antiken Religionen*, 1949.
BUSCH, *Eschatologie*	F. Busch, *Zum Verständnis der synoptischen Eschatologie; Markus 13 neu untersucht*, 1938.
A. T. CADOUX, *Theology*	A. T. Cadoux, *The Theology of Jesus*, 1940.
C. J. CADOUX, *Mission*	C. J. Cadoux, *The Historic Mission of Jesus. A constructive Re-examination of the Eschatological Teaching in the Synoptic Gospels*, 1941.
COLWELL, *Approach*	E. C. Colwell, *An Approach to the Teaching of Jesus*, 1947.
CULLMANN, *Hoffnung*	O. Cullmann, *Die Hoffnung der Kirche auf die Wiederkunft Christi* (Verhandlungen des schweizerischen reformierten Pfarrvereins 83, 1942, 34 ff.).
CULLMANN, *Retour*	O. Cullmann, *Le retour de Christ, espérance de l'Eglise selon le Nouveau Testament*, 1943.
CURTIS, *Teacher*	W. A. Curtis, *Jesus Christ the Teacher*, 1943.
DLZ	*Deutsche Literaturzeitung*.

DAHL, *Volk Gottes*

N. A. Dahl, *Das Volk Gottes. Eine Untersuchung zum Kirchenbewusstsein des Urchristentums* (Skrifter utgitt av Det Norske Videnkaps Akademi i Oslo II. Hist.-filos. Klasse, 1941, No. 2).

DALMAN, *Worte Jesu*

G. Dalman, *Die Worte Jesu mit Berücksichtigung des nachkanonischen jüdischen Schrifttums und der aramäischen Sprache erörtert*, Band I, ²1930.

DELLING,
   Zeitverständnis

G. Delling, *Das Zeitverständnis des Neuen Testaments*, 1940.

DIBELIUS, *Tradition*
   (in German
   Formgeschichte)

M. Dibelius, *From Tradition to Gospel*, 1934 (in German *Die Formgeschichte des Evangeliums*, ²1933).

DIBELIUS, *Jesus*

M. Dibelius, *Jesus* (Sammlung Göschen, Nr. 1130), 1939.

DODD, *Parables*

C. H. Dodd, *The Parables of the Kingdom*, ³1936.

DUNCAN, *Jesus*

G. S. Duncan, *Jesus, Son of Man*, 1947.

EvTh

Evangelische Theologie.

ExpT

The Expository Times.

FLEW, *Church*

R. N. Flew, *Jesus and His Church. A Study of the Idea of the Ecclesia in the New Testament*, ²1943.

GLASSON, *Advent*

T. F. Glasson, *The Second Advent. The Origin of the New Testament Doctrine*, ²1947.

GLOEGE, *Reich Gottes*

G. Gloege, *Reich Gottes und Kirche im Neuen Testament*, 1929.

GRUNDMANN, *Jesus*

W. Grundmann, *Jesus der Galiläer und das Judentum*, 1940.

GUY, *Last Things*

H. A. Guy, *The New Testament Doctrine of the 'Last Things'*, 1948.

HAUCK, *Markus*

F. Hauck, *Das Evangelium des Markus* (Theol. Handkommentar zum N.T., II), 1931.

HAUCK, *Lukas*

F. Hauck, *Das Evangelium des Lukas* (Theol. Handkommentar zum N.T., III), 1934.

JBL

Journal of Biblical Literature.

JEREMIAS,
   Eucharistic Words

J. Jeremias, *The Eucharistic Words of Jesus*, 1955 (Tr. from German of ²1949).

JEREMIAS, *Parables*

J. Jeremias, *The Parables of Jesus*, 1954 (Tr. from German of ³1954).

JEREMIAS, *Weltvollender*

J. Jeremias, *Jesus als Weltvollender*, 1930.

JTS	*Journal of Theological Studies.*
JÜLICHER, *Gleichnisreden*	A. Jülicher, *Die Gleichnisreden Jesu* I². II, 1910.
JÜLICHER, *Itala*	A. Jülicher, *Itala, Das Neue Testament in altlateinischer Überlieferung*, 1938.
KLOSTERMANN, *Markus*	E. Klostermann, *Das Markusevangelium* (Handbuch zum N.T., 3), ³1936 (= ⁴1950).
KLOSTERMANN, *Matthäus*	E. Klostermann, *Das Matthäusevangelium* (Handbuch zum N.T., 4), ²1927.
KLOSTERMANN, *Lukas*	E. Klostermann, *Das Lukasevangelium* (Handbuch zum N.T., 5), ²1929.
KÜMMEL, *Eschatologie*	W. G. Kümmel, *Die Eschatologie der Evangelien. Ihre Geschichte und ihr Sinn*, 1936.
KÜMMEL, *Kirchenbegriff*	W. G. Kümmel, *Kirchenbegriff und Geschichtsbewusstsein in der Urgemeinde und bei Jesus* (Symbolae Biblicae Upsalienses I), 1943.
LEIPOLDT, *Jesus*	J. Leipoldt, *Jesu Verhältnis zu Griechen und Juden*, 1941.
LIDDELL and SCOTT	*A Greek-English Lexicon* compiled by H. G. Liddell and R. Scott, A New Edition . . . by H. S. Jones, 1940.
LIECHTENHAN, *Mission*	R. Liechtenhan, *Die urchristliche Mission. Voraussetzungen, Motive und Methoden*, 1946.
LOHMEYER, *Markus*	E. Lohmeyer, *Das Evangelium des Markus* (Kritischexegetischer Kommentar über das N.T., begründet von H. A. W. Meyer, I, 2), ¹⁰1937 (= ¹¹1951).
MAJOR, *Mission and Message*	H. D. A. Major, T. W. Manson, C. J. Wright, *The Mission and Message of Jesus. An Exposition of the Gospels in the Light of Modern Research*, 1937.
T. W. MANSON, *Sayings*	*The Sayings of Jesus* (Part II of the foregoing reprinted separately), 1949.
W. MANSON, *Jesus*	W. Manson, *Jesus the Mesiah*, 1943.
MEINERTZ, *Theologie*	M. Meinertz, *Theologie des Neuen Testamentes* I, II, 1950.
MEYER, *Prophet*	R. Meyer, *Der Prophet aus Galiläa. Studie zum Jesusbild der drei ersten Evangelien*, 1940.
MICHAELIS, *Matthäus*	W. Michaelis, *Das Evangelium nach Matthäus* I, II (Prophezei, Schweizerisches Bibelwerk für die Gemeinde), 1948, 1949.

MICHAELIS, *Sämann*	W. Michaelis, *Es ging ein Sämann aus zu säen . . . Eine Einführung in die Gleichnisse Jesu über das Reich Gottes und die Kirche*, 1938.
MICHAELIS, *Täufer*	W. Michaelis, *Täufer, Jesus, Urgemeinde. Die Predigt vom Reiche Gottes vor und nach Pfingsten*, 1928.
MICHAELIS, *Verheissung*	W. Michaelis, *Der Herr verzieht nicht die Verheissung. Die Aussagen Jesu über die Nähe des Jüngsten Tages*, 1942.
MINEAR, *Kingdom*	P. S. Minear, *The Kingdom and the Power. An Exposition of the New Testament Gospel*, 1950.
NIKOLAINEN, *Auferstehungsglaube*	A. T. Nikolainen, *Der Auferstehungsglaube in der Bibel und ihrer Umwelt. II. Neutestament-licher Teil* (Annales Academiae Scientiarum Fennicae B. LIX, 3), 1946.
OTTO, *The Kingdom of God* (in German *Reich Gottes*)	R. Otto, *The Kingdom of God and The Son of Man*, 1938 (in German *Reich Gottes und Menschensohr, Eine Religionsgeschichtlicher Versuch*, 1934).
par.	parallels, paralleled by.
RAWLINSON, *Christ*	A. E. J. Rawlinson, *Christ in the Gospels*, 1944.
RB	*Revue Biblique.*
REDLICH, *Mark*	E. B. Redlich, *St. Mark's Gospel*, 1948.
RENGSTORF, *Lukas*	K. H. Rengstorf, *Das Evangelium nach Lukas* (Das N.T. Deutsch. Neues Göttinger Bibelwerk, Teilbändchen 3), [6]1952.
RHPR	*Revue d'histoire et de philosophie religieuses.*
RevHR	*Revue de l'histoire des religions.*
SCHLATTER, *Matthäus*	A. Schlatter, *Der Evangelist Matthäus. Seine Sprache, sein Ziel, seine Selbständigkeit*, [2]1933.
SCHNIEWIND, *Markus*	J. Schniewind, *Das Evangelium nach Markus* (Das N.T. Deutsch. Neues Göttinger Bibelwerk, Teilbändchen 1), 1933.
SCHNIEWIND, *Matthäus*	J. Schniewind, *Das Evangelium nach Matthäus* (Das N.T. Deutsch. Neues Göttinger Bibelwerk, Teilbändchen 2), 1937.
SCHWEITZER, *Quest* (in German *Leben Jesu*)	A. Schweitzer, *The Quest of the Historical Jesus*, [3]1954 (in German *Geschichte der Leben-Jesu-Forschung*, [6]1951).
SHARMAN, *Son of Man*	H. B. Sharman, *Son of Man and Kingdom of God*, [2]1944.

B. T. D. SMITH, *Parables*	B. T. D. Smith, *The Parables of the Synoptic Gospels. A Critical Study*, 1937.
C. W. F. SMITH, *Jesus*	C. W. F. Smith, *The Jesus of the Parables*, 1948.
STAUFFER, *NT*	E. Stauffer, *New Testament Theology*, 1955 (in German *Die Theologie des Neuen Testaments*, [4,5]1948).
STONEHOUSE, *Witness*	N. B. Stonehouse, *The Witness of Matthew and Mark to Christ*, 1944.
STRACK-BILLERBECK	H. L. Strack und P. Billerbeck, *Kommentar zum Neuen Testament aus Talmud und Midrasch*, I–IV, 1922–28.
ST	*Studia Theologica* (Lund).
TAYLOR, *Mark*	V. Taylor, *The Gospel according to St. Mark*, 1952.
TB	*Theologische Blätter.*
TLZ	*Theologische Literaturzeitung.*
TR	*Theologische Rundschau.*
TWNT	*Theologisches Wörterbuch zum Neuen Testament*, hrsg. von G. Kittel und G. Friedrich, Bd. I–IV, Bd. V., Lief. 1–12, 1933–52.
TZ	*Theologische Zeitschrift.*
THEISSING, *Seligkeit*	J. Theissing, *Die Lehre Jesu von der ewigen Seligkeit. Eine Beitrag zur neutestamentlichen Theologie*. Diss. Breslau, 1940.
VOLZ, *Eschatologie*	P. Volz, *Die Eschatologie der jüdischen Gemeinde im neutestamentlichen Zeitalter*, [2]1934.
WAGENFÜHRER, *Kirchenbegriff*	M. A. Wagenführer, *Der Kirchenbegriff des Neuen Testaments* (Germanentum, Christentum, Judentum. Studien zur Erforschung ihres gegenseitigen Verhältnisses II, 1942, 276 ff.).
WALTER, *Kommen*	E. Walter, *Das Kommen des Herrn II. Die Eschatologische Situation nach den synoptischen Evangelien*, 1947.
WEINEL, *Theologie*	H. Weinel, *Biblische Theologie des Neuen Testaments, Die Religion Jesu und des Urchristentums*, [3]1921.
J. WEISS, *Reich Gottes*	J. Weiss, *Die Predigt Jesu vom Reiche Gottes*, [2]1900.
K. WEISS, *Irrtumslosigkeit*	K. Weiss, *Exegetisches zur Irrtumslosigkeit und Eschatologie Jesu*, 1916.

WENDLAND, *Eschatologie*	H.-D. Wendland, *Die Eschatologie des Reiches Gottes bei Jesus. Eine Studie über den Zusammenhang von Eschatologie Ethik und Kirchenproblem*, 1931.
WERNER, *Dogma*	M. Werner, *Die Entstehung des christlichen Dogmas problemgeschichtlich dargestellt*, 1941.
WILDER, *Eschatology*	A. N. Wilder, *Eschatology and Ethics in the Teaching of Jesus*, [2]1950.
ZNW	*Zeitschrift für die neutestamentliche Wissenschaft und die Kunde der Alten Kirche.*
ZTK	*Zeitschrift für Theologie und Kirche.*

INTRODUCTION

THE discussion about the extent, the meaning and the importance of the expectation implicit in Jesus' message that the end was near is today once more in full flood. For a long time it seemed to be completely established that Jesus' preaching was decisively conditioned by the expectation of an imminent end, but that this expectation was not the intrinsic concern of his message, and that Jesus had also declared in some way that God's kingdom was present. This *communis opinio*[1] has been shaken, because in the main three interpretations of Jesus' message, differing widely and indeed excluding each other, have found support. On the one hand stands the *'konsequent'* eschatological view of Albert Schweitzer that Jesus in close connexion with Jewish apocalyptic made the announcement of the imminent end of the world the central theme of his message and expected his appearance as the Son of Man on the clouds of heaven, first in his lifetime, and then in direct connexion with his death. This view has been revived especially by Martin Werner with great vigour.[2] On the other hand Roman Catholic scholars, the 'German-Christian' theologians, and most particularly a very large section of British and American scholars, under the influence of C. H. Dodd, eliminate the 'futurist' eschatology more or less completely from Jesus' preaching, and consider it to be a misunderstanding on the part of the Christian community, a rejudaizing, or a consequence of the

---

[1]Cf. e. g. Wenland, *Eschatologie*; Dibelius, *Jesus*; Flew, *Church*; C. J. Cadoux, *Mission*; W. Manson, *Jesus*; Walter, *Kommen.*—W. Schweitzer, *Eschatologie und Ethik. Eine kurze Übersicht über die Gesprächslage mit einer ausgewählten und mit Anmerkungen versehenen Bibliographie* (Study Department of the World Council of Churches, Geneva, 1951. Order No. Study Dept. 51 G/132) calls this view a synthesis 'which assumes that Jesus fulfilled the old messianic expectations only in part and in an altered form and that at the same time he announced their final fulfilment' (on page 27 Schweitzer places C. J. Cadoux wrongly among the scholars to be named in note 2 instead of in this group).

[2]Werner, *Dogma*. Cf. even earlier F. Buri, *Die Bedeutung der neutestamentlichen Eschatologie für die neuere protestantische Theologie*, 1934 and also U. Neuenschwander, *Protestantische Dogmatik der Gegenwart und das Problem der biblischen Mythologie*, Diss. Bern, 1949, 165 ff. Michaelis, *Täufer*, also supported a purely 'futurist' interpretation of Jesus' eschatology.

penetration of apocalyptic.[3] A third group of researchers either
denies altogether the significance of the conception of time in
Jesus' thought[4] or attempts at least to push to one side the
expectation of an imminent end as an unimportant part of Jesus'
'futurist' expectation of the end.[5]

This great divergence between the conceptions proves that not
only the exegesis of several ambiguous passages is disputed, but
that the sum total of the original evidence for Jesus' eschatological
message is appraised entirely differently, and that therefore a
correct decision can be obtained only by examining the complete
record of Jesus' preaching. Such an examination is all the more
necessary because it is only against the background of Jesus'
preaching concerning the Kingdom of God correctly understood
that the right answers can be given to the questions about the
significance of the person of Jesus in the formation of primitive
Christian thought and about the age and root of the idea of the
Church in the primitive church. Now, such an examination is
particularly essential because the meaning of eschatology, in the
strict sense of the expectation of the end of time, has become a
burning question for systematic theology and for ethics in the
theology of all churches and confessions, and without a clear
insight into the *historical* reality of Jesus' eschatological message
no reliable results can be obtained.

Consequently in what follows I shall consider first of all the
exact facts concerning the tradition of Jesus' eschatological
message, taking account of contemporary exegetical work, and
then against this background I shall seek the historical and the
permanent meaning of the tradition. At the same time the connexion and the contrast with the Jewish range of ideas in Jesus'
lifetime must not be left out of sight, because only thus can the
significance of the 'futurist' expectation of the end contained in

[3]K. Weiss, *Irrtumslosigkeit*; A. Feuillet, *RB* 55, 1948, 481 ff.; 56, 1949,
61 ff., 340 ff.; 57, 1950, 63 ff.—Grundmann, *Jesus*; Leipoldt, *Jesus*; Wagen-
führer, *Kirchenbegriff*;—Dodd, *Parables*; A. T. Cadoux, *Theology*; F. C. Grant,
The Gospel of the Kingdom, 1940; Curtis, *Teacher*, 122 f., 201 f.; J. Knox, *The
Man Christ Jesus*, 1942, 39 f.; J. Knox, *Christ the Lord*, 1945, 23 fi.; Duncan,
Jesus, 45 ff., 179 ff.; Glasson, *Advent*; Guy, *Last Things*; Sharman, *Son of Man*;
Bowman, *Intention*; Bowman, *Maturity*.—H. Clavier, *L'accès au royaume de
Dieu*, 1944, belongs here too.
[4]Delling, *Zeitverständnis*; Duncan, *Jesus*, 186 ff.; Guy, *Last Things*, 49. Cf.
also below page 143, note 4.
[5]Michaelis, *Verheissung*; Cullmann. *Hoffnung*; Cullmann, *Retour*; Busch,
Eschatologie, 146 ff. Cf. also below page 152, note 27.

Jesus' message be correctly determined. In particular cases some exegetical decisions must remain uncertain; this follows from the fact that the oldest tradition can only be drawn out conjecturally from the deposit of the traditions in the gospels. The correctness of the decision in particular cases must therefore hold good within the framework of the picture as a whole.

I

THE IMMINENT FUTURE OF THE KINGDOM OF GOD

1. THE TERMS ἐγγύς AND ἐγγίζειν

HOT debate still centres as much on the texts which speak of the eschatological events as being near in time as on the question whether Jesus in any way expected an imminent consummation of the world and spoke of the Kingdom of God as being present. It therefore seems advisable to start not from the most debated texts, but from an examination of the particular terms which can throw some light on the temporal meaning of Jesus' eschatological pronouncements. It would seem most useful for this purpose to begin with the terms ἐγγύς and ἐγγίζειν. The literal meaning of ἐγγύς in the New Testament is completely unambiguous: it denotes nearness in space. Corresponding with this the verb ἐγγίζειν declares that one has come nearer to a place than before but has not yet reached it (cf. Luke 19.11; Mark 11.1; 14.42 beside 14.43; Luke 18.35 beside 19.1 etc.). There are certainly passages in which one could also translate ἐγγίζειν by 'coming to' (perhaps Luke 15.1; 22.47; 24.15; Acts 21.33); but nothing forces one to conclude that in these passages the literal meaning of 'coming near' has been given up in favour of the sense of 'coming to', 'arriving at', since in all these passages it may simply be a question of a less strict use of language. The same meaning of ἐγγύς and ἐγγίζειν shows itself also in passages where these terms are transferred to a meaning other than temporal, since in these cases also it is always the nearness to, in contrast to the distance from, but not the arrival at the place which is emphasized (e.g. μέχρι θανάτου ἤγγισεν Phil. 2.30 of a man sick unto death, οἵ ποτε ὄντες μακρὰν ἐγενήθητε ἐγγύς Eph. 2.13).

So it is only likely that both terms when used with the transferred temporal meaning are there also intended to denote an event which is near, but has not yet taken place. There is no doubt about this is the case of ἐγγύς. It denotes the nearness of a fixed day which is imminent (John 2.13; 6.4; 7.2; 11.55) as well as the nearness of an event (Heb. 6.8; 8.13; Matt. 26.18 of Jesus' hour of death). Now since in Revelation ὁ καιρὸς ἐγγύς (1.3; 22.10) is used unambiguously to denote the nearness of the end of the world, it is to be presumed to start with that this usage is to be found when ἐγγύς is employed in connexion with eschatological events. It is true that Phil. 4.5 ὁ κύριος ἐγγύς is not a positive proof, but as it is said a little earlier (3.20): σωτῆρα ἀπεκδεχόμεθα κύριον Ἰησοῦν Χριστόν, so in 4.5 ἐγγύς can hardly be interpreted otherwise than as meaning an imminent coming.[1] So when Paul (Rom. 13.11) writes in the course of an exhortation to cast off at last the works of darkness: νῦν γὰρ ἐγγύτερον ἡμῶν ἡ σωτηρία ἢ ὅτε ἐπιστεύσαμεν, it undoubtedly means that the day of salvation at the parousia has drawn nearer than it was at the time when Paul and the other Christians first believed. It is true that Michaelis[2] has objected to this exegesis on the ground that here the last day is indeed thought of as being near, but argues that Paul does not deduce so much 'that the last day will take place at a time, fixed though unknown to himself' as that 'the fact of his conversion which lies in the past is for the apostle the pledge of the nearness of the last day'. Nevertheless this argument is not in the least convincing; for if it is affirmed that salvation is now *nearer* than when they first believed and if this is made the *basis* of the assertion that it is time to arise from sleep, then the period until salvation appears is considered to be shorter than when they first believed. New Testament usage is therefore completely uniform as regards the temporal use of ἐγγύς: it denotes that an event will happen soon, by which it is meant or presumed that there will not be a long time to wait before it happens.

It is against this background that we can now consider the only text in which Jesus uses the word ἐγγύς in an eschatological sense, Mark 13.28 f. par. Matt. 24.32 f.; Luke 21.29–31. Here the conclusion which everyone would draw as a matter of course from the observation that the fig tree was putting forth its leaves, ὅτι ἐγγὺς τὸ θέρος ἐστίν, is used as the basis for the summons: οὕτως καὶ ὑμεῖς, ὅταν ἴδητε ταῦτα γινόμενα, γινώσκετε ὅτι ἐγγύς ἐστιν ἐπὶ

---

[1] W. Michaelis, *Der Brief an die Philipper*, 1935, 67 considers also that nearness experienced in fellowship with the Lord is meant here, but Rom. 10.8 (=Deut. 30.14) and Ps. 144.18 LXX are hardly sufficient authority for such a 'mystical' usage, since in both these passages it is a question of God and God's word as being near at hand.

[2] Michaelis, *Verheissung*, 55 f.

θύραις. This is preceded (Mark 13.26 f.) by the prediction of the parousia of the Son of Man with the gathering of the elect, and there follows in 13.30 a saying which sums up the whole of the eschatological events. Now as in the parable (13.28) the budding of the fig tree points to the conclusion that the summer is near, so in the application (13.29) ταῦτα γινόμενα must in the same way denote happenings which guarantee the nearness of an expected event. It follows from this that ἐγγύς ἐστιν ἐπὶ θύραις cannot refer to the parousia mentioned in 13.26 f.; moreover since in 13.30 likewise a fresh start is made which cannot refer back only to 13.26 f., 13.28 f. must be a detached saying. Therefore the subjects to be presumed for ταῦτα and ἐγγύς ἐστιν cannot be deduced from the connexion with 13.26 ff., 30. But it can nevertheless safely be concluded from the clear parallelism of the parable and its application[3] that ταῦτα must signify some kind of *premonitory signs* of the end, whilst as the subject of ἐγγύς ἐστιν, the end, the parousia, the entry of the Kingdom of God must be presumed.[4] So this gives us a reliable proof of the fact that Jesus expected the eschatological consummation in the near future and knew its imminent coming to be announced by premonitory signs in the present.[5]

[3]Lohmeyer, *Markus*, 280 wishes to strike out the two introductory sentences ἀπὸ δὲ τῆς συκῆς μάθετε τὴν παραβολήν and οὕτως καὶ ὑμεῖς because they are not precisely formulated. But that is not necessary, since the introductions to the parables are known to lack precision.

[4]Bultmann, *Urchristentum*, 1949, 98, 243 note 50 conjectures no doubt correctly that Mark and Matthew suppose the 'Son of Man' previously mentioned to be the subject of 'is nigh', while the detached saying has rather in mind the βασιλεία τοῦ θεοῦ which Luke 21.31 completes. C. W. F. Smith, *Jesus*, 240 ff. also points correctly to the fact that Jesus' own presence and his deeds are to be estimated as *signs* that God's reign 'is beginning to make its progress known'.

[5]So there is therefore no evidence for the assertion of Dodd, *Parables*, 137 note 1 that it is 'surely more pointed', if Jesus in this parable summons men to recognize the significance of the *present* situation (so also B. T. D. Smith, *Parables*, 91; Taylor, *Mark*, 520); for in that case the parallelism with the picture in 13.28 is completely lost. And when A. Feuillet, *RB* 56, 1949, 82 f. (similarly K. Weiss, *Irrtumslosigkeit*, 144; Sharman, *Son of Man*, 98 f.) interprets the parable by saying that Jesus was pointing to the new world which would follow on the destruction of Jerusalem, it is impossible to refer ταῦτα to the destruction of Jerusalem, and the subject of ἐγγύς ἐστιν becomes completely nebulous. Finally M. Hermaniuk, *La Parabole Évangélique*, Univ. Cath. Lovaniensis, Diss. II, 38, 1947, 198 completely misses the parallelism between the picture and what it represents, when he denies that the fig tree is being compared with the signs of the end and declares the comparison to be between the disciples' ability to understand the sign of the fig tree and the ability demanded of them to recognize the premonitory signs of the approaching end.

Now Mark 13.28 has concerning this matter a parallel[6] in Luke
12.54–56 where Jesus reproaches his disciples that they infer the
occurrence of natural events from premonitory signs, but cannot
deduce from the characteristics of the present the conclusion
which obtrudes itself. It is not stated what Jesus meant by the
characteristics of the present nor what conclusion should be
drawn from them, but in view of Mark 13.28 f. we can surely
consider that Jesus wishes the present to be understood as a
pointer to the imminent eschatological consummation.[7] But if
this is so, these two passages support each other and there is not
the least reason to doubt that Mark 13.28 f. belong to the oldest
tradition and therewith to the authenticated sayings of Jesus.
This therefore provides a certain proof of the important fact concerning the term ἐγγύς that Jesus expected the eschatological consummation in the near future, and the assessment of the texts
containing the verb ἐγγίζειν must be materially influenced by
this.

There can be no doubt that ἐγγίζειν, when its use is transferred
to a temporal meaning normally denotes 'to come near' in con-
formity with the literal usage. This applies to the obviously rare
profane passages[8] as well as to the prevailing eschatological usage
of the Septuagint.[9] In the New Testament too this meaning is
quite certain in a number of passages (Luke 21.20, 28; 22.1; Rom.
13.12 ἡ νὺξ προέκοψεν, ἡ δὲ ἡμέρα ἤγγικεν; Heb. 10.25; James 5.8
ἡ παρουσία τοῦ κυρίου ἤγγικεν ; I Peter 4.7). On the other hand
Matt. 26.45 ἰδοὺ ἤγγικεν ἡ ὥρα καὶ ὁ υἱὸς τοῦ ἀνθρώπου παραδίδοται
εἰς χεῖρας ἁμαρτωλῶν might perhaps be translated 'The hour is
come and the Son of Man is being betrayed into the hands of
sinners', especially as in his source Mark 14.41 ἦλθεν ἡ ὥρα
is said. But this assumption would probably be incorrect, because

[6] So rightly Schniewind, *Markus*, 166.

[7] C. J. Cadoux, *Mission*, 269 thinks that Luke 12.54–56 means that Jesus'
Jewish contemporary would interpret the signs of his time as foretelling an
imminent war with Rome (similarly also Sharman, *Son of Man*, 77), since 'the
ordinary intelligent Jew' could not infer from the signs of the time that the
eschatological judgment was imminent. But Jesus had always assumed that
only 'those who see' could recognize the signs of the time (Matt. 13.16 f.;
11.3–6).

[8] J. H. Moulton and G. Milligan, *The Vocabulary of the Greek New Testament*,
Part III, 1919, 178 quote only Pap. Oxyrh. IX, 1202, 8 ἐνγίζοντος τοῦ ἑκάστου
ἔτους ἀγῶνος; H. Preisker, *TWNT* II, 329 mentions Epictetus, *Diss.* III,
10, 14 τί γάρ ἐστι τὸ κακῶς ἔχειν; ἐγγίζειν τῷ διαλυθῆναι τὴν ψυχὴν ἀπὸ τοῦ
σώματος; Liddell and Scott have no references.

[9] References in H. Preisker, *TWNT* II, 330, 26 ff.

Matthew would hardly have replaced the clear ἦλθεν with the ambiguous ἤγγικεν if he had wished to retain the meaning 'is come'. It is much more likely that Matthew made this change because he relates ὥρα with the hour of death, while Mark applies it to the arrest. Therefore Matt. 26.45 should assuredly be translated 'the hour has come near'.[10] There is less certainty about the translation of Matt. 21.34, where in the parable of the wicked husbandmen, after the vineyard has been handed over to the husbandmen and the householder has departed on his journey, it is said. 'ὅτε δὲ ἤγγισεν ὁ καιρὸς τῶν καρπῶν'. Here one *might* indeed translate 'when the time of the harvest had come'.[11] But there is no necessity for this translation, since the servants could be sent off to collect the fruits even before the arrival of the harvest; so that it would be better to translate here also 'when the time of the harvest had come near'.[12] Apart from the passages already mentioned the verb ἐγγίζειν occurs also in the summary of Jesus' preaching in Mark 1.15 par. Matt. 4.17 ἤγγικεν ἡ βασιλεία τοῦ θεοῦ, and as a saying of Jesus in the missionary charge to the disciples Matt. 10.7 = Luke 10.9 (in Luke ἤγγικεν ἐφ' ὑμᾶς ἡ βασιλεία τοῦ θεοῦ), and in view of the usage discussed above, the usual translation here also is: 'The Kingdom of God is coming near'. This has recently been contested by C. H. Dodd who wishes to translate 'The Kingdom of God has come'.[13] He brings forward the following argument for this: in the Septuagint ἐγγίζειν is used as well as φθάνειν to

[10]So also all the Latin versions and the Sinaitic Syriac (Curetonian is missing). The Peshitta has wrongly *mṭt* = is come.

[11]The Peshitta (*mṭ'*) translates it thus, and this is no doubt also the meaning of the Sinaitic Syriac (*ḥw'*).

[12]So the Syriac Curetonian (*qrb*) and the Old Latin versions together with the Vulgate (*adpropinquasset* or *adpropiasset*, see Jülicher, *Itala*, 154). Similarly Luke, 21.8 in the passage about the false prophets ἐγώ εἰμι, ὁ καιρὸς ἤγγικεν could only be translated 'the time has come near'; for it is quite clearly concerned with the prediction of the judgment in the style of Celsus' 'prophets' (in Origen *c. Celsum* VII, 9); here also *all* the Syriac versions read *qrb*.

[13]Dodd, *Parables*, 44 f. This translation is accepted as probable by R. H. Lightfoot, *History and Interpretation in the Gospels*, 1935, 65, 107. The same translation is given by Leipoldt. *Jesus*, 117; A. T. Cadoux, *Theology*, 46; Duncan, *Jesus*, 41 f.; Redlich, *Mark*, 50 f., 73; M. Barth, *Augenzeuge*, 91; K. G. Kuhn, *Achtzehngebet und Vaterunser und der Reim*, 1950, 42. Also M. Black, 'The Kingdom of God has come', *ExpT* 63, 1951/52, 289 f. (quoting in support P. Joüon, *Recherches de Science Religieuse* 17, 1927, 538) would like to assume as the original text *qrbt* in the sense of 'has come', because *qrb can* have this meaning occasionally in the Old Testament. But even Black does not explain how the gospel tradition could come to such a mistaken translation as ἤγγικεν when the original Aramaic wording used *qrb*, which almost always denotes nearness.

translate *nagha'* and *m^{e}tā'*, both of which mean 'to arrive', so that probably both the sayings of Jesus ἤγγικεν ἡ βασιλεία τοῦ θεοῦ (Luke 10.9 ἤγγικεν ἐφ' ὑμᾶς) and ἔφθασεν ἐφ' ὑμᾶς ἡ βασιλεία τοῦ θεοῦ (Matt. 12.28 = Luke 11.20) are intended to reproduce the same Aramiac expression and are both to be translated 'The Kingdom of God has come'. But this argument cannot be sustained. For to begin with there are no grounds at all for the supposition that ἤγγικεν in Mark 1.15; Matt. 10.7 and ἔφθασεν 12.28 must represent the same Aramaic verb with no 'futurist' meaning;[14] for only really compelling reasons would allow the assumption that within the same stratum of tradition (Matt. 10.7 and 12.28 both belong to Q) one and the same central idea has been translated differently in such a way that the one translation (ἤγγικεν) is employed, contrary to its usage elsewhere, in the sense of the other translation. Furthermore J. Y. Campbell and K. Clark have shown[15] that in the Septuagint also in the preponderating number of cases ἐγγίζειν bears the same meaning of 'coming near' and that the few passages (e.g. Jonah 3.6 ἤγγισεν ὁ λόγος πρὸς τὸν βασιλέα) quoted against this by Dodd[16] only prove that the translators of the Septuagint occasionally stretch the meaning of ἐγγίζειν to the marginal case of 'approaching to'. As references in profane writings for ἐγγίζειν = 'to approach' seem to be completely lacking, it is unlikely that in the tradition of detached sayings the verb ἐγγίζειν was used with a quite unusual meaning to translate an Aramaic expression the sense of which could be reproduced unambiguously; besides this unusual sense of ἐγγίζειν is deduced in the few Septuagint passages from the context only. And finally the evangelists, as has been shown, used the word ἐγγίζειν in other passages *without exception* in the sense of 'coming near', so if in Mark 1.15 etc. they wished to express the idea of 'having come', they must have been guilty either of an extremely grave misunderstanding of Jesus' fundamental message concerning the coming of the Kingdom of God or of an incomprehensible inconsistency in their use of words.[17] There can therefore be no doubt that according to the detached saying in the

[14]So also C. C. McCown, 'Jesus, Son of Man', *Journal of Religion* 28, 1948, 7.
[15]J. Y. Campbell, *ExpT* 48, 1936/37, 9 f.; K. Clark, *JBL.* 59, 1940, 367 ff. Cf. also C. J. Cadoux, *Mission*, 198 note 4.
[16]C. H. Dodd, *ExpT* 48, 1936/37, 140 f.
[17]C. T. Craig, 'Realized Eschatology' *JBL* 56, 1937, 20 emphasizes rightly that the *perfect* ἤγγικεν when used of time can only refer to the near future. Cf. also Taylor *Mark*, 167.

Q tradition and the summary in Mark 1.15 Jesus proclaimed that the Kingdom of God had come near.[18]

2. WHAT IS SAID ABOUT THE 'COMING' OF THE *ESCHATON*

What has been deduced from the usage of ἐγγύς and ἐγγίζειν is confirmed by the statements which presume or expressly mention not the nearness but the futurity of the Kingdom of God. That is undoubtedly the case in the second petition of the Lord's prayer ἐλθάτω ἡ βασιλεία σου (Matt. 6.10 = Luke 11.2), for the parallels in the Jewish prayers[19] very seldom use the verb 'to come', but frequently 'to be manifested' or 'to bring about the reign'. This usage shows clearly that this petition expects the Kingdom of God to come into existence in the future; therefore Jesus can be applying it only to the future coming of the Kingdom of God. The verb ἔρχεσθαι for the appearance of the βασιλεία generally bears the same meaning. It is true that the phrase, the 'coming' of the kingdom, which the rabbis seldom employ, is not often attested in the case of Jesus either. The clearest instance is Mark 9.1 ἀμὴν λέγω ὑμῖν, ὅτι εἰσίν τινες ὧδε τῶν ἑστηκότων οἵτινες οὐ μὴ γεύσωνται θανάτου ἕως ἂν ἴδωσιν τὴν βασιλείαν τοῦ θεοῦ ἐληλυθυῖαν ἐν δυνάμει. As the special introduction shows, it is clearly a case of a detached saying, which Mark, or the tradition he has adopted, has attached to the preceding series of sayings about following Jesus.[20] This saying must therefore be explained without regard to the context. One thing is clear: it is declared of definite people that

---

[18]Sharman, *Son of Man*, 99 ff. attemps to prove that Mark 1.15 does not reproduce Jesus' preaching correctly, since Mark 13.29 and 9.1 do not refer to the Kingdom of God, but to the destruction of Jerusalem; but this completely overlooks Matt. 10.7, quite apart from the mistaken interpretation of Mark 9.1.

[19]See Dalman, *Worte Jesu*, 88, 310 ff.; Strack-Billerbeck I, 418 f.—C. H. Dodd, *History and the Gospel*, 1938, 177 also refers this petition not to the eschatological future, but to the present; but to prove this he can only offer the reflection that the present alone can be brought into the context of God's redemptive action (similarly E. Pfennigsdorf, *Der Menschensohn*, 1948, 182). And Sharman, *Son of Man*, 133, explains simply that the second petition has nothing to teach about the nature of the Kingdom of God or that its meaning is defined by the third! Finally C. J. Cadoux, *Mission*, 201 and most particularly E. Lohmeyer, *Das Vaterunser*, ²1947, 68 ff. emphasize the exclusively 'futurist' eschatological meaning of the second petition.

[20]Cf. e.g. Lohmeyer, *Markus*, 171; Hauck, *Markus*, 105; C. J. Cadoux, *Mission*, 199; Taylor, *Mark*, 380.

they will not need to die, because the Kingdom of God will have come ἐν δυνάμει whilst they are still alive.[21] It has been questioned whether ἐν δυνάμει is not merely an addition of the evangelist, who (as in Rom. 1.4) wishes to distinguish the entry of the King-dom of God 'with power' from its previous hidden existence. But this assumption is arbitrary, since ἐν δυνάμει even without empha-sizing the antithesis, might simply denote the powerful manifes-tation to which at present nothing comparable corresponds (cf. Mark 13.26 ὄψονται τὸν υἱὸν τοῦ ἀνθρώπου ἐρχόμενον ἐν νεφέλαις μετὰ δυνάμεως πολλῆς καὶ δόξης).[22] But ἕως ἂν ἴδωσιν . . . ἐληλυθυῖαν be-side οὐ μὴ γεύσωνται can only have the meaning of a *futurum exactum*: death will not come to these people before a particular occurrence in the future; they are not to die because the Kingdom of God will previously have been made known to them.[23] Since therefore ἕως ἂν ἴδωσιν describes a future event and τὴν βασιλείαν is the direct object of ἴδωσιν, the coming of the Kingdom of God must *also* still lie in the future for Jesus. It is true that C. H. Dodd disputes this.[24] He wishes to translate: ' . . . until they have seen that the Kingdom of God has come with power'; those who stood round were promised that some of them before their death will recognize that the Kingdom of God *has* come. So in that case it would not be a question of the future coming of the Kingdom of God, but only of the recognition which still lies in the future of its having come.[25] But this attempt to strike out the *future* coming of the Kingdom of God from Mark 9.1 is untenable. For

---

[21]Thus J. Weiss, *Reich Gottes*, 41 f.; Klostermann, *Markus*, 85.

[22]Barrett, *Spirit*, 73 f. emphasizes that Mark 9.1 and 13.26 show Jesus' characteristic contrast between the hidden present and the manifest future.

[23]It is correct that the wording of the saying does not exclude the idea that the τινές will yet die later (thus M. Barth, *Augenzeuge* 89); but it is only pos-sible to understand it in this way by wrongly referring the arrival of the βασιλεία with power to historical events. See below note 25.

[24]Dodd, *Parables*, 42, 53 f.; Dodd, *ExpT* 48, 1936/37, 141 f. Likewise Bowman, *Maturity*, 250 f.

[25]Similarly K. Weiss, *Irrtumslosigkeit*, 165 f. (some will recognize the mani-festation of Jesus' kingly glory by the infliction of Israel's punishment); Duncan, *Jesus*, 182 f. (Jesus is convinced that the beginning of the new order will be realized visibly during the lifetime of some of the disciples); Glasson, *Advent*, 112 (Jesus expected at first that some would have to die with him before the Kingdom of God came with power; but then he went alone to the Cross and 'a few weeks later the Kingdom of God came with power'); Sharman, *Son of Man*, 99, likewise Walter, *Kommen*, 96 (Mark 9.1 refers to the destruction of Jerusalem which Jesus expected soon); Bowman, *Maturity*, 251 (the Kingdom of God comes when many of this generation acknowledge Jesus' lordship); M. Barth, *Augenzeuge*, 90 (certain people will see the Son of Man appearing before their death, for 'the appearing of the Son of Man and

firstly it has been correctly pointed out by different scholars that ἴδωσιν τὴν βασιλείαν . . . ἐληλυθυῖαν could not describe the becoming aware of a fact that had long existed, but only the experience of one that had just appeared.[26] And next the addition of ἐν δυνάμει means either that Jesus himself spoke of the *open appearance* of the Kingdom of God or that the evangelist had so understood him. Now since Matthew in 16.28 in his reproduction of Mark 9.1 (ἕως ἂν ἴδωσιν τὸν υἱὸν τοῦ ἀνθρώπου ἐρχόμενον ἐν τῇ βασιλείᾳ αὐτοῦ) is also thinking of the eschatological *appearance* of the Messiah, which he clearly regards as equivalent to the coming of the Kingdom of God,[27] he *and* Mark must have completely misunderstood Jesus' saying if in fact the wording of Mark (with ἐν δυνάμει) should not be Jesus' own. But, as we saw, there is no reason to assume such a change in the interpretation of a traditional saying of Jesus. It may therefore be safely asserted that Mark 9.1 bears the meaning that some of Jesus' hearers will live to see the appearance of the Kingdom of God in the comparatively near future and therefore will not fall victims to death.

Yet it is difficult to determine the precise significance of this saying. That it belongs to the oldest tradition is likely, if only because the fact that this prediction was not realized must have caused such serious difficulties that they would hardly have been created.[28] It is equally clear that Jesus says of a limited number of

---

the dawn of God's reign were already even in Daniel described as *one* event'). In all these exegeses the emphasis is laid, contrary to the way the sentence is composed, on ἴδωσιν instead of on ἐληλυθυῖαν.

[26]See J. Y. Campbell, *ExpT* 48, 1936/37, 93 f.; J. M. Creed, *ibid.*, 184 f.; C. T. Craig, *JBL* 56, 1937, 20; K. Clark, *JBL* 59, 1940, 372 f.; Taylor *Mark*, 385.

[27]Bowman, *Maturity*, 253 f. assumes that Matt. 16.28 like Mark 9.1 is thinking only of the corporate 'Son of Man', i.e. of the Church, in which case surely this corporate interpretation of the term 'Son of Man' is highly questionable (similar to Bowman also Taylor, *Mark*, 386). Glasson, *Advent*, 72 takes the opposite view that according to Matt. 16.28 the parousia is wrongly introduced into Mark 9.1 (cf. note 25). And Meinertz, *Theologie* I, 62 refers the 'coming of the Kingdom of God' in Mark 9.1 to 'the powerful development of God's reign already on earth'.

[28]'There are therefore no sufficient grounds for the assumption that we are concerned with a saying 'formulated by the early Church as a word of consolation for the non-appearance of the parousia' (Bultmann, *Tradition*, 128). The same view is taken by K. Kundsin, *Das Urchristentum im Lichte der Evangelienforschung*, 1929, 15; E. Fuchs, *Verkündigung und Forschung*, 1947/8, 1949, 76; G. Bornkamm, 'Die Verzögerung der Parusie,' *In Memoriam E. Lohmeyer*, 1951, 118 f.

persons only (τινὲς) that they will live to see the coming of the
Kingdom of God; yet there is no reason for the assumption that
this was intended (later?) to weaken the promise of its coming in
this generation (Mark 13.30),[29] because it is obvious that within
a group of people only some individuals will remain alive until a
definite date in the somewhat distant future. Lastly who is meant
by τινὲς ὧδε τῶν ἑστηκότων? The obvious assumption, adopted
already by Matthew and Luke, that simply a few of the people
happening to stand near Jesus were in mind, is contradicted only
by the striking position of ὧδε. Since however only Codex B
offers this reading and this Codex is known to be faulty,[30] it
cannot be called well attested[31] and it must therefore be considered
very doubtful. But if it is nevertheless thought to be authentic, as
being the *lectio difficilior*, this order of words can easily be
explained by the fact 'the participle is often separated from the
word it qualifies'.[32] In any case however Mark 9.1 says that some
of those standing near Jesus are to experience in their lifetime the
entry of the Kingdom of God.[33] This not only confirms again the
expectation of a future Kingdom of God in Jesus' thinking, but
also establishes the fact that this futurity is thought of as restricted.
Yet the absence of an unrestricted promise to all Jesus' contemporaries to experience the Kingdom of God implies that it cannot

[29]Thus Hauck, *Markus*, 106; M. Goguel, 'Eschatologie et apocalyptique
dans le christianisme primitif', *RevHR* 105, 1932, 396; against this C. J.
Cadoux, *Mission*, 291 note 1. Even more wide of the mark is the assertion
of R. Meyer, *Prophet*, 124 that in Mark 9.1 under the impression of his failure
Jesus was expecting the dawning of the Kingdom of God no longer for himself, but only for some of the disciples. And the assumption of A. T. Cadoux,
Theology, 30 is quite untenable that Jesus in Mark 9.1 and 13.30 assumed still
more generations after the appearance of the Kingdom of God, so that its
coming in power would not be 'the final consummation of the kingdom, but
only an important event in its progress'. But then no reasons are given for
this strange exegesis!

[30]See Herm. v. Soden, *Die Schriften des Neuen Testaments in ihrer ältesten
erreichbaren Textgestalt* I, 2, 1907, 906 ff.

[31]That D* also attests this position is a mistake which has been carried from
Tischendorf through von Soden to S. C. E. Legg, *Novum Testamentum
Graece secundum textum Westcotto-Hortianum, Evangelium secundum Marcum*,
1935, ad loc. and Taylor, *Mark*, 384. Actually ὧδε is missing in D altogether,
as Huck-Lietzmann, *Synopse*, ⁹1936 states correctly. For the reading in B
recently Taylor, loc. cit.

[32]Cf. Bl.-Debr. §474, 5c with appendix.

[33]Michaelis, *Verheissung*, 34 ff. suggests as a hypothesis that ὧδε might be
translated 'thus' and οἱ ἑστηκότες be interpreted as 'those who stand' in
contrast with those who fall; then of course it would refer to the last generation before the end and not to that of Jesus. This translation is untenable and
Michaelis describes it as merely possible.

be expected within a very short period. Thereby A. Schweitzer's view that Jesus expected the coming of the Kingdom of God before his death is already proved to be impossible.[34] Yet we shall have to return to this question.

Jesus speaks in the synoptic gospels twice more of the 'coming' of the Kingdom of God, as well as three times of the coming of eschatological 'days'. It is true that these three texts (Luke 17.22; 21.6; 23.29) arouse critical doubts. The eschatological discourse, Luke 17.22–37, which is paralleled in part in Matt. 24.26 ff., is introduced by the saying in 17.22 which occurs in Luke only: ἐλεύσονται ἡμέραι ὅτε ἐπιθυμήσετε μίαν τῶν ἡμερῶν τοῦ υἱοῦ τοῦ ἀνθρώπου ἰδεῖν καὶ οὐκ ὄψεσθε. This saying might have been framed by Luke as an introduction.[35] The clumsy juxtaposition of ἡμέραι and αἱ ἡμέραι τοῦ υἱοῦ τοῦ ἀνθρώπου favours this and so especially does the fact that the plural αἱ ἡμέραι τοῦ υἱοῦ τοῦ ἀνθρώπου is found only in Luke, and in 17.26, in accordance with the parallelism, denotes the time *before* the parousia and in 17.22 the parousia itself, for which in other passages (17.24, 30) the singular ἡμέρα is used. It would therefore be possible that Luke has here adopted the rabbinical technical expression, met with nowhere else in Jesus' mouth, for the 'Days of the Messiah' (which were thought to be limited in time).[36] But these facts are no compelling proof of a secondary origin of the sentence which could therefore also belong to the oldest tradition. In this case the saying presumes that Jesus on the one hand reckoned on the future appearance of the 'days of the Son of Man' and on the other hand expects that his disciples will one day ardently await this appearance for which they long. This must surely mean that Jesus foresees a time when he will have left his disciples without the hoped-for parousia having occurred or become clearly visible.[37] Luke 21.6 (ἐλεύσονται ἡμέραι) is on the contrary doubtless a secondary expansion of Mark 13.2; and Luke 23.29 f. (ἰδοὺ ἔρχονται ἡμέραι ἐν

[34]Michaelis, *Verheissung*, 43; Cullmann, *Retour*, 24, against Schweitzer, *Quest*, 357 ff. (in German *Leben Jesu*, 405 ff.).
[35]Bultmann, *Tradition*, 138. The saying certainly does not betray 'disappointed hopes of the early Church' (against P. Wernle, *Die synoptische Frage*, 1899, 77).
[36]See Strack-Billerbeck IV, 2, 1928, 826 ff.
[37]So correctly C. J. Cadoux, *Mission*, 303; Liechtenhan, *Mission*, 14 f. It is impossible to deny that the hope of the parousia here refers to the future, either by taking this saying to be merely a warning against apocalyptic hope (Sharman, *Son of Man*, 81 ff.) or simply by declaring that it cannot be interpreted with certainty (Glasson, *Advent*, 87).

αἷς ἐροῦσιν . . .) is a prediction of final terrors and its place in the
oldest tradition must remain doubtful.[38]

The two texts which speak of the 'coming' of the Kingdom of
God are all the more important. In Luke 22.18 the first cup-word
at the Last Supper reads: οὐ μὴ πίω ἀπὸ τοῦ νῦν ἀπὸ τοῦ γενήματος
τῆς ἀμπέλου ἕως οὗ ἡ βασιλεία τοῦ θεοῦ ἔλθῃ. This word corresponds in its essentials with the word in Mark 14.25 par. Matt.
26.29 spoken to conclude the action at the meal; οὐ μὴ πίω ἐκ τοῦ
γενήματος τῆς ἀμπέλου ἕως τῆς ἡμέρας ἐκείνης ὅταν αὐτὸ πίνω καινὸν ἐν
τῇ βασιλείᾳ τοῦ θεοῦ. Now there is, as we know, much debate about
the length of Luke's original account and consequently about the
literary nature of its first half (22.15–18). If, contrary to a wide-
spread opinion,[39] the complete passage (Luke 22.15–20) is to be
regarded as the original account of the Last Supper in the gospel,[40]
the question remains how the double account in Luke 22.15–18
and 19, 20 is to be explained. The second half of this account, the
two eucharistic words (22.19, 20), is most closely associated with
the tradition reproduced by Paul (I Cor. 11.24 f.) but equally with
Mark 14.23 f. par. Matt. 26.27 f. as regards the general structure
of the words. The verses Luke 22.19, 20 are therefore a special
third form of the liturgical tradition of the eucharistic words.[41]
The double eschatological passover word (22.15–18) which
corresponds essentially with Mark 14.25 springs either from
another tradition which Luke has accepted or is placed by Luke
himself in front of the traditional liturgical form of the eucharistic words. J. Jeremias[42] has recently tried to show that Luke 22.
15–18 presents 'the original duplication of the eschatological
prospect', although in this case Mark 14.25 is earlier than Luke

---

[38]According to Bultmann, *Tradition*, 37 f., 121 f. this is a Christian prophecy
put into Jesus' mouth; this is not certain, but it is undoubtedly possible;
C. J. Cadoux, *Mission*, 277 on the contrary considers it a genuine prediction of
Jesus about the siege of Jerusalem for which there are no indications.

[39]Cf. the supporters in Jeremias, *Eucharistic Words*, 100 note 1 (in German
75 note 2); in addition J. Behm, *TWNT* III, 731; W. Manson, *Jesus*,
136 f.

[40]Thus recently convincingly Jeremias, *Eucharistic Words*, 87 ff. (in German
67 ff.) (see there 106 note 1 (in German 79 note 4) for further supporters of
this view), in addition G. Schürmann, 'Luke 22, 19b–20 als ursprüngliche
Textüberlieferung', *Biblica* 32, 1951, 364 ff., 522 ff.; K. G. Kuhn, *TLZ* 75,
1950, 404.

[41]See Jeremias, *Eucharistic Words*, 69, 102 f. (in German 56, 77 f.).

[42]*Eucharistic Words*, 115 f., 165 ff. (in German 86 f., 118 ff.); likewise K. G.
Kuhn, 'Über den ursprünglichen Sinn des Abendmahls und sein Verhältnis
zu den Gemeinschaftsmahlen der Sektenschrift', *ETh* 9150/51, 515.

in wording and order. In proof of this he argues that Luke *must* have followed a separate source since he rejects transpositions and parallelism. But firstly it is not unlikely that Luke might have undertaken an insignificant transposition, such as placing the eschatological word first, since we know that he made slight transpositions in 6.17–19 and 8.19–21 as compared with Mark.[43] It is also true that Luke frequently excised Semitic parallelisms,[44] but yet also occasionally created some himself;[45] if he had, as Jeremias supposes, placed 22.15–18 and 22–19, 20 derived from two sources side by side, then he would *actually* have a parallelism which Mark-Matthew do not have. But the assumption that Luke 22.15–18 is an original duplication of the 'eschatological prospect' taken over by Luke is decisively refuted by the fact that, except for the emphasis placed on the Last Supper as a passover meal, there is nothing in Luke 22.15–18 but what is in the saying Mark 14.25; and the formation of this simple saying out of the double saying of Luke would be completely inexplicable. So it is still the most probable assumption that we have in Luke 22.15–18 a reshaping for historical purposes,[46] and therefore it is essentially more probable that Mark 14.25 gives the oldest form of the eschatological eucharistic saying, and that Luke, apart from the mention of the passover, actually says no more than Mark 14.25. But this saying (Mark 14.25), as Jeremias has convincingly proved,[47] is a vow of abstinence: Jesus declares that he will not drink wine any more until he can partake of the messianic meal with his disciples. From this it follows that Jesus expects the coming of the Kingdom of God to be in the near future, and that he feels it to be so near that he can impress its proximity on his disciples by limiting his abstinence to the dawning of the King-

[43]Thus correctly Jeremias, *Eucharistic Words*, 69 (in German 56).

[44]Jeremias, *Eucharistic Words*, 116 note 4 (in German 87 note 2) refers rightly to E. Norden, *Agnostos Theos*, 1913, 357 ff.

[45]See E. Norden, op. cit. 360 alluding to Luke 6.27 f. compared with Matt. 5. 44; Luke 10.8 ff. compared with Matt. 10.13 ff.; Luke 10.16 compared with Matt. 10.40.

[46]See the references in Dibelius, *Tradition*, 210 f. (in German *Formgeschichte*, 211 f.) and also the scholars quoted in Jeremias, *Eucharistic Words*, 116 note 1 (in German 86 note 2), also A. Oepke, *ST* 2, 1948/50, 143 note 3; H. Vogels, 'Mark 14.25 und Parallelen', '*Vom Wort des Lebens,*' *Festschrift f. M. Meinertz* 1951, 95. K. G. Kuhn, op. cit., in note 42, 515, can only raise against this the objection that it is difficult to imagine this process.

[47]Jeremias, *Eucharistic Words*, 165 ff. (in German 118 ff.). For the view that Jesus himself drank of the cup, Vogels (loc. cit. note 46) 96 ff. can only adduce patristic evidence (Taylor, *Mark* 547 asserts: 'the text implies this'!).

dom of God. And it is equally clear that Jesus foresees between his imminent death and this eschatological 'coming' a certain interval of time about the length of which nothing is said in this word.[48] With this the question of an interval in time between Jesus' death and the parousia is posed; it can be carried further only in a later connexion.

There still remains the text from the material peculiar to Luke, Luke 17.20 f.: to the Pharisees' question about the day appointed for the coming of the Kingdom of God Jesus declares: 'The Kingdom of God cometh not μετὰ παρατηρήσεως; neither shall they say, Lo here, or there; for the Kingdom of God is ἐντὸς ὑμῶν.' The lack of connexion with what goes before and after proves that we have here a detached saying in which Luke has probably introduced the traditional words of Jesus with a question as in a Greek *chria*.[49] But Luke may yet have named the questioners correctly. The meaning of ἐντὸς ὑμῶν, the subject of much debate, can be won only from the rejected antitheses οὐ μετὰ παρατηρήσεως and οὐδὲ ἐροῦσιν. ἰδοὺ ὧδε ἢ ἐκεῖ. It is clear what οὐ μετὰ παρατηρήσεως means, for the Hellenistic word παρατήρησις which is not found elsewhere in the Greek Bible designates observation especially of premonitory signs and symptoms. So here a future time for the Kingdom of God which can be more or less definitely determined is clearly rejected. The second negative antecedent sentence aslo speaks of a future happening the entry of which is disputed. 'Lo, here, Lo, there' is an immediate reminder of the warning within the synoptic apocalypse: 'And if then any man shall say unto you Lo, here is the Christ; or Lo, there, believe it not (Mark 13.21 par. Matt. 24.23).' This warning doubtless means that the

[48]That this interval of time is expected to be very short does not follow from Mark 14.25 (against C. J. Cadoux, *Mission*, 327). It is completely errone-ous for Wagenführer, *Kirchenbegriff*, 218 to assert that Jesus' death 'interrupts for a short time the fellowship of God's reign with the disciples embodied in the meal, and that after the completion of his life's work Jesus will dwell again in spirit among the congregation.' The evasion suggested by Glasson, *Advent*, 113 that Jesus expects 'some future reunion with His disciples' or some great development to result from his death is also impossible, and so is the assumption of A. T. Cadoux, *Theology*, 47, who wishes to translate καινόν as 'novel, of a new sort' as the designation of heavenly wine (similarly also Dodd, *Parables*, 56; Michaelis, *Verheissung*, 28 f.). Vogels, op. cit. in note 46, 101 ff., inclines to the eschatological exegesis and then strangely considers that the question cannot be decided!

[49]Cf. Bultmann, *Tradition*, 24 and Dibelius, *Formgeschichte*, 162. The history of the exegesis of Luke 17.20, 21 has been carefully compiled by B. Noack, *Das Gottesreich bei Lukas, Eine Studie zu Lk. 17.20–24* (Symbolae Biblicae Upsalienses 10), 1948, 3 ff.

desire to search for a Messiah (cf. also Matt. 24.26 = Luke 17.23) who is presumably already present somewhere is to be rejected as foolish. In keeping with this Luke 17.21 also declares the uselessness of speculating about the coming of the Kingdom of God at a future time or of seeking for its appearance in some place or other. So the desire to calculate the date of the Kingdom of God and the search for it are rejected in two different forms; for neither the time nor the place of its coming can be recognized if it is thus wrongly sought. Now there can be two alternatives to this wrong search for the expected Kingdom of God; either it is presumed that the Kingdom of God is indeed in the future, but cannot be calculated in advance nor will it appear secretly, or it is presumed that the reason why it cannot be calculated in advance nor sought for some day is that it is already now in existence. The decision between these two alternatives depends fundamentally upon what ἐντὸς ὑμῶν means here. ἐντός does not occur again in Luke, and in the New Testament it appears only in Matt. 23.26 with the unambiguous meaning of 'inside' (τὸ ἐντός τοῦ ποτηρίου); one must therefore seek for possible different meanings in other Greek usage and from this it appears without doubt that ἐντός can mean 'inside, inwards' as well as 'within, amongst'.[50] Consequently the translation of Luke 17.21 can be based only upon the interpretation of the text as a whole. Now the translation 'within you' could only be understood to mean that the Kingdom of God has a quality of inwardness (*Innerlichkeit*).[51] It is not a positive

---

[50] See Liddell and Scott, and Bauer, *Wörterbuch*, s.v. ἐντός. P. M. S. Allen, *ExpT*, 49, 1937/38, 476 f.; 50, 1938/39, 233 ff. and C. H. Roberts. 'The Kingdom of Heaven (Luke 17, 21)', *Harvard Theol. Rev.* 41, 1948, 1 ff. have contested that ἐντός could ever stand for 'amongst'. But this meaning is undoubtedly found in Xenophon, *An.* I, 10, 3 (τᾶλλα ὁπόσα ἐντὸς αὐτῶν καὶ χρήματα καὶ ἄνθρωποι ἐγένοντο πάντα ἔσωσαν) and in Herodotus VII, 100, 3 (ὁ δ' ἐντὸς τῶν πρῳρέων πλέων ἐθηεῖτο καὶ τοῦ αἰγιαλοῦ = 'as he drove between the ships' prows and the shore'), Ps. 87.6 Symmachus (ἐντὸς νεκρῶν ἀφεθείς). And A. Sledd, *ExpT* 50, 1938/39, 235 ff. has rightly remarked that ἐντός with an object *in the plural* often means 'within, amongst' according to the context.

[51] This interpretation assumes the recasting of the saying in the Oxyrhynchus-logion 654, 3 ἡ βασ[. . .] ἐντὸς ὑμῶν [ἐ]στι[ν] . . . [καὶ ὅς ἐὰν . .] γνῷ, ταύτην εὑρή[σ]ει (see for this J. Jeremias, *Unbekannte Jesusworte*, [2]1951, 20 f.) and it is attested by all the Latin translations (*intra vos*) and the Peshitta (*lgw mnkwn*). The translation 'inwardly in you' is also supported by K. Weiss, *Irrtumslosigkeit*, 163; P. Feine, *Theologie des Neuen Testaments*, [5]1931, 79; B. H. Streeter, *The Four Gospels*, [5]1936, 290; M. Nielen, 'Der Mensch in der Verkündigung des Evangeliums' (in *Das Bild des Menschen*, F. Tillmann zum 60. Geburtstag, 1934), 17; Leipoldt, *Jesus*, 120; A. T. Cadoux, *Theology*, 50 f.;

objection to this explanation that the declaration 'the Kingdom of God is in your hearts' does not fit the Pharisees, because it is after all not completely certain that the saying was originally addressed to them. But on the one hand it is noteworthy that the rare ἐντός instead of the frequent ἐν is not likely to have been used by Luke or his tradition without a purpose; and on the other hand it must be observed that to calculate the Kingdom of God in advance or to search for it in the future can hardly be contrasted with 'in you' as a matter of a place, but only as one of time. Therefore the translation 'amongst you' must be preferred.[52] Now this translation can, as we have seen, be interpreted as referring to the present or to the future. If to the future the meaning would be: 'the Kingdom of God does not come in such a way that one can calculate it in advance or search for it, but it will (suddenly) be present amongst you'.[53] The ἐστίν of the Greek text cannot be used as an objection to this meaning, since, as is well known, it is usual in Aramaic for the copula to be missing; but this interpretation makes sense only if an unexpected, sudden future revelation is contrasted with a

---

Curtis, *Teacher*, 120 f.; A. T. Olmstead, *Jesus in the Light of History*, 1942, 171 f.; A. P. Wikgren, Proceedings in *JBL* 67, 1948, xiii; H. Clavier, *L'accès au royaume de Dieu*, 1944, 13 f.; Meinertz, *Theologie*, I, 34 f.—Dodd, *Parables*, 84 note 1 translates 'within you', but explains it very obscurely by saying that the Kingdom of God belongs to the spiritual order, not to time and space. And Liechtenhan, *Mission*, 26 f. understands ἐντὸς ὑμῶν in the sense that 'to belong or not to belong' lies hid 'in the innermost being of men' and will break through into the open unexpectedly at the dawning of the Kingdom of God. But that meaning is undoubtedly intruded into it. The text is dissolved into philosophy even more when it is said to declare that the Kingdom of God is 'in no sense present' either in the future or now (thus E. Fuchs, *Verkünd. u. Forsch.* 1947/48, 1949, 76).

[52]Both the Old Syriac versions already exhibit this translation *byntkwn* and this form of expression is already attested rabbinically in Siphre Num. 5.3 §1 (p. 4, 10 f. Horovitz, p. 12 Kuhn), where the comment on Num 5.3 'in the midst whereof I dwell' reads: 'Beloved are the Israelites, for even when they are unclean, the Shekina dwells among them' (*haḥbibhim b ney yisra'el sh' 'ᵖp shᵉhem tᵉme'im shᵉkhinah beyneyhem*).

[53]Thus, in addition to those named in Kümmel, *Eschatologie*, 12 note 23, also W. Wrede, *Vorträge und Reden*, 1907, 111: D. Völter, *Die Grundfrage des Lebens Jesu*, 1936, 43 f.; T. W. Manson, *Sayings*, 304; C. T. Craig, *The Beginning of Christianity*, 1943, 79. J. Héring, *Le royaume de Dieu et sa venue*, 1937, 42 f., translates similarly: 'for it will be said: "the Kingdom of God is in the midst of you".' But there are no reasons for interpreting Luke 17.21 that the Kingdom of God will be fulfilled 'in the midst of you' 'if you are obedient to the approaching God' (thus Ackermann, *Jesus*, 79).

future coming that is calculated in advance or hidden. But there is nothing in the text of this detached saying to suggest the word 'sudden' which must therefore be rejected as an intrusion. So the interpretation referring to the present alone remains: 'the Kingdom of God will not come according to calculations made in advance, nor will a search have to be made for it; for lo, the Kingdom of God is present in our midst'. This interpretation leaves only the manner of its presence obscure. But since Jesus, as has still to be shown, does not recognize any present development of the Kingdom of God, there remains only the interpretation that the Kingdom of God has already become effective in advance in Jesus and in the present events appearing in connexion with his person.[54] This interpretation of the difficult text stands naturally only as a hypothesis;[55] but if it is correct, we see here for the first time in statements about the 'coming' of the Kingdom of God an eschatological statement of Jesus which speaks not of

---

[54]Thus, in addition to those named in Kümmel, *Eschatologie*, 13 note 24, Rengstorf, *Lukas*, 202; J. Kaftan, *Neutestamentliche Theologie*, 1927, 43; R. A. Hoffmann, *Das Gottesbild Jesu*, 1934, 52 note 1; P. Wernle, *Jesus*, 1916, 288; E. Stauffer, *TWNT* III, 117 note 369; id. *NT Theology*, note 394; Delling, *Zeitverständnis*, 140; Busch, *Eschatologie*, 141; L. Ragaz, *Die Bergpredigt Jesu*, 1945, 26; Rawlinson, *Christ*, 48; C. J. Cadoux, *Mission*, 130; P. M. Bretscher, *Concordia Theological Monthly* 15, 1944, 730 ff. (according to the extract in W. N. Lyons and M. M. Parvis, *New Testament Literature* I, 1948, No. 1621); Walter, *Kommen*, 19 ff.; E. Pfennigsdorf, *Der Menschensohn*, 1948, 47.—Dibelius, *Jesus*, 63 f. (similarly C. W. F. Smith, *Jesus*, 242) would prefer to speak of the signs of the Kingdom and translates: 'for lo, God's reign is to be felt in your midst'.—C. H. Roberts (loc. cit. in note 50) would translate on the basis of two quotations from papyri 'with you, in your possession, if you want it, now' and interprets 'the Kingdom is not something external to man, but a conditional possession'. But H. Riesenfeld and A. Wikgren, *Nuntius Sodalicii Neotestamentici Upsaliensis* 2, 1949, 11 f. and 4, 1950, 27 f. have made it probable that in the two papyri references the ἐντός with the genitive stands elliptically for 'in the house, in the dwelling', so that, if we accept this meaning, Luke 17.21 should be translated 'in your domain'. This would amount essentially to the same sense as the translation 'amongst you', whilst that proposed by Roberts is neither confirmed by authorities, nor could it be inferred with any degree of certainty from the text. And J. G. Griffiths, 'ἐντὸς ὑμῶν (Luke 17.21)', *ExpT* 63, 1951/52, 30 f. has shown that the papyrus quotations cited by Roberts are examples of the local meaning 'on this side of'.

[55]B. Noack, op. cit. in note 49, 39 ff., wishes to prove that Luke by placing 17.20 f. and 17.22 f. together shows that he also understands ἐντός to mean 'amongst'; the happy present in which the Kingdom of God is there amongst the disciples is contrasted with the gloomy future in which this present has once more disappeared. But this supposed contrast between the two sayings does not follow from the text, so that nothing can be gathered from the context for the interpretation of 17.21.

the future, but of the present. It must still be examined whether the facts really demand that Jesus, beside expecting the Kingdom of God to come in the future, connected the future closely also with his earthly presence.

3. WHAT IS SAID ABOUT THE ESCHATOLOGICAL 'DAY'

The examination of the texts with ἐγγύς, ἐγγίζειν and ἔρχεσθαι has already established the fact that Jesus expected the near future to bring in the Kingdom of God. This can be confirmed and defined more precisely by considering a few more terms. Let us first direct our attention to ἡμέρα. That Jesus used this word with a 'futurist'-eschatological meaning is certain on the authority of Mark as well as on that of the Q tradition.[56] The prediction ἀνεκτότερον ἔσται γῇ Σοδόμων καὶ Γομόρρων ἐν ἡμέρᾳ κρίσεως ἢ τῇ πόλει ἐκείνῃ is found in Matt. 10.15 in connexion with Jesus' direction to his disciples about their attitude towards the cities which did not accept their missionary preaching; instead of ἐν ἡμέρᾳ κρίσεως Luke 10.12 has ἐν τῇ ἡμέρᾳ ἐκείνῃ. Matthew with his mention of the day of judgment has preserved the more primitive saying; already in Q (= Luke 10.12) it evidently formed the conclusion of a group of sayings about the attitude of the cities to the missionary preaching of the disciples who were to proclaim that the Kingdom of God was near; further in the parallel saying threatening Chorazin and Bethsaida (Matt. 11.22 = Luke 10.14) ἡμέρα κρίσεως (Matt.) replaces κρίσις (Luke).[57] And finally in Mark 13.32 par.

---

[56] The age of Matt. 7.22 πολλοὶ ἐροῦσίν μοι ἐν ἐκείνῃ τῇ ἡμέρᾳ is doubtful because its continuation shows, in view of Luke 13.26, that it was reshaped by the early Church. Matt. 11.24 γῇ Σοδόμων ἀνεκτότερον ἔσται ἐν ἡμέρᾳ κρίσεως ἢ σοί is lacking in Luke's parallel passage 10.15 and is therefore probably framed as a loose parallel to Matt. 11.22. The age of the texts which speak of the 'coming' of the eschatological 'day' (Luke 17.22; 21.6; 23.29) has already been discussed (page 29). Luke 21.34 προσέχετε ἑαυτοῖς μήποτε βαρηθῶσιν ὑμῶν αἱ καρδίαι ἐν κραιπάλῃ . . . καὶ ἐπιστῇ ἐφ' ὑμᾶς αἰφνίδιος ἡ ἡμέρα ἐκείνη not only shows clear Lucan peculiarities of style (προσέχειν ἑαυτοῖς, ἐφιστάναι), but has also such strong Hellenistic colouring as regards its contents, that the saying cannot be derived from the old tradition (see Bultmann, *Tradition*, 126; Hauck, *Lukas*, 257). The age of the texts from the synoptic apocalypse (Mark 13.17, 19, 20, 24 and par.) which speak of the time before the final eschatological act as 'that day' can only be ascertained in connexion with the discussion of the apocalypse. All these texts must therefore be left out of consideration here.

[57] It is therefore inadmissible from the point of view of method to interpret the appended saying threatening Capernaum, Matt. 11.23 = Luke 10.15: 'Shalt thou be exalted unto heaven? thou shalt go down unto Hades' as a

Matt. 24.36 ἡ ἡμέρα ἐκείνη occurs and there can be no doubt that in this Jesus is alluding to a current prophetic-apocalyptic usage which by 'that day', 'the day of judgment' etc. denotes the final historical event.[58] Jesus also uses this term invariably for the end of time in the future; on that judgment day according to Jesus not only will the universal judgment about men's behaviour take place (Matt. 12.36), but questions will also be asked about men's attitude towards the appearance of Jesus in history (Matt. 10.15 = Luke 10.12 beside Matt. 10.14 = Luke 10.10 f.; Matt. 11.21 f. = Luke 10.13 f.).[59] Consequently the present time, being marked out by Jesus' actions and message, stands out in a *particular* relation to the coming day of judgment. Besides this, that day will un-doubtedly coincide with the entry of the Kingdom of God (Mark 14.25 οὐ μὴ πίω . . . ἕως τῆς ἡμέρας ἐκείνης ὅταν αὐτὸ πίνω καινὸν ἐν τῇ βασιλείᾳ τοῦ θεοῦ); for this promise which predicts Jesus' absence from the common meal of the disciples until the coming of the Kingdom of God surely presumes that this coming will coincide in time with 'that day' and cannot be thought to be far distant.

Furthermore it is clear that this eschatological 'day' stands in an even more real relation to the present than has already been shown, inasmuch as 'that day' is also described as αἱ ἡμέραι τοῦ υἱοῦ τοῦ ἀνθρώπου (Luke 17.26) or ἡ ἡμέρα αὐτοῦ (i.e. of the Son of Man, Luke 17.24). Both these texts are probably originally independent detached sayings[60] which Luke

prediction of the massacre by the attacking Roman legions, and to base on it the view that Matt. 11.22 and 10.15 are also a prophecy of the coming Roman war (against C .J. Cadoux, *Mission*, 268). Matt. 11.23 can hardly refer to 'two possibilities within the historical development' (Michaelis, *Matthäus* II, 128), but must be applied to the day of judgment (thus T. W. Manson, *Sayings* 77). But even if this exegesis did not prove to be correct, Matt. 11.23 could not help us to understand 11.21, 22.

[58] See Volz, *Eschatologie*, 163 f.—Dodd, *Parables*, 81 ff., disputes without proof the realistic quality of the saying of Jesus (against this correctly C. T. Craig, *JBL* 56, 1937, 20 f.).

[59] Glasson, *Advent*, 128 f. maintains that the mention of Sodom in Luke 10.15 forbids the thought of the day of judgment, as Sodom will not be judged again a second time; it is rather a warning to the unbelieving cities of a fate similar to the one that Sodom experienced in the past. But Glasson does not say how in that case he explains Σοδόμοις . . . ἀνεκτότερον ἔσται.

[60] Cf. Bultmann, *Tradition*, 123, 128; he conjectures correctly that the parallel passage, Luke 17.28–30, dealing with the days of Lot which introduces nothing essentially fresh, is a new secondary development. (It is true that Bultmann, *Urchristentum*, 243 note 46 quotes Luke 17.30 also as Jesus' opinion.)

has clearly applied to the parousia by inserting them between 17.22 and 17.30. But that may also have been their original meaning. In Luke 17.23 f. = Matt. 24.26 f. the contrast is drawn between the possibility that men, being wrongly informed, will search somewhere for the Son of Man and his sudden appearance in the future: 'For as the lightning when it lighteneth out of the one part under the heaven shineth unto another, so shall the Son of Man be in his day'; and Luke 17.26 f. = Matt. 24.37–39 compares with the carefree conduct of Noah's contemporaries the carefree behaviour of mankind today who will just as un-expectedly be surprised by ruin: 'As it came to pass in the days of Noah, even so shall it be in the days of the Son of Man'. It follows from the juxtaposition of these two statements that the singular ἡ ἡμέρα τοῦ υἱοῦ τοῦ ἀνθρώπου has the same meaning as the plural αἱ ἡμέραι τοῦ υἱοῦ τοῦ ἀνθρώπου ;[61] and also that the coming day of judgment will be marked by the appearance of the Son of Man who is clearly represented as judge in Luke 17.26 f.[62] Both texts completely correspond in their emphasis on the threatening and incalculable nature of the eschatological day with Jesus' attitude already familiar to us, so that there is no need to doubt their belonging to the oldest tradition.[63] If in these words the relation-

[61]Noack, op. cit. in note 49, 42 f., emphasizes correctly that the plural as well as the singular simply denotes the time of the future appearance of the Son of Man (cf. also Minear, *Kingdom*, 251, note 14).

[62]It is arbitrary to cut out the allusion to the Son of Man, because in Luke 17.24 B D it ἐν τῇ ἡμέρᾳ αὐτοῦ is omitted, because 17.31 could be applied only to a sudden danger, not to the last judgment, and because the whole passage Luke 17.22–37 points to the prediction of the horrors of war (Glasson, *Advent*, 83 ff.; similarly C. J. Cadoux, *Mission*, 274 f., 322 note 2; A. Feuillet, *RB* 56, 1949, 358).

[63]Matthew has in the parallel passages (24.27, 37, 39) ἡ παρουσία τοῦ υἱοῦ τοῦ ἀνθρώπου (but cf. also 24.3 τὸ σημεῖον τῆς σῆς παρουσίας). As this expression, distinctive of primitive Christianity since Paul, occurs in the synoptic gospels only in the passages named, Matthew has without doubt introduced here an idea from the theology of the early Church. This is supported by the fact that we cannot know for certain whether in the Aramaic world of ideas expressed in Jesus' language there was any equivalent to the Greek idea of παρουσία. For apart from two texts probably edited by Christians only two passages are found which may go back to a Semitic origin: *Assumptio Mosis* 12, 12 *usque ad adventum illius*, which probably refers to the arrival of God, and *Apoc. Baruch* 30, 1 'when the time of arrival (*m'tyt'*) of the Messiah shall be fulfilled and he returns in glory'. But we do not know in either case whether the Latin translation or the Greek one, on which the Syriac is based, had not first introduced the *terminus technicus* of *adventus* or παρουσία; and for *Apoc. Bar.* 30, 1 Volz, *Eschatologie*, 43 f. conjectures a Christian interpolation for reasons which deserve consideration. Since it must therefore remain open to question whether a Palestinian-Jewish *terminus technicus* with this meaning

ship of Jesus to the coming Son of Man is not mentioned, that by
no means justifies the assumption that Jesus used them 'just of
the Son of Man and not of himself'.[64] For not only in the passage
about to be discussed (Mark 8.38) did Jesus speak of the coming
Son of Man in a way that points to the relationship of this figure
to himself without clarifying it distinctly; in Matt. 8.20; 11.19 he
also related the 'Son of Man' unmistakably to his person without a
clear definition.[65] Therefore the words in Luke 17.24, 26 agree with
what Jesus expressed elsewhere; for he connects the present with
the expected future in a double sense: the eschatological Day of
Judgment will judge a man according to the attitude he has taken
up towards Jesus in his present guise, and it is the same Jesus,
with whom a man has to establish a relationship in the present,
before whom he will have to justify himself in the future. So this
makes it clear already that the eschatological prediction of Jesus
does not bear a purely speculative-apocalyptic character, but
receives its meaning from the significance of the person of Jesus
which confronts men and which both in the present and the future
is decisive for the fate of mankind.

It is certainly all the more striking that this same Jesus now
emphasizes so strongly that the time fixed for the expected
eschatological 'day' is unknown. We saw this hinted at already in
the saying Luke 17.24 = Matt. 24.27 in which the sudden coming
of the Son of Man is illustrated by the sudden coming of the
lightning. The same is shown in Matt. 25.13; 'Watch therefore,
for ye know not the day nor the hour'. This saying is appended
as an interpretation to the parable of the ten virgins, but it is
formulated in such a general way, that it is uncertain whether it
belonged originally to the parable, especially as the parable

---

in fact existed, it is all the more certain that Matthew introduced a term from
the language of the early Church into the passages quoted (cf. on the question
of the origin of the term παρουσία in primitive Christianity M. Dibelius, *An
die Thessalonicher I, II; An die Philipper*, ³1937, 15; A. Meyer, *Das Rätsel des
Jakobusbriefes*, 1930, 160; Volz, *Eschatologie*, 64; K. Deissner, 'Parusie', *Die
Religion in Geschichte und Gegenwart IV*, ²1930, 979; Glasson, *Advent*, 31, 85 f.).

[64]Thus Bultmann, *Tradition*, 128; similarly M. Dibelius, *Gospel Criticism and
Christology*, 1935, 47 f. According to J. Knox, *Christ the Lord*, 1945, 41 ff. Jesus
had assumed a unique relationship between himself and the coming Son of
Man, but not an identity.

[65]Thus also Wilder, *Eschatology*, 57: 'It appears more likely . . . that he
was content . . . simply to insist upon the direct relation between himself
and the future Son of Man'.

summons not to watchfulness, but to preparedness. The assumption that the saying has been added to the parable only by the
evangelist is therefore very likely; but it does not in the least
follow from this that the saying was shaped altogether by him on
the model of Mark 13.35.[66] Yet since the age of the saying must
remain doubtful, it affords no certainty that it was the opinion of
Jesus that the eschatological date was quite unknown to men;
this would contradict the statement made earlier that the date of
the appearing of the Kingdom of God was expected within the
lifetime of the generation of Jesus' contemporaries. But this
thought is also found in the striking saying of Mark 13.32: 'But
of the day or hour knoweth no one, not even the angels in heaven,
neither the Son, but the Father'. This is a detached saying showing no connexion with what precedes or follows it. Its difficulty in
the first place does not lie in the statement that even Jesus does
not know the time fixed for 'the day', but in the mention of the
'Son' and the 'Father'. This use of the word 'Son' is found in the
synoptic gospels apart from Mark 13.32 only in Matt. 11.27;
besides there is a story about a son in the parable of the wicked
husbandmen (Mark 12.6 and par.). Now the parable (Mark 12.1 ff.
and par.) presents considerable difficulties in other respects also,
and these are to be discussed later (see pages 82 f.); the question
whether Jesus by indicating himself in this way could have
described himself as 'the Son' cannot therefore be answered from
this parable. The saying in Matt. 11.27 par. Luke 10.22 belongs
as regards its meaning and its origin to the most controversial
texts in the gospels;[67] yet only a few problems can be dealt with
here. Since the fundamental work of E. Norden it is widely
accepted that Matt. 11.25–30 forms a tripartite unity, the
separate parts of which must then be explained by the general
tenor of the whole group of passages.[68] The absence of Matt.

[66] Jeremias, *Parables*, 41, 88 (in German 39, 87); Bultmann, *Tradition*, 191;
Klostermann, *Matthäus*, 201.

[67] Besides E. Norden, *Agnostos Theos*, 1913, 277 ff., J. Weiss, *Neutest. Studien
f. G. Heinrici*, 1914, 120 ff. and W. Bousset, *Kyrios Christos*, ²1921, 45 ff.,
recently: J. Schniewind, *TR, NF* 2, 1930, 169 f.; Bultmann, *Tradition*,
171 f.; Dibelius, *Tradition*, 279 ff. (in German *Formgeschichte*, 279 ff.); V. Völter,
Die Grundfrage des Lebens Jesu, 1936, 167 ff.; T. Arvedson, *Das Mysterium
Christi. Eine Studie zu Matt. 11.25–30*, 1937; Grundmann, *Jesus*, 209 ff.; W.
Manson, *Jesus*, 71 ff.; Stonehouse, *Witness*, 212 ff.; H. Schulte, *Der Begriff
der Offenbarung im Neuen Testament*, 1949, 13 ff.; Michaelis, *Matthäus II*, 129 ff.;
J. Bieneck, *Sohn Gottes als Christusbezeichnung der Synoptiker*, 1951, 75 ff.

[68] Cf. e.g. Dibelius, Grundmann, Arvedson, Schulte, Bieneck, loc cit. in
note 67; A. Oepke, *ST* 2, 1948/50, 152 f.

11.28–30 in Luke is in this case explained as an omission by Luke. But since this omission is really inexplicable, the passage in Matt. 11.25–27 appears all the more to be composite.[69] While 11.25, 26 is a prayer of thanksgiving, which shows Jesus in conflict with the intellectual arrogance of the Jewish teachers of his time,[70] the saying about revelation, 11.27, employs the typically Hellenistic thought of mutual recognition: 'all things have been delivered unto me of my Father and no one knoweth the Son save the Father; neither doth any know the Father save the Son, and he to whomsoever the Son willeth to reveal him'.[71] Here the function of the Son as the revealer rests clearly on the fact that the Father recognizes him and that he therefore knows the Father. But that is an idea of Hellenistic mysticism quite foreign to Judaism.[72] An explanation of Matt. 11.27 according to Jewish ideas involves either disputing the fact that the recognition between the Father and the Son is mutual[73] or striking out the sentence 'and no one knoweth the Son save the Father' on dubious grounds of textual criticism.[74] As neither of these alternatives is satisfactory, it must be said that Matt. 11.27 drops out of the tradition of Jesus' sayings for reasons based on the history of religion. And this is confirmed by the realization that for Jesus to speak of the 'Son' is hardly possible, because 'Son of God' was

---

[69]See especially Bultmann and Michaelis, loc. cit. in note 67; Klostermann, *Matthäus*, 101 f.

[70]Grundmann, *Jesus*, 212 f. emphasized this correctly.

[71]Doubtless οὐδεὶς ἔγνω τὸν υἱόν must be read with the early Fathers of the Church since the time of Justin (see Norden, op. cit. in note 67, 75 note 1 and 301); on the other hand only the order τὸν υἱὸν εἰ μὴ ὁ πατήρ and τὸν πατέρα . . . εἰ μὴ ὁ υἱός can be original according to the evidence of nearly all the MSS. against Justin, the Gnostics and a few later Fathers and MSS.; see the evidence in Th. Zahn, *Geschichte des Neutestamentlichen Kanons* I, 2, 1889, 555 f. and *The Liège Diatessaron*, ed. D. Plooij and C. A. Phillips II (= *Verhandelingen der Koninkl. Akad. van wetenschappen te Amsterdam, Afd. Letterkunde*, NR XXIX, 6), 1931, 154. For the saying offers reasons why the Son alone knows the Father and can reveal Him to others; namely because the Father recognizes the Son; the extra-canonical reading rests on a misunderstanding of the text (thus correctly Norden, op. cit., 286 f.; Arvedson, op. cit., 109 ff.; J. Bieneck, op. cit. note 67, 82; probably also H. Schulte, op. eit. in note 67, 15; against J. Weiss, op. cit., 126; Dibelius, op. cit., 280 note 2 [in German 281 note 1] etc.).

[72]References in Norden, op. cit., 287 f. and Bousset, op. cit., 48 ff.

[73]Michaelis, op. cit., 132; Stonehouse, op. cit., 213, note 12; J. Bieneck, op. cit. in note 67, 84.

[74]Grundmann, *Jesus*, 222; also W. Manson, op. cit., 74 assumes 'considerable elaboration, both in form and in substance', but does not define its extent.

not a Jewish title for the Saviour.[75] Therefore if Matt. 11.27
cannot be claimed as part of the oldest Jesus tradition, it is all the
more questionable whether the mention of the 'Son' in Mark
13.32 can be an authentic tradition of a saying of Jesus. In view
of this un-Jewish way of speaking of the Messiah as the 'Son', it
has been conjectured that the text Mark 13.32 arose first in the
early Church, when the delay of the parousia began to make itself
felt.[76] But this conjecture is unlikely because there was no need to
create an even greater difficulty by ascribing to Jesus ignorance
of the final date in order to remove the difficulty of the delay of
the parousia.[77] Since the wording 'the Son' by itself is without
doubt extremely unusual within the framework of Jewish conceptions, it has been conjectured that the end of the saying 'neither
the Son, but the Father' is a Christian addition to an original
saying of Jesus.[78] But then there would be very little reason to
mention the angels in the rest of the saying. So, since it would be
difficult to account for a later origin of the whole saying, the
assumption that its wording has not remained intact, but that its
main thought reproduces a saying from the oldest tradition is still
the most probable.[79] In that case here also Jesus refuses to make
any apocalyptic calculations about the date of the eschatological
consummation awaited in the future.[80] Therefore it can be

[75]See my remarks in *Mélanges M. Gougel* (*Aux sources de la tradition
chrétienne*), 1950, 129 f. (for the literature on this question). J. Bieneck loc. cit.
in note 67, has not contributed anything to elucidate this question. See also
J. Jeremias, *TWNT* V, 680 note 196 and Jeremias, *Parables*, 57 (in
German 56).

[76]Cf. W. Bousset, *Kyrios Christos*, [2]1921, 43 f.; C. Clemen, *Religionsgeschichtliche Erklärung des Neuen Testaments*, [2]1924, 77.

[77]Thus correctly recently Flew, *Church*, 33; E. Lohmeyer, *Das Vaterunser*,
[2]1947, 31; Taylor, *Mark*, 439 places Mark 13.32 rightly in this respect beside
10.40.

[78]Thus Dalman, *Worte Jesu*, 159; Bultmann, *Tradition*, 130 considers the
saying originally without its final enlargement to be actually a Jewish saying.

[79]This is the opinion of Hauck, Lohmeyer, Schniewind, *Markus*, ad loc.,
also V. Taylor, *Jesus and His Sacrifice*, 1937, 34 f.; W. Grundmann, *Die Gottes-
kindschaft in der Geschichte Jesu*, 1937, 160; Flew, *Church*, 33 f.; Michaelis,
Verheissung, 17; Cullmann, *Retour*, 22; Colwell, *Approach*, 92 f.; Duncan,
Jesus, 106; C. J. Cadoux, *Mission*, 33; Glasson, *Advent*, 97; E. Pfennigsdorf,
Der Menschensohn, 1948, 52, 67, etc.

[80]Glasson, *Advent*, 97 f. avoids this by stating that the meaning of the
phrase 'that day and that hour' cannot be ascertained; and Bowman, *Intention*,
61 simply denies that the end of the world is spoken of, 'that day' is said to
refer to the 'day of the Lord' of the Old Testament, at the same time it
remains completely obscure what the concrete meaning of this might be in
Jesus' mouth. A. Feuillet, *RB* 56, 1949, 87 refers 'that day' to the historical

asserted again on the basis of the sayings which speak of the eschatological 'day' that the Kingdom of God is expected as a future reality in Jesus' message and that this is attested with such certainty that there are no possible grounds for denial.

4. THE COMING JUDGMENT

We have already seen when considering the pronouncements about the 'day' that for Jesus the future appearance of the Kingdom of God coincides with the judgment.[81] This fact can be established even more firmly by examining the terms κρίσις and κρίμα and some other texts. Jesus did not only say in quite general language that the judgment will come upon men (Matt. 5.21 f. ἔνοχος ἔσται τῇ κρίσει, Matt. 7.1 f. κριθήσεσθε = Luke 6.37 καταδικασθῆτε, Mark 12.40 par. Luke 20.47 λήμψονται περισσότερον κρίμα, Matt. 23.33 πῶς φύγητε ἀπὸ τῆς κρίσεως τῆς γεέννης).[82] He also clearly expects that this judgment will take place at the appearance of the Son of Man (Luke 17.34 f. about two on one bed (Matt. 24.40 in one field), or at one mill, one shall be taken, the other left).[83] The judgment which will then be held will extend over the whole

---

event of the judgment on Jerusalem which is indeed to take place in this generation, but which lies in the initiative not of Jesus, but of the Father. All these interpretations overlook the fact that Jesus has spoken elsewhere of 'that day' or used similar words, and that Mark 13.32 must also be interpreted in connexion with this usage (thus correctly Taylor, *Mark*, 522).

[81]Cf. for the following Wilder, *Eschatology*, 94 ff. (There are further references to the judgment as an ethical theme, which however it would serve no useful purpose to quote here owing to their ambiguity as regards time.)

[82]According to Glasson, *Advent*, 74 the saying in Matt. 23.33 is transferred from the Baptist's saying in Matt. 3.7 to Jesus; but apart from the address 'offspring of vipers' the wording in the two passages is completely different.

[83]From the literary point of view Luke 17.26–35 is a secondary grouping. But even if, as has already been stressed in note 60, 17.28–30 is presumably a secondary formation, yet there is no need to doubt that ταύτῃ τῇ νυκτί, which is applied in 17.30 by Luke to the day of the appearance of the Son of Man, applied in the original grouping of the logion 17.34 f. also to his appearance; especially since Matt. 24.40 f. shows the same application which therefore no doubt goes back to Q. To apply Luke 17.34 f. to the horrors caused by the invading soldiery (C. F. Cadoux, *Mission*, 274) is therefore arbitrary.—Also Luke 21.36 'Watch ye at every season, making supplication that ye may prevail to escape all these things that shall come to pass, and to stand before the Son of Man' can be applied only to the final judgment by the Son of Man and not to an eternal judgment which takes place during the course of human history (against Duncan, *Jesus*, 175); but it is unlikely that the saying is old, see Hauck, *Lukas*, 257.

of mankind. Consequently it presupposes the general resurrection
of the dead. (Matt. 12.41 f. par. Luke 11.31 f. 'the Ninevites and
the Queen of Sheba shall rise up in the judgment with the men of
this generation and shall condemn them'.) Since Jesus speaks here
of the rising up of 'this generation' also, it is clearly expected that
at least many of Jesus' contemporaries will die before the rising
up and the judgment come.[84] This confirms the fact established
by Mark 9.1 that Jesus expected the coming of the *eschaton* to be at
hand but yet not very near. We must ask how the two conceptions,
of nearness and at the same time of a certain remoteness of the end,
are related to each other. It is not only that the judgment takes
place at the appearance of the Son of Man, but also that it is he
himself, the Son of Man, who holds it, and in this we see afresh
the relationship already observed between the present and the
eschaton. These facts follow with certainty from Mark 8.38: 'For
whosoever shall be ashamed of my words in this generation, the
Son of Man shall be ashamed of him, when he cometh in the
glory of his Father with the holy angels'. This saying is transmitted both in Mark 8.38 par. Luke 9.26[85] and in Q (Matt. 10.32 f.
=Luke 12.8 f.). In both cases the context is clearly secondary, so
that no doubt we have here a detached saying. The version in Q
('Every one, who shall confess me before men, him shall the Son
of Man confess before the angels of God; but he that denieth me
in the presence of men shall be denied in the presence of the
angels of God' Luke 12.8 f.) shows that the saying was originally
a double one. To start with it tells of the confession before men,
then of the denial before men; the comparison of Mark 8.38 with
Luke 12.8 shows in addition that the confession and denial of the
Son of Man corresponded originally with the confession and
denial of Jesus, so that the version in Matt. 10.32 ('who shall

[84]Of course if the wording of Matt. 12.41 f. is taken strictly, it follows that
'the whole generation of contemporaries' will die and rise again (Bultmann's
objection, *TLZ* 72, 1947, 271). But Mark 9.1 does allow a restriction to
the greater part of the contemporary generation (thus correctly Liechtenhan,
Mission, 14). Glasson, *Advent*, 128, appealing to J. Wellhausen, *Das Evangelium Matthaei*, [2]1914, 63 (likewise Michaelis, *Matthäus*, II, 41 f.) wishes to
translate ἀναστήσονται and ἐγερθήσεται merely by 'appearing' to be judged and
denies that there is any mention of a future day of judgment. But this weakening is very unlikely and moreover contradicts the usage of κρίσις in the combination ἡμέρα κρίσεως (see above pages 36 f.).
[85]Matt. 16.27 has only reproduced the second half of the saying in Mark
and has added to it Ps. 62.13; that is doubtless secondary (thus correctly
Glasson, *Advent*, 127 f.).

confess me . . . him will I confess') represents a Christian interpretation.[86] Although therefore the original wording of the saying cannot be reconstructed, yet the meaning is clear: whoever declares himself for or against Jesus by open support or denial, will meet with a corresponding fate when the Son of Man appears in glory with the angels for the judgment. Here therefore is clearly expressed what could only be inferred from Luke 17.24, 26, that a man's attitude to Jesus in the present time is decisive for the sentence he will receive at the final judgment.

Here also the relation between the Son of Man and the Jesus who is speaking is not expressed without ambiguity. But no doubt this is a 'riddle', the solution of which is suggested from the text itself, because the recognition or the denial by the Son of Man as judge is linked in an altogether unusual way to the preceding recognition or denial of the man Jesus.[87] The identification of Jesus with the Son of Man obtrudes itself of course all the more when it is known that Jesus designated himself in veiled language as 'man'. It is true that this fact has again recently been vigorously debated.[88] Some have denied that Jesus ever spoke of himself as

[86]Thus correctly Bultmann, *Tradition*, 177; C. J. Cadoux, *Mission*, 100; Taylor, *Mark*, 383 f. Dodd, *Parables*, 93 ff. eliminates from the Q version the mention of the Son of Man and retains only the acknowledgment 'before my Father in heaven' or 'before the angels of God'; but the elimination of the eschatological meaning of the saying is impossible, because the rendering in Luke 12.9 ('he that denieth me in the presence of men' shall be denied in the presence of the angels of God') is clearly a variant abbreviation of Luke 12.8 ('him shall the Son of Man also confess before the angels of God'). It is equally impossible simply to declare the Q version to be the original one as compared with Mark 8.38 in order to assert that there was originally no mention in the saying of the future coming of the Son of Man (Duncan, *Jesus*, 175; Sharman, *Son of Man*, 12 f.; V. Taylor, *ExpT* 58, 1946/47, 12; Taylor, *Mark*, 384; Liechtenhan, *Mission*, 15; Glasson, *Advent*, 74 f.); for the differentiation between 'I' and 'Son of Man', which leaves the identity of the Son of Man open is doubtless original contrasted with the unambiguous rendering of Matt. 10.32; and the allusion to the parousia in Mark 8.38 does not in fact say anything different from the confession and denial 'before the angels of God'.—The work of G. Bornkamm, 'Das Wort Jesu vom Bekennen', *Monatsschr. f. Pastoraltheologie* 34, 1938, 108 ff. does not help us with this passage.

[87]Cf. Schniewind, *Markus*, 114. E. Lohmeyer, *Gottesknecht und Davidssohn*, Symb. Biblicae Upsalienses 5, 1945, 125 f. emphasizes correctly that Jesus alone may speak of the Son of Man, 'but, because he has full authority to speak, when he speaks, it sounds as if a bond bordering on identity is uniting the speaker, sent in the present, with the judge of the end of time still hidden from all the world'.

[88]See the report of C. C. McCown, 'Jesus, Son of Man, A Survey of Recent Discussion', *Journal of Religion* 28, 1948, 1 ff.

the Son of Man as a term denoting sovereignty,[89] others admit that he did so, but consider that the title is to be understood collectively as the designation of the holy nation of which Jesus is the head.[90] But most particularly has it been denied that Jesus spoke of himself as the coming Son of Man and the judge; instead it has been asserted that when Jesus spoke of the future coming of the Son of Man, the coming of the Kingdom of God was always meant collectively;[91] or an attempt has been made to prove that the statements about the eschatological coming of the Son of Man belong to Jesus' earlier period and might therefore have been intended collectively.[92] But the interpretation of the conception of the Son of Man in the collective sense suffers shipwreck just on the eschatological pronouncements such as Mark 8.38, Luke 17.24 and most particularly on the texts still to be discussed Matt. 10.23; 24.44; 25.31. And that Jesus applied this veiled ascription of sovereignty to himself is shown indubitably by Mark 2.10, 28 and Matt. 8.20; 11.19; and the objections raised against these texts will not hold water.[93] While it is not possible to discuss this difficult question any further here, it may be said that Mark 8.38 shows afresh that the *eschaton* is linked by Jesus to the present in a completely new way: the present is not only, as the present *always* is, the time in which a man decides in advance by

---

[89]Thus, e.g. in different ways W. Grundmann, *Die Gotteskindschaft in der Geschichte Jesu und ihre religionsgeschichtlichen Voraussetzungen*, 1938, 155 ff.; Meyer, *Prophet*, 146; Duncan, *Jesus*, 135 ff.; Curtis, *Teacher*, 135 ff.; Bowman, *Maturity*, 255 ff.; R. Parker, 'The Meaning of "Son of Man",' *JBL* 60, 1941, 151 ff.; J. Y. Campbell, 'The Origin and Meaning of the Term Son of Man', *JTS* 48, 1947, 145 ff.; Ackermann, *Jesus*, 107 f.

[90]T. W. Manson, 'The Son of Man in Daniel, Enoch and the Gospels', *Bulletin of the John Rylands Library* 32, 1949/50, 171 ff.; C. J. Cadoux, *Mission*, 100; V. Taylor, 'The Son of Man Sayings Relating to the Parousia', *ExpT* 58, 1946/47, 12 ff.; Taylor, *Mark*, 384, 386.

[91]H. H. Rowley, *The Relevance of Apocalyptic*, [2]1947, 121; Bowman, *Maturity*, 257.

[92]See V. Taylor, loc. cit. in note 90.

[93]Correctly recently M. Black, 'The "Son of Man" in the Teaching of Jesus', *ExpT* 60, 1948/49, 32 ff.—The assumption frequently accepted that there is in Mark 2.10, 28 a mistaken translation for 'man' (recently e.g. C. J. Cadoux, *Mission*, 75 f., 95 f.; J. Jeremias *TLZ* 74, 1949, 528; Ackermann, *Jesus*, 107) overlooks the fact that Mark 2.10 has no meaning unless the complete authority of the Son of Man *on earth* is to be emphasized, and that Mark 2.28 clearly represents an intensification of 2.27 (see recently Taylor, *Mark* 199 f., 219). Matt. 8.20 makes sense only if Jesus is speaking of his own fate, and Matt. 11.19 is an original comparison between *Jesus* and the Baptist, for the good reason that the early Church never saw the contrast between them as clearly as this.

his actions the sentence to be passed on him at the final judgment, but the presence of Jesus is in itself already an eschatological hour of decision, because in *this* present, the man Jesus has appeared who confronts men with denial or confession; by their actions they determine in advance the sentence of the 'Son of Man' at the final judgment. An eschatological valuation of the present has therefore an essential connexion with Jesus' expectation of the end.[94]

Finally the same fact appears also in the promise to the disciples: 'Verily I say unto you, that ye which have followed me, in the regeneration, when the Son of Man shall take his seat on the throne of his glory, ye also shall sit upon twelve thrones judging the twelve tribes of Israel' (Matt. 19.28 = Luke 22.28, 30). The saying which undoubtedly in this version of Matthew represents the more original form is in its essence a saying of Jesus, a promise to the group of the twelve, which represents Jesus' claim to win the whole nation.[95] According to this the judgment is not only carried out by the Son of Man when he appears, but also the most intimate group of Jesus' disciples is to have a share in it as accusers, witnesses and fellow rulers.[96] So the coming final judgment is again linked with the present and again what obviously matters is the attitude adopted towards the person of Jesus in the

---

[94]F. Büchsel, *Jesus*, 1947, 46 even wishes to discover in the idea of the last judgment the real core of Jesus' proclamation of the Kingdom of God, but this is probably an exaggeration.

[95]See the remarks in Kümmel, *Kirchenbegriff*, 31, 56 and the reservations below on page 92 note 19. V. Taylor, op. cit. in note 90, 12 (likewise Taylor, *Mark*, 622) and Glasson, *Advent*, 142 again prefer the Lucan version in which the mention of the parousia is lacking; and M. Goguel, *RevHR* 123, 1941, 32 f. thinks the saying could not originate with Jesus, because he could not have expressed himself so openly about his coming messianic kingdom to his disciples; according to Sharman, *Son of Man*, 32 it is even impossible that in view of Mark 10.42 ff., 9.33 ff. Jesus promised the Twelve better places than the other disciples. But the saying does not speak of a special reward for the Twelve, but of Jesus' claim on his nation, which appears from their office as judges; and besides, Jesus did not in this saying speak *openly* of his messianic office as judge, since in fact the reference to the 'Son of Man' is ambiguous.

[96]That the judging in this case 'is a function of the office of kingship' is rightly emphasized by Theissing, *Seligkeit*, 55; Stauffer, *NT Theology*, note 637; M. Goguel, op. cit. in note 95, 32 note 3; A. Fridrichsen, *The Apostle and His Message*, 1947, 18 note 12; against this G. Schrenk, *Die Weissagung über Israel im Neuen Testament*, 1951, 17 f. Glasson, *Advent*, 141 ff. interprets Luke 22.30 symbolically to mean the promise of the new Israel and thus arbitrarily removes every eschatological reference. Taylor *Mark*, 622 wants to apply the rule of the king to a kingdom in history 'in the expected community of the Son of Man'.

present, because that will decide the verdict in the final eschato-logical judgment. So not only is the personal confession or denial of Jesus in question, but it is assumed that a group of men has gathered round this Jesus, which derives its significance entirely from its relation to Jesus, and just for that reason receives an eschatological promise. Thus here too the coming final judgment is linked with the present in so far as the present also receives an eschatological stamp through the group of the twelve gathered round Jesus and proclaiming the message of the Kingdom by his commission; for the condition of the coming final judgment by the Son of Man round whom the twelve are to gather is being secretly prepared beforehand in the present. The fact that for Jesus the present is linked in an unusual way with the coming eschatological event, giving the present an eschatological stamp, is clearly attested here also.

Jesus undoubtedly spoke of the judgment in other ways as well. But most of the texts are worded so generally that nothing can be gathered from them about the time or the manner of the expected judgment (cf. Matt. 7.13 f.; 23.15; Matt. 25.30 = Luke 19.27; Mark 3.29; Luke 12.16 ff.). Some have interpreted other sayings of Jesus to his Jewish hearers as predictions of the impending war with Rome and of its terrors as judgment within this world.[97] But the texts quoted for this do not in any way justify this assump-tion; Luke 13.1 ff. (the allusion to the Galileans murdered by Pilate and the men on whom the tower of Siloam fell) threatens a corre-sponding fate, but not a national catastrophe; Luke 13.6 ff. (the parable of the barren fig-tree) speaks only of the judgment to be expected for the impenitent; Luke 12.57 ff. (the exhortation to be quit of the adversary before judicial proceedings begin) is pre-sumably an exhortation to be converted before the judgment day arrives, in any case it contains not the least hint of an impending national catastrophe. On the other hand the question whether Jesus predicted the destruction of the temple as an event within this world or one in the strict sense eschatological must be discussed later in detail, taking into account Mark 13.2; Matt. 23.34 ff. (see below pp. 100 ff.). But it can be stated already here that there can be no question of Jesus having expected a national catastrophe which he deduced from the political situation.

[97]C. J. Cadoux, *Mission*, 266 ff.; Bowman, *Intention*, 61 f.

5. OTHER PRONOUNCEMENTS ABOUT THE FUTURE OF THE KINGDOM OF GOD

The expectation of a future Kingdom of God is confirmed by additional texts.[98] The future eschatological events are to be introduced by the coming of the Son of Man on the clouds of heaven. So Jesus declares in answer to the question of the High Priest about his Messiahship in the trial scene (Mark 14.62) in the words of Dan. 7.13: 'I am, and ye shall see the son of man sitting at the right hand of power, and coming with the clouds of heaven'.

[98] I pass over here the beatitudes (Matt. 5.3 ff. = Luke 6.20 ff.), because their 'futurist'-eschatological meaning does not appear from the wording, but only from their connexion with the rest of Jesus' eschatological pronouncements (correctly also Walter, *Kommen*, 68); the assertion of Wilder, *Eschatology*, 108 f. about Matt. 5.4, 6 (Blessed are the mourners and they that hunger) that they are described as *being already* comforted and filled and that completion only is awaited cannot be justified by the text.—It cannot be stated with certainty whether Jesus employed the well-known Jewish usage in mentioning the pair of opposites 'this age—the coming age' or spoke of 'the end of the age'. In a number of passages these expressions have no doubt been inserted secondarily, as the synoptic parallels show (thus Matt. 12.32; 24.3; Luke 20.35); other passages must be described as late because of their content; Matt. 13.39, 40 is a secondary interpretation of a parable (see below pages 132 f.); Matt. 28.20 is a saying of the risen Lord; Mark 10.30 par. Luke 18.30 is also probably secondary, since the juxtaposition of a hundredfold recompense in this time and of eternal life in the age to come is contrary to Jesus' thought, which does not describe where God's forgiveness will take place (cf. Matt. 6.4, 6, 18; thus Hauck, Klostermann, Lohmeyer, *Markus*, ad loc.; Bultmann, *Urchristentum*, 243; differently R. M. Grant, 'The coming of the Kingdom', *JBL* 67, 1948, 297, but without evidence, and Taylor, *Mark*, 434 f., who wishes to interpret καὶ ἐν τῷ αἰῶνι τῷ ἐρχομένῳ ζωὴν αἰώνιον as an addition and the hundredfold recompense as figurative). C. J. Cadoux, *Mission*, 235, following Clement of Alexandria, wishes to read the text with Wellhausen, *Das Evangelium Marci*, ²1909, 81 f. so that *only* a hundredfold recompense in the beyond is in question; but the text of Clement (copied in H. J. Vogels *Übungsbuch zur Einführung in die Textgeschichte des Neuen Testaments*, 1928, 27) is doubtless corrupt; thus also Taylor, *Mark*, 435. On the other hand Matt. 13.49 οὕτως ἔσται ἐν τῇ συντελείᾳ τοῦ αἰῶνος in the parable of the fish-net could belong to the old tradition, since the parable itself must certainly go back to Jesus; but as συντέλεια τοῦ αἰῶνος is elsewhere found only in texts formulated by Matthew, it is unlikely that Matt. 13.49 reproduces a traditional *wording* (cf. Jeremias, *Parables*, 67 f. [in German 66 f.]). It is therefore very questionable whether the mention of the 'coming age' may be traced back to Jesus himself (against this e.g. Dalman, *Worte Jesu*, 126 ff.; Bultmann, *Urchristentum*, 242 f.; supporting this J. Weiss, *Reich Gottes*, 107 f.; Michaelis, *Täufer*, 55; C. J. Cadoux, *Mission*, 200).—I leave on one side Matt. 5.18 and 16.19 as being undoubtedly late texts which presume a future appearance of the *Eschaton* (on the question of the age of these texts cf. my detailed discussion in *ZNW* 33, 1934, 127 f. and *Kirchenbegriff*, 32 ff.; see also below pages 139 f.).

Nowadays indeed the whole trial scene is generally considered to be a secondary formation by the community, because proceedings by night before the Sanhedrin are repugnant to Jewish law and also because no witnesses of them can be named, since they were not held in public.[99] But there is of course no difficulty in assuming that Christians could obtain enlightenment from some member of the Sanhedrin about the events there which were so decisive for them; and it is also nowhere clearly stated that the hearing reported in Mark 14.53 ff. was a formal legal proceeding, so Goguel's assumption is altogether probable that it was only a meeting of the Sanhedrin at which no verdict was to be pronounced, but merely an expression of opinion in readiness for Pilate.[100] Besides this Lohmeyer has pointed out correctly that Jesus' reply has 'no later analogy', so that it is unlikely that this unfulfilled prediction originated later.[101] It can therefore be said with considerable certainty that according to a good tradition Jesus, in the course of the hearing before the Sanhedrin after his arrest, gave his assent to the question about his Messiahship and illustrated it by pointing to the future coming of the Son of Man in divine glory. Without doubt it follows from this that Jesus expected that his future installation into the full messianic office would be the necessary preliminary to his participation in the coming judgment.[102] This judgment to be executed by the Son of

[99]Thus e.g. H. Lietzmann, 'Der Prozess Jesu', *Sitzungsbericht d. Berliner Akad. Philos.-histor. Klasse* 1931, 315 ff.; Klostermann, *Markus*, 154; Bultmann. *Tradition*, 290 f.; M. Dibelius, 'Das historische Problem der Leidensgeschichte,' *ZNW* 30, 1931, 199 f.; J. Finegan, *Die Überlieferung der Leidens- und Auferstehungsgeschichte*, 1934, 72 f.; F. C. Grant, *The Earliest Gospel*, 1943, 177 f.; M. Buber, *Zwei Glaubensweisen*, 1950, 109 f.; Ackermann, *Jesus*, 113.

[100]M. Goguel, *La vie de Jésus*, 1932, 495; M. Goguel, 'A propos du procès de Jésus', *ZNW* 31, 1932, 298 f. Cf. also Dodd, *Parables*, 91, note 1; Taylor, *Mark*, 565, 570; for other supporters of this view see J. Blinzler, *Der Prozess Jesu*, 1951, 7 f. Blinzler himself in 59 ff. considers Mark 14.53 ff. to be the report of a legal sentence on Jesus, as the law of the Mishna was not at that time in force.

[101]Lohmeyer, *Markus*, 330 f.; similarly W. Manson, *Jesus*, 115; M. Black, *ExpT* 60, 1948/49, 35; J. Blinzler, op. cit. in note 100, 143.

[102]Attempts have been made to evade these facts by interpreting Mark 14. 62 on the authority of the parallels Matt. 26.64 ἀπ' ἄρτι ὄψεσθε and Luke 22.69 ἀπὸ τοῦ νῦν ἔσται . . . καθήμενος to mean that Jesus will be exalted after his death to heavenly glory, so that it is the exaltation, not the parousia, which is in question and that ὄψεσθε means spiritual experience (K. Weiss, *Irrtumslosigkeit*, 174 ff.; Duncan, *Jesus*, 175 f., 181; Stonehouse, *Witness*, 240 f.; A. Feuillet, *RB* 56, 1949, 72; V. Taylor, *ExpT* 58, 1946/47, 13 f.; Walter, *Kommen*, 90 explains it as referring to the present experience of the exaltation

Man is described by its results. The unrighteous will be con-
demned to darkness or the fiery furnace, the effect of which
Matthew pictures with the stereotyped formula 'weeping and
gnashing of teeth', which however is not original in every case
(Matt. 8.12 = Luke 13.28; Matt. 13.42, 50; 22.13; 24.51; 25.30).
Of those deemed righteous it is said on the other hand that they
may take part in the messianic feast (Matt. 8.11; Luke 14.24;
cf. also the 'drinking in the Kingdom of God' Mark 14.25).[103]
Indeed it has actually been supposed that Jesus taught his disciples

---

and the future witnessing of the parousia). Glasson, *Advent*, 63 ff. goes a
step further and postulates with the Sinaitic Syriac version for Mark 14.62
a 'henceforth' and interprets the quotation of Dan. 7.13 used by Jesus as the
coming of the Son of Man to God in accordance with the continuation of the
verse which Jesus did not quote (thus likewise also Bowman, *Maturity*,
248 ff.). But there are no reasons at all on grounds of textual criticism for pre-
ferring the Matthew-Luke wording or for actually introducing their reading
into Mark, and to transfer ὄψεσθε to a spiritual experience is as arbitrary as to
contest that Dan. 7.13 points to an eschatological cosmic event. The interpretation of ἀπ' ἄρτι in Matt. 26.64 as ἀπαρτί = 'certainly' (thus W. Michaelis,
'Exegetisches zur Himmelsfahrtpredigt', *Kirchenblatt f. d. ref. Schweiz* 108,
1952, 115 referring to A. Debrunner, *Conjectanea Neotestamentica* XI, 1947,
48) is unlikely, since Luke 22.69 with his ἀπὸ τοῦ νῦν probably expresses the
same need to make an alteration as Matthew does with ἀπ' ἄρτι.—E. Stauffer,
'Der Stand der neutestamentlichen Forschung', *Theologie und Liturgie*, ed. by
L. Hennig, 1952, 50 f. makes the suggestion that the Amorean Abbahu
offers 'the authentic Jewish contruction of the words used in Jesus'
trial, the official interpretation, which formed the basis of the grounds
for the verdict' when he says: 'If a man says to you: "I am God", he lies; "I
am the Son of Man", he will regret it; "I will ascend into heaven", he speaks
but will not achieve it' (Jer. Ta'an 65b l. 68 ff.). In this controversy the allusion
is said to be not to John 8.28, but to Mark 14.62, and accordingly the
ἐγώ εἰμι in Jesus' answer is not a simple affirmation, especially as Jesus elsewhere adopts a very reserved attitude towards the messianic claim, but Jesus
wished to use, as in Ex. 3.14, 'the highest form of divine self-revelation'. But
from the point of view of method it is not permissible to identify, *'ani'el* of the
Talmud text with *'eh'yeh 'asher 'eh'yeh* of Ex. 3.14 and by this means to find in
the Amorean saying an allusion to Mark 14.62. Although the saying of
Abbahu is probably in fact an attack on the Christian estimation of Jesus
(thus e.g. also Dalman, *Worte Jesu*, 202 f.; R. T. Herford, *Christianity in Talmud
and Midrash*, 1903, 62 f.; A. Meyer, *Handbuch zu den Neutestamentlichen Apok-
ryphen*, ed. by E. Hennecke, 1904, 61 f.), no connexion of any kind with
Mark 14.62 appears probable.

[103]C. J. Cadoux, *Mission*, 243 f., 341 f. (warns against a purely figurative
interpretation). It is entirely arbitrary to deny that Jesus spoke of the messianic feast etc. when referring to Matt. 12.24 f. (thus Sharman, *Son of Man*f
128) or to apply the feast described in Luke 14.21 ff. to the present reality o,
Jesus' ministry (thus Guy, *Last Things*, 47). Liechtenhan, *Mission*, 28 wishes
to find this idea also in Luke 22.29 f. which he claims as an authentic saying
of Jesus. But cf. note 95 against this assumption.

in his model prayer to ask for a share in the eschatological feast;[104] but even if ἐπιούσιος should mean 'for tomorrow', the application to the messianic feast is excluded by the sequence of thought in the prayer as well as by Jewish parallels. But it is very significant that further detailed descriptions of the punishments of the wicked or of the gifts to the righteous are lacking,[105] that on the other hand the reality of obtaining the Kingdom of God is further described by a number of expressions which mark it out as an event of the future. That is certainly true of the phrase 'to enter into the Kingdom of God'. This phrase which occurs frequently[106] is often expressed in the future tense (Mark 10.15, 23; Matt. 5.20). Its future meaning is also assured by the contrast, used as an alternative to it, between εἰσελθεῖν εἰς τὴν ζωήν and ἀπελθεῖν εἰς τὴν γέενναν, which presupposes the last judgment to be a preliminary condition of entering into the Kingdom of God (Mark 9.43 ff.).[107] Now the expression 'to enter into the Kingdom of God' has its rabbinical parallel in the expression 'to reach the coming aeon',[108] but the expression used by Jesus is not found anywhere else in the same form and seems therefore to be typical of Jesus' language. Yet Jesus links his teaching, as Windisch has

[104]This interpretation of ἐπιούσιος = *panem crastinum, id est, panem quem daturus es nobis in regno tuo* has since Jerome again and again found supporters (the latest A. Schweitzer, *The Mysticism of Paul the Apostle*, 1931, 239) (in German *Die Mystik des Apostels Paulus*, 1930, 233 ff.); Jeremias, *Weltvollender*, 88 f.; E. Littmann, 'Torrey's Buch über die Evangelien', *ZNW* 34, 1935, 29; Michaelis, *Matthäus II*, 318 ff.; E. Lohmeyer, *Das Vaterunser*, ²1947, 92 ff. ('in the daily bread, the bread to come').

[105]The description of the eschatological condition of the righteous as 'shining forth as the sun' in Matt. 13.43 cannot be proved to be old, because it belongs to the allegorical explanation of the parable of the tares.

[106]Mark 10.15, 23–25; 9.43–47; Matt. 5.20; 7.21 (19.17) 23.13 (25.46); of these passages Matt. 7.21 and 19.17 appear from the parallels to be formulated by Matthew. Cf. also Matt. 21.31 οἱ τελῶναι καὶ αἱ πόρναι προάγουσιν ὑμᾶς εἰς τὴν βασιλείαν τοῦ θεοῦ.

[107]For the 'futurist' meaning of the phrase 'to enter into the Kingdom of God' cf. Michaelis, *Täufer*, 65 ff.; C. J. Cadoux, *Mission*, 231 f.; Sharman, *Son of Man*, 123 ff. simply declares in opposition to this that these statements do not have a distinct 'futurist' meaning and that the question about the time of the entry is irrelevant in view of the depth of this conception! Bowman, *Maturity*, 76 denies the future meaning of the 'entry into the Kingdom' by appealing in error to the Mishna Ber. 2.2.—That I Thess. 4.16 f. contains a genuine saying of Jesus which promises the martyred disciples that they shall be the first to take part in the resurrection and are to 'meet' the Lord (thus Jeremias, *Unbekannte Jesusworte*, ²1951, 62 ff.) is incredible in view of the fact that the saying not only contains the Pauline phrase ἐν Χριστῷ, but it is also formulated in the name of the Christian Church.

[108]See Dalman, *Worte Jesu* 95; Strack-Billerbeck I, 252 f.

shown,[109] with the conception of the rabbis and apocalyptists, according to which a man must fulfil certain conditions in order to partake of the eschatological glory. This connexion confirms that for Jesus the Kingdom of God is a future event the nature of which can be paraphrased as $\zeta\omega\eta$ without describing the state in greater detail.

So Jesus also speaks, as an exact parallel to the phrase 'to enter into the Kingdom of God', of $\kappa\lambda\eta\rho o\nu o\mu\epsilon\hat{\iota}\nu$ eternal life (Mark 10.17 par. Luke 18.18),[110] and the future sense of this phrase is evident owing to the promise of the judge of the world in Matt. 25.34 to the 'blessed of my father': $\kappa\lambda\eta\rho o\nu o\mu\dot{\eta}\sigma\alpha\tau\epsilon$ $\tau\dot{\eta}\nu$ $\dot{\epsilon}\tau o\iota\mu\alpha\sigma\mu\dot{\epsilon}\nu\eta\nu$ $\dot{\upsilon}\mu\hat{\iota}\nu$ $\beta\alpha\sigma\iota\lambda\epsilon\dot{\iota}\alpha\nu$ $\dot{\alpha}\pi\dot{o}$ $\kappa\alpha\tau\alpha\beta o\lambda\hat{\eta}\varsigma$ $\kappa\dot{o}\sigma\mu o\upsilon$. Finally the future meaning of $\beta\alpha\sigma\iota\lambda\epsilon\dot{\iota}\alpha$ is also confirmed by the promise in Luke 12.32: 'Fear not, little flock, for it is your father's good pleasure to give you the kingdom'.[111] Now it is true that the future character of the $\beta\alpha\sigma\iota\lambda\epsilon\dot{\iota}\alpha$ is not clearly indicated by this wording;[112] and since it is a detached saying inserted here owing to the catchword $\beta\alpha\sigma\iota\lambda\epsilon\dot{\iota}\alpha$ the meaning cannot be ascertained precisely from the context. But the 'futurist'-eschatological meaning of the 'giving' can hardly be doubtful on that account, because the fear of 'the little flock' can only express itself through its not daring to confess Jesus openly. In contrast to this fear which must be overcome, in the texts already discussed (Mark 8.38 and par.; Matt. 10.32 f. and par.) it is promised to him who confesses Jesus before men, that he will be recognized by the Son or Man at his appearance in glory; so there can be no doubt that in Luke 12.32 also 'the little flock' of the present is promised the gift of the $\beta\alpha\sigma\iota\lambda\epsilon\dot{\iota}\alpha$ in the eschatological future. And thereby it is proved afresh that the promise of

[109]H. Windisch, 'Die Sprüche vom Eingehen in das Gottesreich', *ZNW* 27, 1928, 163 ff.

[110]In Matt. 19.29 $\kappa\lambda\eta\rho o\nu o\mu\dot{\eta}\sigma\epsilon\iota$ is used for $\lambda\dot{\alpha}\beta\eta$ in Mark 10.30; Luke 18.30 is secondary; and Luke 10.25 $\tau\dot{\iota}$ $\pi o\iota\dot{\eta}\sigma\alpha\varsigma$ $\zeta\omega\dot{\eta}\nu$ $\alpha\dot{\iota}\dot{\omega}\nu\iota o\nu$ $\kappa\lambda\eta\rho o\nu o\mu\dot{\eta}\sigma\omega$; is a new Lucan version of the introduction to the question concerning the greatest commandment.

[111]Matt. 21.43 'the Kingdom of God shall be taken away from you and shall be given to a nation bringing forth the fruits thereof' is clearly a secondary interpretation of the parable of the husbandmen (cf. Klostermann, *Matthäus*, 173; Dahl, *Volk Gottes*, 150).—It is completely arbitrary to explain Luke 12.32 as a corruption of Matt. 6.34 (Sharman, *Son of Man*, 132) or, as it is a question of *confessing* Jesus, as 'a word of comfort from the risen Lord to the primitive community' (E. Fuchs, *Verkünd. und Forsch.* 1947/48, 77).

[112]Therefore Guy, *Last Things*, 45 and (with hesitation) C. J. Cadoux, *Mission*, 132 f. deduce from this passage a present meaning of the Kingdom of God.

the coming Kingdom of God makes the present appear already decisive as an eschatological present; for the 'little flock' receives the promise because it gathers as believers round Jesus and thereby enters into relation with the promised *eschaton* already in the present. In Jesus' thought the expectation in the future of the Kingdom of God and of the salvation given with it is closely connected with the certainty that the promise has already in some way been fulfilled, although the futurity of the promised gift is not affected.

6. THE PRESSING IMMINENCE OF THE END

Before we can clarify this question further, the meaning of Jesus' message about the future appearing of the Kingdom of God must be elucidated further. We saw at the beginning that Jesus predicted its coming to be near, indeed to be arriving within the lifetime of his generation. Can this statement be confirmed or defined more precisely? That Jesus felt the end to be critically near is seen also in the calls for watchfulness. We are concerned here with a very intricate complex of the tradition from the literary point of view. On the one hand are found general calls for watchfulness (βλέπετε, ἀγρυπνεῖτε, οὐκ οἴδατε γὰρ πότε ὁ καιρός ἐστιν Mark 13.33, 37; 'let your loins be girded and your lamps burning' Luke 12.35); on the other hand the tradition contains in several variations the parable of the absent householder, for whose return the servants are to wait (Mark 13.34–36; Luke 12.36–38; Matt. 24.42, 45–51 = Luke 12.42–46); then there is the parable of the master of the house who would have watched, had he known when the thief was coming, with the application 'be ye ready, for in the hour that ye think not the Son or Man cometh' (Matt. 24.43 f. = Luke 12.39 f.); finally the parable of the ten virgins admonishes: 'watch therefore, for ye know not the day nor the hour' (Matt. 25.1–13). Without going into all the literary problems posed by these texts, the following may yet be said: the first-named general calls to watchfulness are passages of transition about which nothing certain as to their independent traditional origin can be said.[113] The parable of the absent householder is

[113]In Mark 13.33 we meet with the term καιρός which only occurs again as a designation of the eschatological date in Luke 21.8 in a secondary Lucan addition. As the term in the Septuagint renders the most varied ideas of time in the original text (see G. Delling, *TWNT* III, 459 f.) and besides has no specific Aramaic equivalent, it hardly goes back to an old tradition. In

handed down in its essentials in two forms (in Luke 12.36–38 the servants are to be found watching by their lord when he returns from the marriage feast; in Matt. 24.42, 45–51 = Luke 12.42–46 the lord has given the servants definite tasks for the period of his absence and when he returns unexpectedly he will ask about their performance). Both forms are characterized by a strong predominance of metaphorical features which are meant to suggest the application of the picture language to the relationship of the returning Jesus to his disciples. But there is no ground for denying on principle that these allegorizing features were Jesus' own.[114] The undoubted meaning of this imagery is that the disciples must at all times be ready for the arrival of the Lord. Indeed the term ἔρχεσθαι points already, as we have seen, to the expectation of the coming eschatological day, and the 'coming' of the man Jesus who is still living on earth cannot be mentioned at all except with the 'futurist' eschatological expectation in mind. So there is no doubt that these parables are intended to urge preparedness for the day of the appearance of the parousia which may occur at any time and is therefore pressing.[115] The parable of the master of the house who would have watched for the thief, had he known when he was coming (Matt. 24.43 f. = Luke 12.39 f.) cannot be understood in any other way. For the deduction drawn from the imagery with its application by

Luke 12.35 the exhortation 'let your lamps be burning' can be interpreted as an allusion to the parable in Matt. 25.1 ff. (thus in my first edition); but this is by no means necessary and so this saying may belong to the original tradition.

[114]It is not correct that the texts present as a problem the failure of the parousia to appear and thereby are shown to be framed by the Church (thus Bultmann, *Tradition*, 125). Michaelis, *Verheissung*, 5 ff. has proved that the references to the different night-watches in which the lord may come and the reflection of the servant 'my lord tarrieth' belong to the imagery of the parable and are not due to the problem arising out of the delay of the parousia. W. Foerster, *Herr ist Jesus*, 1924, 231 f., 268 ff. has emphasized rightly that the parables under discussion do not speak fortuitously of the coming of the lord, but are proved just by this metaphorical trait to be parables of the parousia, which undoubtedly originated with Jesus himself. Yet in no case should the imagery be turned so far into allegory as to explain the servants to be the apostles under the leadership of Peter. (Thus A. Feuillet, *RB* 56, 1949, 89 and 57, 1950, 66.)

[115]The parables lose all real meaning if the wakefulness for the unexpected coming of the lord is interpreted as readiness for the judgment which is always in process (Duncan, *Jesus*, 181; C. W. F. Smith, *Jesus*, 251 ff.; Glasson, *Advent*, 95) or the coming of the lord as the return of Jesus at the end of the life of each apostle, and the waking and watching as the preservation of the first ardour (A. Feuillet, loc. cit. in note 114).

contrast: 'therefore be ye also ready' is associated unambiguously
with the expectation of the parousia by the reason given in Matt.
24.44b = Luke 12.40b 'for in the hour that ye think not the Son
of Man cometh'; moreover the imagery of the coming of the thief
can hardly admit of any interpretation other than the *coming* of the
Son of Man.[116] Thus this parable also stresses the ignorance of the
date and at the same time the pressing imminence of the expected
eschaton.

The parable in Luke 12.58 f. also probably points in the same
direction. This instruction to be reconciled with one's adversary
before the beginning of legal proceedings, because one might
otherwise be obliged to pay the last mite, is clearly added in Matt.
5.25 f., attracted by a catchword, to the exhortation to be reconciled before offering a gift, and in this position cannot be understood as anything but a prudential maxim. But Luke, by placing
12.57 'Why even yourselves judge ye not what is right?' in front
of it, clearly understood the text as a parabolic exhortation: as one
should be reconciled on the way to the judge even at the last
moment, so one should know that it is a matter of importance to
be ready now at the last moment for the coming judgment. Since
this interpretation yields a meaning free from objection, it corresponds undoubtedly with the original meaning of this text, which
must therefore be understood as a pointer to the necessity of preparedness in view of the pressing imminence of the end.[117]

This applies finally also to the parable of the ten virgins (Matt.
25.1 ff.). The proceedings at a rural wedding assumed here
obviously cannot be interpreted with certainty as to detail,[118] but
there is no doubt that the parable enjoins readiness for an event of
which the time is not known, but is certainly very near. That it is
intended to point to the parousia of the Son of Man appears quite
certainly from the metaphorical words of the bridegroom (= the
judge of the world): 'I know you not' (25.12) and in the
appended exhortation to await the day and the hour. This
explanatory exhortation (25.13) was presumably added by the
evangelist, as it emphasizes wrongly watchfulness instead of pre-

---

[116]Here too all meaning is taken from the imagery if it is given the interpretation that the unexpected character of the Kingdom of God demands
constant readiness (C. W. F. Smith, *Jesus*, 248).

[117]Thus Bultmann, *Tradition*, 101, 185 f.; Klostermann, *Matthäus*, 44 f.;
Hauck, *Lukas*, 177; especially Jeremias, *Parables*, 31 f., 126 f. (in German 28 f.,
129 f.).

[118]Cf. the plausible explanation of Michaelis, *Sämann*, 162 ff. for the details.

paredness.[119] But the parable does not receive an allegorical colour by this addition alone; and it is erroneous to regard it as a summons not to desist from preparedness although the parousia has not yet arrived, which would show the parable, at any rate in the form handed down to us, to have been formulated by the Church.[120] Owing to the allegorical features of the parable (Jesus is the bridegroom, the speech of the bridegroom is that of the world's judge, etc.) others have conjectured that a simpler parabolic story underlies the traditional form, but that this can no longer be reconstructed.[121] Now it is not absolutely necessary to consider the figure of the bridegroom in this parable to be a metaphor and to apply it to Jesus as the messianic bridegroom; but since the messianic age is often described as a wedding feast,[122] the metaphorical meaning of the bridegroom in the parable is very likely.[123] Yet this metaphor no more turns it into 'a formation by the Church completely overgrown with allegory' (Bultmann) than do the metaphorical words of the bridegroom which are paralleled in the metaphorical conclusions of the parables in Mark 4.29;

[119]See above pages 39 f.

[120]Thus Klostermann, *Matthäus*, 199 f.; Bultmann, *Tradition*, 125, 190 f.; G. Bornkamm, 'Die Verzögerung der Parusie,' *In memoriam E. Lohmeyer*, 1951, 120 ff. Also J. Jeremias, *TWNT* IV, 1098 and *Parables*, 41 (in German 39) also considers 25.13 to be a postcript of the evangelist and that the parable originally had no allegorical features.

[121]Thus Jülicher, *Gleichnisreden* II, 456 f.; T. W. Manson, *Sayings*, 243 ff.; similarly J. Wellhausen, *Das Evangelium Matthaei*, ²1914, 121 ff. —According to C. W. F. Smith, *Jesus*, 165 f. the parable ended originally with 25.10 (thus also Sharman, *Son of Man*, 38 f., who wishes to show that the parable thus shortened was even a reshaping of Mark 13.35–37 par. Luke 12.35, 38; 13.25!).

[122]Jeremias, *Weltvollender*, 22 ff.

[123]J. Jeremias, *TWNT* IV, 1094 ff. and *Parables*, 41 f. (in German 39 f.) has disputed that Jesus designated himself allegorically as the messianic bridegroom. But even though Jeremias is probably right in saying that late Judaism does not know the messianic title of 'bridegroom', yet Mark 2.19a 'Can the sons of the bridechamber fast while the bridegroom is with them?' can hardly be weakened so much as to mean only: can the friends of the bridegroom fast during the wedding celebrations? (Bultmann, *Tradition*, 107 note 1; Dodd, *Parables*, 116 note 2; B. T. D. Smith, *Parables*, 95 also interpret it similarly.) For in connexion with the accusation against the disciples that they do not fast, the words about the bridegroom and his friends can only be applied metaphorically to Jesus and the disciples. So the designation 'bridegroom' can hardly be only for Mark 'a name with a messianic sound' (W. Wrede, *Das Messiasgeheimnis in den Evangelien*, ²1913, 19). On the contrary, Jesus is here making an affirmation concerning himself in terms which veil his meaning (thus recently Taylor, *Mark*, 210) and perhaps first grew out of the picture of the messianic marriage feast, and which may therefore very likely be intended as well in Matt. 25.1 ff. See also below pages 75 ff.

Matt. 22.13a; 24.51a = Luke 12.46b; Matt. 25.30a and which are thereby seen to be customary in Jesus' style. On the contrary it is rather a question of a parable urgently directing the hearer by means of its metaphorical features to a correct interpretation: the eschatological coming of the Son of Man is completely incalculable, but is very near, therefore it is important to hold oneself in readiness for it. It follows from this that the problem of the delayed parousia is in no way suggested in the parable, since the trait 'while the bridegroom tarried' (25.5) belongs only to the vivid embellishment of the picture half. It follows equally that the parable by means of its metaphorical features enforces the interpretation to be prepared for the eschatological coming of the Son of Man. It is therefore completely mistaken for Dodd[124] to interpret the parables just discussed (the waiting servants, the faithful and unfaithful servant, the thief in the night and the ten virgins) not as summons to be prepared for the future coming of the Son of Man, but as an exhortation to be on the alert for possible developments in the supreme crisis of history introduced by Jesus' coming. For this interpretation does not only necessarily water down the parables to general truths,[125] but even in Matt. 25.1 ff. pushes to one side those metaphorical passages which demand the interpretation that the parousia is to be expected; thus no explanation is given why in all these parables the 'coming' of the master, the bridegroom, the thief is constantly mentioned. On the contrary it

[124]Dodd, *Parables*, 154 ff. in agreement with J. Jeremias, *TWNT* IV, 1097. Quite similarly for the parable of the ten virgins Glasson, *Advent*, 93; C. W. F. Smith, *Jesus*, 169 ff.—A. Feuillet, *RB* 57, 1950, 71 ff. wishes to refer it to the last judgment at the end of each human life and to identify the bride with the virgins and the Church!

[125]For this purpose Dodd must e.g. in Matt. 24.45 ff. set aside the departure and return of the master as unimportant and interpret the parable as intending to pillory the leaders of the Jews as God's unfaithful servants. In the parable of the waiting servants (Luke 12.35 ff. = Mark 13.33 ff.) the waiting for the return of the master is watered down to the 'idea . . . of alertness and preparedness for any emergency'. The exhortation deduced from the parable of the thief at night to be prepared for a coming event (Matt. 24.43 f.) is directed towards preparedness for the imminent persecution of Jesus and his disciples, the destruction of Jerusalem and the Jewish nation. The parable of the ten virgins also is only intended to give warning against the consequences of not being prepared for the imminent events during Jesus' ministry. Similarly Glasson, *Advent*, 93 wishes to apply the parable of the ten virgins to the blindness of the Jews who do not recognize the crisis in their history, and C. W. F. Smith, *Jesus*, 169 to a situation in which some could see what the occasion demanded and others could not see it! C. J. Cadoux, *Mission*, 313 ff. rightly turns away from these weakening interpretations.

follows also from all these exhortations to be on the alert and to be prepared that Jesus describes the coming of the Son of Man and therewith the entry of the Kingdom of God as possibly very imminent, and in any case pressingly near, although its actual date was completely unknown.

Finally this fact is confirmed by some other detached sayings. To the parable of the widow who importunes the unjust judge (Luke 18. 1–6), by means of an introduction undoubtedly formulated by himself (Luke 18.6 εἶπεν δὲ ὁ κύριος), Luke appends an interpretation which promises that God will listen to the elect who pray without ceasing: λέγω ὑμῖν ὅτι ποιήσει τὴν ἐκδίκησιν αὐτῶν ἐν τάχει (18.8a). The parable appears to emphasize only the efficacy of continuous prayer and therefore many consider that its application, namely that the prayer for justification on the last day will be answered, is a secondary addition to the parable.[126] But this assumption is not in the least necessary.[127] For on the one hand the interpretation 18.6–8a is in no way a re-interpretation, since the parable, as a metaphor, can bear a particular as well as a general application and can scarcely do without one altogether; on the other hand the decision of the judge 'to avenge' the woman is probably a metaphorical feature which is intended to suggest an application to the justification procured by God for the elect. But if there is no necessity to detach 18.6–8a from the original parable, there need also be no hesitation in recognizing the promise that God will avenge ἐν τάχει as original. In that case this text also shows the expectation of the eschatological judgment and the coming of the Kingdom of God after a short delay.

Two further texts indicate that this short delay was understood by Jesus to have a definite limit. In Mark 13.30 par. Matt. 24.34; Luke 21.32 there is appended to the parable of the fig tree, which has already been discussed and which illustrated the proximity of the end, the saying: ἀμὴν λέγω ὑμῖν ὅτι οὐ μὴ παρέλθῃ ἡ γενεὰ αὕτη μέχρις οὗ ταῦτα πάντα γένηται. It appears from the

---

[126]Thus Jülicher, *Gleichnisreden* II, 284 ff.; Bultmann, *Tradition*, 189; B. T. D. Smith, *Parables*, 152 f.; C. J. Cadoux, *Mission*, 303; Glasson, *Advent*, 90 f.; Sharman, *Son of Man*, 64 f. That 18.8b is a secondary addition is probably correct (thus recently Jeremias, *Parables*, 84 (in German 84 f.); Guy, *Last Things*, 37). E. Fuchs, *Verkünd. u. Forsch.* 1947/48, 77 wants to ascribe the whole passage 18.1–8a to the primitive Church.

[127]Cf. Hauck, *Lukas*, 219; W. Michaelis, *Das hochzeitliche Kleid*, 1939, 256 ff.; Liechtenhan, *Mission*, 15, 18.—The idea of K. Weiss, *Irrtumslosigkeit* 220 that in Luke 18.8a 'speedily' applies to help after the final distress and the prayer during that time is quite impossible!

introduction to the saying and the catchword-link with the next
verse that this is a detached saying fitted on to ταῦτα γινόμενα
13.29 by the catchword ταῦτα γένηται. In this parable the
meaning of ἡ γενεὰ αὕτη and ταῦτα πάντα is much debated.
In the context of Mark ταῦτα πάντα designates clearly the whole
of the eschatological happenings including the final parousia
(Mark 13.26); this meaning can in any case be given to the
original detached saying, since πάντα refers most readily to the
eschatological happenings as a whole. Michaelis has indeed
asserted[128] that ταῦτα πάντα refers back to ταῦτα in 13.29 where
ταῦτα indicates events *before* the end; in that case the limited
proximity of the *end* would certainly not be clearly mentioned in
13.30. But this exegesis overlooks the fact that according to Mark
also ταῦτα πάντα need not necessarily take up the ταῦτα in 13.29,
and moreover it is wrong to attempt to derive the exegesis of the
saying from the *immediate* context given by Mark, which the
original independence of the saying does not justify. Finally it
would be a remarkable statement that *definite* events *previous* to the
end will be limited to the period of this γενεά, without making a
pronouncement about the actual moment of the end which alone
is of importance. There can therefore be no doubt that Mark
13.30 is intended to mean: the events leading up to the end will
occur before the period of this γενεά has ended.[129] This is usually
understood without more ado as a prediction that the end will
come during the lifetime of the present generation. But this
natural explanation has been disputed and two other translations

[128]Michaelis, *Verheissung*, 30 ff.—In a letter Michaelis raised the question
whether ταῦτα πάντα could not also be referred back to 13.4 i.e. to the destruction of Jerusalem; but a logion with such a limited meaning could
scarcely have been handed down in isolation, and the destruction of Jerusalem is of course in Jesus' thought also a strictly eschatological event. That
Mark, 13.30 was originally identical with Mark 9.1 and only developed away
from it secondarily is a completely arbitrary assumption (against G. Lindes-
kog, 'Logia-Studien', *ST* 4, 1950/52, 181).

[129]Sharman, *Son of Man*, 98 f., wishes to refer ταῦτα πάντα to 13.5–23, to the
events before the destruction of Jerusalem, K. Weiss, *Irrtumslosigkeit*, 109 ff.
and A. Feuillet, *RB* 56, 1949, 84 to the destruction of Jerusalem, which will
take place during the lifetime of this generation; Walter, *Kommen*, 83 wishes
to interpret it as the destruction of Jerusalem *and* the final judgment, and
Taylor, *Mark*, 521 assumes that ταῦτα πάντα has secondarily 'replaced a
reference to some definite event, probably the destruction of the Temple and
the fall of Jerusalem'. But quite apart from the question whether this would
even catch the meaning of the saying in Mark's context, the detached saying
does not admit of such a limitation (cf. also note 128 and T. W. Manson,
Sayings, 333 f.).

have been proposed. According to one of them γενεά here denotes 'nation', as 'in all other sayings of Jesus in which the expression occurs'; then the saying would mean that the Jewish nation would not perish till the end had come.[130] According to the other translation γενεά here denotes 'the type' and the saying declares that 'this type, namely the perverse and faithless . . . nature of man will continue to the last day'.[131]

But in the other passages in the synoptists where this word occurs it usually indicates distinctly the men of Jesus' generation (Matt. 11.16 = Luke 7.31; Mark 8.12 par. Luke 11.29; especially Matt. 23.36 = Luke 11.51) and also in Matt. 12.39, 45; 16.4 this meaning is by no means excluded. So ἡ γενεὰ αὕτη in Mark 13.30 can hardly be rightly understood otherwise than as referring to 'this generation'.[132] In that case the coming of the end during the lifetime of this generation is predicted unambiguously in Mark 13.30 which signifies, as in Mark 9.1, that at any rate some of the men alive at present will witness the *eschaton* in their lifetime.

Thus Mark 13.30 corroborates what has already been concluded from Mark 9.1; but the meaning of Matt. 10.23 is essentially more difficult to determine. The connexion of the saying is very loose. In the missionary charge to the disciples in 10.17–25 Matthew includes a prediction that they will be persecuted. First 10.17–22 deals with their accusation before councils, and these verses correspond largely with Mark 13.9–13, which section Matthew has left out in chapter 24. To the prediction that the disciples will be hated for Jesus' sake there is attached in 10.23a the instruction preserved only in Matthew: 'But when they persecute you in this city, flee into the next'. According to the context this can only indicate that the disciples must endure persecution in their missionary work, that they should not expose themselves to this danger, but should flee to another city, of course to continue their mission there (cf. Matt. 10.14). Now to this is attached Matt. 10.23b ἀμὴν γὰρ λέγω ὑμῖν, οὐ μὴ τελέσητε τὰς πόλεις τοῦ Ἰσραὴλ ἕως ἔλθῃ ὁ υἱὸς τοῦ ἀνθρώπου. After verse 23a this can only mean: in your flight you will not reach all the cities of Israel before

---

[130]Thus Schniewind, *Markus*, 167; Busch, *Eschatologie*, 133 f.; H. Bietenhard. *Das tausendjährige Reich*, Diss Bern, 1944, 121; Meinertz, *Theologie* I, 61.

[131]Michaelis, *Verheissung*, 30 ff.

[132]Thus also Cullmann, *Hoffnung*, 36 f.; Cullmann, *Retour*, 24; G. Schrenk, *Die Weissagung über Israel im Neuen Testament*, 1951, 65 note 4; M. Albertz, *Die Botschaft des Neuen Testamentes* I, 1, 1947, 79; Walter, *Kommen*, 81.

the Son of Man appears in glory. But τελέσητε can hardly signify 'to come to the end of anything'; it connotes the completion of a task ('to bring to an end, to discharge', cf. Luke 12.50). The saying therefore probably deals with the completion of the missionary task and declares that the disciples cannot fulfil it with regard to their nation before the parousia appears.[133] As 10.23b is by no means smoothly attached to 10.23a, we must ask whether 23a in fact represents the original introduction to 23b, especially since 10.24 f. deals with the relation between master and disciples; according to 10.25b this probably means that the disciple is not to fare better than his master. Since this saying occurs in Luke 6.40 in a quite different connexion in which it is certainly not applied to suffering like the master, it follows that 10.23b was also not originally connected with 10.24 f. These considerations prove, in spite of all objections, that the logion 10.23b is a detached saying which in its essentials fits very well into the missionary charge, but has no firm connexion with its surroundings. Now, as we know, A. Schweitzer[134] interpreted 10.23 in its place in the missionary charge to mean that Jesus 'did not expect his disciples back in this age', and that, as this prediction was not fulfilled because the disciples did after all return to Jesus, 'the non-fulfilment of Matt. 10.23 signifies the first postponement of the parousia'; 'the missionary charge is historical as a whole and down to the smallest detail'. After the return of the disciples Jesus' endeavours are now according to Schweitzer directed to escaping from the people (Mark 6.30 ff.); in his view Jesus wishes to go to Jerusalem at once in order to take upon himself there the remaining final tribulation through his death at the hand of the authorities, and thereby to compel the coming of the Kingdom of God. M. Werner[135] has taken up Schweitzer's exegesis and declares it to be its merit that 'it alone . . . makes it intelligible to us that Jesus on the occasion of sending out his disciples should really have pronounced this discourse essentially as Matthew's gospel records it'. Now it is of course correct that it is possible for Schweitzer to explain Matt. 10.23 strictly within the situation when the discourse sending out the disciples was held as recorded by Matthew. But he makes this possible only by tacitly combining the circumstances of Matt. 10 with those of Mark 6. Thus Matthew does

---

[133]See Michaelis, *Matthäus II*, 94 f.; G. Schrenk, op. cit. in note 132, 14 f.
[134]Schweitzer, *Quest*, 357 ff. (in German *Leben Jesu*, X, 405 ff.).
[135]Werner, *Dogma*, 71 ff.; Werner, *Schweiz. Theol. Umschau* 12, 1942, 49 ff.

indeed presume as the occasion for his missionary charge the dispatch of the disciples on a mission (10.5 ff.), but Schweitzer then transfers the charge at once to the situation described in Mark 6.6 ff., so that now the return of the disciples and Jesus' endeavour to separate himself from the crowd (Mark 6.30 ff.) appear as the sequel in time to the mission, although Matt. 14.13 paralleled in Mark 6.30 in fact omits the return of the disciples. This combination produces therefore an *artificial* connexion between the missionary discourse and the disciples' return; and to this it must be added that nothing in the sources affords grounds for the assertion that Jesus was disappointed that the disciples came back without the end of the world having appeared. Matt. 10.23b must rather be interpreted, contrary to Schweitzer's exegesis, as an isolated logion.[136] Then the meaning of the saying appears clearly to be: the parousia of the Son of Man will arrive before the disciples have finished proclaiming the Kingdom of God in Israel.[137] Thereby the coming of the Kingdom of God is transferred here also to the lifetime of Jesus' disciples, and moreover it is presumed as well that this coming may happen at any time and suddenly within this period. But how is it to be explained in the face of this prediction that the disciples nevertheless return to Jesus (Mark 6.30 par. Luke 9.10, cf. also Luke 10.17)? It is very open to question whether we ought to ask this. For firstly it does indeed seem within the frame of the Marcan account that the return to Jesus of the commissioned disciples was final; but it is by no means certain that the information used by Mark does not presuppose that the disciples, or some of them, set out again to proclaim their message anew. And then Matt. 10.23b in no way assumes that the expectation of an early coming of the Son of Man excludes the return of the disciples to Jesus in the course of their missionary activity. Therefore the information that

---

[136]Werner's demand that the problem of the missionary charge as a whole must be solved if objections are raised to Schweitzer's exegesis (*Umschau*, 51), overlooks completely the literary results of the analysis of the discourse as to the composite character of the tradition recorded there.

[137]The assertion that the saying could not go back to Jesus (Duncan, *Jesus*, 182; Sharman, *Son of Man*, 29; K. Kundsin, *Das Urchristentum im Lichte der Evangeliumforschung*, 1929, 15; Glasson, *Advent*, 103 f.; C. J. Cadoux, *Mission*, 95, 143; T. W. Manson, *Sayings*, 182; probably also Wilder, *Eschatology*, 39 f.; against this V. Taylor, *ExpT* 58, 1946/47, 14), can be proved only by arguing very unconvincingly that the experience of the primitive Church shows itself here or that Jesus made no such temporal predictions.

Jesus sent out disciples on a missionary errand and that these
disciples returned to him again does not in any way contradict the
assumption that Jesus promised his disciples that the Kingdom of
God would come before the *complete* discharge of their missionary
commission. So Matt. 10.23 confirms the conclusion already
obtained that Jesus reckoned on the coming of the Kingdom of
God and of the Son of Man in glory within the lifetime of the
generation of his hearers.[138] This may conclude the discussion of
all the relevant texts which show that Jesus proclaimed the
proximity of the *eschaton* (within a limited time) or at least its
coming *in the future*.[139]

7. THE EXPECTATION OF AN INTERVAL BETWEEN JESUS' DEATH AND THE PAROUSIA

Attempts have been made to evade in various ways what this
exegesis has established. W. Michaelis[140] asserts the meaning of
Matt. 10.23 to be that the disciples are not to hold out under

[138]It is not possible to prove the assertion that for Jesus the coming of the
Son of Man was not identical with the coming of the Kingdom, but only with
the last act of God's royal rule in history (thus Flew, *Church*, 32). Equally
impossible is the assertion that 'the coming of the Son of Man' did not concern the world, but Israel alone, and that the prediction was fulfilled by the
destruction of Jerusalem in the year 70 (thus P. Benoit, *L'évangile selon Saint
Matthieu*, 1950, 74).

[139]J. Jeremias quotes as a further authority for Jesus' imminent expectation
Mark 9.13 par. Matt. 17.12, where the Baptist is designated as Elias who has
already come and in whom the predicted suffering has been fulfilled (*TB*
20, 1941, 216; *TWNT* II, 938). This text is today usually regarded as
a formulation by the Church (cf. Bultmann, *Tradition*, 131 f.; Dibelius,
Tradition, 226 f. (in German *Formgeschichte*, 228 f.); Klostermann and Lohmeyer, *Markus* ad loc.). But at least as regards 9.11, 13 there is no compelling
need for this (see Taylor, *Mark*, 394 f.; that Jesus argues here from an
apocryphal quotation, as 9.13 presumes, does not refute the assumption that
the tradition is primitive, see E. Stauffer, *NT Theology*, note 267). But
neither does the text prove that Jesus also supported the rabbinical dogma
that Elias would come *immediately* before the Messiah, so this text had better
be omitted as an authority for Jesus' imminent expectation (he certainly does
not say that the Messiah and the day of Jahve have already appeared, thus
Guy, *Last Things*, 48).

[140]Michaelis, *Verheissung*, 63 f.; W. Michaelis, *Irreführung der Gemeinde?*,
1942, 18 ff.; 29 ff.; similarly also Schniewind, *Matthäus*, 127 f.—K. Weiss,
Irrtumslosigkeit, 189 applies Matt. 10.23 to the non-conversion of the cities of
Palestine, on account of which the disciples are not to run the risk of martyrdom; the obduracy of Israel will last till the judgment on Jerusalem. This
exegesis can certainly not be reconciled with the wording. Walter, *Kommen*,
97 wishes to discover in the saying only a mysterious hint that the conversion
of the Jews is a lengthy process!

persecution thinking by this means to compel the conversion of Israel, since it will after all only be ended on the Last Day. But M. Werner has correctly emphasized[141] with regard to this that the idea of converting the whole of Israel plays no part in the missionary discourse, and moreover in Matt. 10.23a there is no question at all of a desire to compel it even under persecution; and apart from this the original connexion of 23a and 23b is uncertain. Therefore others have wished to deny that any particular point of time is mentioned in Matt. 10.23;[142] but the wording of 23b is contradicted as much by explaining away the 'coming' of the Son of Man as a *unique* event in time as by reducing this wording to mean a development which cannot be limited in time in the spread of the Christian message. If both these interpretations are without more ado to be considered exegetically untenable, I must next examine in more detail the view supported by various means according to which Jesus associated the coming of the Son of Man and the dawn of the Kingdom of God closely in time with his imminent death. According to A. Schweitzer,[143] when the disciples returned from their missionary journey without the end of the world having appeared, Jesus expected that his return in glory would follow immediately upon his death and resurrection. Similarly W. Michaelis[144] understood as part of the parousia the resurrection which Jesus expected for himself: 'Jesus will just become the Messiah through the resurrection as part of the parousia'. O. Cullmann[145] suggested that Jesus in Matt. 10.23

---

[141]*Schweiz. Theol. Umschau* 12, 1942, 53 f.

[142]Busch, *Eschatologie*, 135 (Matt. 10.23 declares that the Son of Man 'comes without the gathering of the messianic nation, even in a struggle against them through hardship and the cross', wherefore 'even in Matt. 10.23 "when" is not the decisive factor'); Minear, *Kingdom*, 129 ff. (the coming of the Son of Man is not on one and the same day for all men, but the disciples will receive the reward for their sufferings and their missionary work in due season; 'the coming of the Son of Man signals the completion of the task of the Church, and the task of the members of that body', 133). Meinertz, *Theologie I*, 63 ('the Son of Man comes even amidst persecutions and sufferings; i.e. the messianic reign makes its way openly. This does not depend on the completion of the missionary work among the people of Israel; the reign of God is not tied to a particular people').

[143]Schweitzer, *Quest*, 364, 387 note 1 (in German *Leben Jesu*, 414, 433 note 1); A. Schweitzer, *The Mysticism of Paul the Apostle*, 1931, 59 f. (in German *Die Mystik des Apostels Paulus*, 1930, 61). After him Werner, *Dogma*, 75.

[144]Michaelis, *Täufer*, 100 ff. Similarly Dahl, *Volk Gottes*, 166.

[145]Cullmann, *Hoffnung* 37, 40; Cullman, *Retour*, 26. Thus also probably Glasson, *Advent*, 114.—Differently later O. Cullmann, *Christ and Time*, 1951, 149 (in German *Christus und die Zeit*, 1946, 131).

(as well as in Mark 9.1; 13.30) 'pointed to his death and resurrec
tion as the beginning of the Kingdom of God'. According t
J. Jeremias,[146] on the other hand, Jesus thought that the thir
day predicted for the resurrection was at the same time the day o
the coming of the Son of Man, because the resurrection, as wel
as the rebuilding of the temple, was to take place after three days
so that 'Jesus saw the day of the Son of Man and with it the nev
age of God's grace to be extremely near'. E. Lohmeyer[147] als
presumes the immediate connexion in time of the resurrection an
the parousia, when he interprets the promise which associate
Jesus' going before into Galilee with the resurrection (Mar
14.28; 16.7) as 'a transition from the resurrection to the parousia'
And lastly various methods have been used to prove that Jesu
did not think of an interval between his resurrection and th
parousia;[148] that in particular Matt. 10.23 shows that Jesu
expected the parousia to follow directly on his passion,[149] or tha
he anticipated immediately after his death his 'coming' which wa
fulfilled in his resurrection.[150] Similarly C. H. Dodd[151] contest
that Jesus expected a period of time between his resurrection an
parousia since he actually considered that the Kingdom of Go
had dawned and did not look for the parousia in the future at all
Finally others have thought the coming of the Son of Man in
collective sense to be equated with the dawn of the Kingdom o
God, and have therefore interpreted the beginning of the Churcl
as the coming of the Son of Man and the dawn of the Kingdom o
God.[152] Now it has already been pointed out that it is impossible
to interpret the title of the Son of Man in a collective sense and
that Matt. 10.23 in particular supports this opinion.[153] Besides,
Matt. 10.23 in no way suggests a connexion with the passion and

[146]*TB* 20, 1941, 219 f. Similarly C. J. Cadoux, *Mission*, 293 ff.; Barrett.
Spirit. 155, 160.

[147]E. Lohmeyer, *Galiläa und Jerusalem*, 1936, 10 ff.

[148]Thus also R. Bultmann, *TLZ* 73, 1948, 663; E. Fuchs, 'Warum for-
dert der Glaube von uns ein Selbstverständnis?', *ZTK* 48, 1951, 346.

[149]H. W. Bartsch, 'Parusieerwartung und Osterbotschaft', *EvT* 1947,
120.

[150]Stonehouse, *Witness*, 240 ff. points out that in Matt. 10.23; 16.28,
in contrast to Matt. 24.30; 25.31, nothing is said about the coming of
the Son of Man on the clouds of heaven in power; yet Stonehouse wishes
nevertheless to retain the later coming of the Son of Man on the clouds of
heaven.

[151]Dodd, *Parables*, 51 ff., 81 ff., 97 ff.

[152]Bowman, *Maturity*, 254 f.; V. Taylor, *ExpT* 58, 1946/47, 13 f.

[153]See above page 46.

death of Jesus, and that it describes the same event as Matt. 16.28 (the Matthaean recasting of Mark 9.1) and as Matt. 24.30 also cannot be doubted. To distinguish between a 'coming' of the Son of Man at the resurrection and a later 'coming' on the clouds of heaven is therefore completely impossible. Consequently Matt. 10.23 does not in any way point to a connexion in time between the resurrection and the parousia, and the other references quoted in support are equally unconvincing. The resurrection and the parousia are said to be associated in Mark 9.9 par. Matt. 17.9 compared with Matt. 16.20, because Jesus' Messiahship is disclosed at the resurrection and then there is no longer any need to keep silence about his messianic office.[154] But Mark 9.9 is undoubtedly an ending formulated by the evangelist and not part of the old tradition, and Matt. 16.20 is an elucidation (probably essentially correct) of Mark's charge in 8.30 to be silent, attached to the pericope of the messianic confession; so nothing can be learned from these texts about Jesus' own point of view. In the saying before the high priest, Mark 14.62 'ye shall see the Son of Man sitting at the right hand of power and coming with the clouds of heaven', resurrection and parousia are considered to be very closely connected and imminent,[155] but mistakenly, because Mark 14.62 gives no indication at all of the time when the Son of Man will be seen and makes no mention whatever of the resurrection. Similarly no conclusion can be drawn from the fact that Jesus' resurrection, just like the rebuilding of the temple, is to take place 'in three days', wherefore 'originally the third day is the day of the Son of Man'.[156] For firstly the prediction of the resurrection 'in three days' is to be found only in the three predictions of the passion which in the form handed down to us are undoubtedly formulated by the tradition (Mark 8.31; 9.31; 10.33; in the parallel passages Matthew and Luke have each time 'on the third day' which can hardly denote a material difference).[157] Secondly the time specified 'after three days' or 'within three days' (thus Mark 14.58 par. Matt. 26.61; Mark 15.29 par. Matt. 27.40) is such a very familiar designation of a short period[158] that this

[154]Michaelis, *Täufer*, 102.

[155]J. Jeremias, *TB* 20, 1941, 219 f.

[156]Loc. cit.

[157]Cf. e.g. Dibelius, *Tradition*, 225 f. (in German *Formgeschichte* 227 f.); F. C. Grant, *The Earliest Gospel*, 1943, 179 note 5; C. J. Cadoux, *Mission*, 254.

[158]Cf. M. Goguel, *La foi à la résurrection de Jésus dans le Christianisme primitif*, 1933, 164 f. and C. J. Cadoux, *Mission*, 287.

indication of time in round numbers could easily be used quite independently in different contexts.

Likewise Matt. 12.39 f. (Jesus will give this evil generation only the sign of Jonah; 'for as Jonah was three days and three nights in the belly of the whale, so shall the Son of Man be three days and three nights in the heart of the earth') cannot prove that Jesus designated his death and resurrection as the only great sign that he would give to men.[159] For although this setting of the saying by Matthew is again and again maintained to be the original one,[160] it can hardly be doubted that Matt. 12.40 offers an unnatural parallel between Jonah and Jesus, foreign to Jesus' original saying. It is also completely uncertain whether in Luke 11.30 ('for even as Jonah became a sign unto the Ninevites, so shall also the Son of Man be to this generation') the early Church has not added particulars to the original saying preserved in Mark 8.12.[161] On the other hand it is also unlikely that the shortest wording in Mark 8.12 'There shall no sign be given unto this generation' represents the oldest form of the saying,[162] since the enigmatic addition 'but the sign of Jonah' could hardly have been added only subsequently. So Luke 11.29 = Matt. 12.38 must be the oldest version ('this evil generation seeketh after a sign, and there shall no sign be given to it but the sign of Jonah'). It is hardly possible to discover a certain interpretation of it. If the future tense δοθήσεται implied a future event (Jesus will return like Jonah to proclaim the judgment),[163] there is the objection that the comparison between Jonah as the announcer of the judgment and the Son of Man as the judge is scarcely obvious. The comparison might therefore most readily be understood in this way: as Jonah preached repentance immediately before the judgment, so Jesus preached repentance immediately before the judgment; Jesus, the preacher of judgment, is therefore the sign that will be given to

[159]Cullmann, *Retour*, 26.

[160]Michaelis, *Matthäus II*, 165 f.; Nikolainen, *Auferstehungsglaube*, 49; Barrett, *Spirit*, 90; Schniewind, *Matthäus*, 157; Schlatter, *Matthäus*, 416.

[161]A different view in J. Jeremias, *TWNT* III, 412 f. who takes the original meaning of the saying from Luke 11.30 to be that Jonah by his delivery from death is certified as God's ambassador in the same way as Jesus, so that the resurrection would be the one sign that Jesus will give to his generation.

[162]Thus J. Wellhausen, *Das Evangelium Matthäi*, ²1914, 62; Lohmeyer, *Markus*, 156 note 4; Sharman, *Son of Man*, 14 f.

[163]Thus the first edition, also Bultmann, *Tradition*, 124; Klostermann, *Matthäus*, 111 f.; Hauck, *Lukas*, 158.

this generation.[164] In any case the saying about the sign of Jonah does not prove that Jesus described his resurrection as 'the sign of the Son of Man' and thereby brought it into very close temporal connexion with the parousia.

Moreover it is not part of the clearly attested preaching of Jesus that he spoke of the coming of the Kingdom of God as being ushered in by his death, thereby connecting very closely the resurrection and the parousia.[165] A series of old detached sayings affords sound evidence that Jesus expected his death. In the reply to the request of the sons of Zebedee for places on the right hand and on the left hand of Jesus in his glory (Mark 10.35–40 par. Matt. 20.20–23) Jesus promises both disciples that they shall drink the cup that he must drink and shall undergo the baptism with which he must be baptized. These two metaphors undoubtedly indicate suffering and death;[166] and it is also difficult to deny that this is a real prediction by Jesus, since the Church is able to report the martyrdom of John by a remote tradition only, so that this can hardly be a *vaticinium ex eventu*.[167] Thus here Jesus was clearly prepared for his future suffering and death. And from the request of the disciples as well as from Jesus' refusal of

[164]C. T. Craig, *The Beginning of Christianity*, 1943, 80, 186; Jeremias, *Parables*, 130 note 29 (in German 133 note 5); Minear, *Kingdom*, 156; Meyer, *Prophet*, 122; S. E. Johnson, 'Jesus and First Century Galilee', *In Memoriam E. Lohmeyer*, 1951, 87; Taylor, *Mark*, 361, 363; E. Pfennigsdorf, *Der Menschensohn*, 1948, 51. Similarly also Bowman, *Intention*, 175. It is as unnatural to identify John the Baptist, the preacher of judgment, with the sign that will be given (Colwell, *Approach*, 31; C. H. Kraeling, *John the Baptist*, 1951, 136 f.), as to place Jonah and Jesus side by side as preachers to the Gentiles (C. J. Cadoux, *Mission*, 153).

[165]Cullmann, *Retour*, 26.

[166]It has recently often been affirmed that Jesus spoke in Mark 10.38 and Luke 12.50 of his imminent suffering as a baptism because he understood his own baptism as an anticipation of his death on the cross (O. Cullmann, *Die Tauflehre des Neuen Testaments*, 1948, 13 ff.; W. F. Flemington, *The New Testament Doctrine of Baptism*, 1948, 31 f.; somewhat differently H. W. Bartsch, 'Die Taufe im Neuen Testament', *EvT* 1948/49, 85 ff.). But the exegesis of the account of Jesus' baptism which this presumes is as much open to question as the transference of this exegesis into Mark 10.38; Luke 12.50, where the symbolism of being baptized = dying is simply *presumed* (cf. my exposition in *TR* NF 18, 1950, 37 ff. and Barrett, *Spirit*, 117). This symbolism need certainly not have originated first 'on Hellenistic speech terrain, (against A. Oepke, *TWNT* I, 536).

[167]Cf. recently W. Manson, *Jesus*, 125 f. and Taylor, *Mark*, 441. The age of the text cannot be impugned by pointing to the behaviour of the disciples at the passion (thus M. Goguel, 'Deux notes d'exégèse', *RevHR* 123, 1941, 42), nor may it be deduced from it that the two disciples 'are to share the fate of their master . . . in the crisis which lies immediately before them'

it ('to sit on my right hand or on my left is not mine to give, but it is for them for whom it has been prepared'), it is equally clear that Jesus reckoned with his resurrection and his appearance in glory, although no conclusion can be drawn from this about the relationship in time between the 'sitting on my right hand' and Jesus' death. Similarly Luke 12.50 ('I have a baptism to be baptized with; and how am I straitened till it be accomplished') shows that Jesus looks forward to suffering and death as an inevitable necessity; for the hint that Jesus shrinks from the suffering shows that this saying too can hardly be a *vaticinium ex eventu*.[168]

Whilst this saying does not betray any hope of the resurrection or the parousia, this hope appears clearly in Luke 17.25: 'But first must he suffer many things and be rejected of this generation'. This is no doubt a detached saying which Luke has appended to the saying already discussed about the coming of the Son of Man like lightning (Luke 17.23 f. = Matt. 24.26 f.).[169] Yet the πρῶτον shows that the saying must have stood originally in a pertinent connexion with a promise of the parousia. Now Bultmann[170] has pointed out that in Luke 17.25 suffering-resurrection and the parousia are found combined; further that the synoptists

---

(against Dodd, *Parables*, 59); for the text contains no indication of the time when the disciples are to drink the cup. To interpret Mark 10.35 ff. in a collective sense ('It is plain from Mark 10.35-45 that the inner circle of disciples expected a *corporate* triumph and . . . a corporate tribulation first', thus T.W. Manson, 'The New Testament Basis of the Doctrine of the Church', *Journal of Ecclesiastical History* 1, 1950, 6) is impossible in view of 10.38.

[168]Thus correctly Otto, *The Kingdom of God*, 360 (in German *Reich Gottes*, 311); W. Manson, *Jesus*, 126; M. Buber, *Zwei Glaubensweisen*, 1950, 104 note 1; Glasson, *Advent*, 110 ff.; J. Jeremias, *The Servant of God*, 1957, 102 f. (in German *TWNT* V, 712). That Luke 12.50 is a secondary development of 12.49 is as unconvincing as the attempt to explain 12.49 f. from the Gnostic myth of a saviour (against Bultmann, *Tradition*, 165 f.). If E. Benz, 'Der gekreuzigte Gerechte bei Plato, im Neuen Testament und in der alten Kirche', *Abhandl. d. Akad. d. Wissenschaften und Literatur in Mainz*, Geistes- und sozialwissenschaftliche Klasse 12, 1950, 1044, does not regard Luke 12.50 as a prediction by Jesus of his death, because baptism first acquired its connexion with the death and resurrection of Christ through the theology of the early Church, but as 'a pointer to the impending heavy trial', then this symbolism of 'being baptized' would be very far from lucid.

[169]But it ought not to be concluded from the fact that the saying is appended that it is historically secondary (against Sharman, *Son of Man*, 82 note 11; Duncan, *Jesus*, 141 note 1).

[170]*TB* 20, 1941, 278 f.; Bultmann, *Theology of the New Testament* I, 1952, 30; in German *Theologie des Neuen Testaments*, I, 1948, 30.

record two types of predictions: the Hellenistic ones of suffering, dying and rising again, and the Palestinian ones of the suffering of the Son of Man; that these two types were foreign to each other and that their combination in Luke 17.25 is 'of course secondary'. While it is in fact correct that a promise of the resurrection and of the parousia does not appear elsewhere side by side in the same saying of Jesus, others have wished to see in this a further proof that Jesus considers the resurrection to be one with the parousia.[171] But firstly there is no proof that the predictions of suffering and resurrection must have a Hellenistic source (the idea of the suffering of the Son of Man is not of *Hellenistic*-Jewish origin either and Bultmann offers no proof of this) and therefore there is also no proof that the two types of prediction were of different origin according to the history of religion, and therefore came from sources alien to each other. And besides, Luke 17.25 contains no mention of Jesus' resurrection, though such a mention is characteristic of the later predictions of suffering. It is on the contrary so indefinite that it can scarcely be explained as a *vaticinium ex eventu*.[172] It is therefore an unwarranted deduction that resurrection and parousia *could* not have been named together in the same saying and so there is no valid reason against the assumption that Luke 17.25 is a reliable old tradition. In that case the saying declares that Jesus awaits suffering and rejection from his contemporaries, but that he reckons with appearing in glory *thereafter*. Here therefore not only is suffering, but also an interval between suffering and parousia clearly presumed; therefore the suffering, and the resurrection thought to be connected with it, on the one hand and the parousia on the other are not placed side by side in point of time. Finally Luke 13.31–33 also shows that the passion and the resurrection are expected. Now it may only be a conjecture that vv. 32 and 33 consist of two parallel sayings, of which the second did not originally belong here,[173] yet the first

[171]J. Jeremias, *TB* 20, 1941, 220; C. J. Cadoux, *Mission*, 293 f.; Duncan, *Jesus*, 140 f.; according to Taylor, *Mark*, 116 f. both statements came out of Jesus' mouth, but the prediction of the parousia was 'less explicit and apocalyptic than 8.38 and 13.26 would suggest'.

[172]Thus correctly M. Goguel, *La vie de Jésus*, 1932, 188, 373 f.; Otto, *The Kingdom of God*, 361 (in German *Reich Gottes*, 312); M. Black, 'The "Son of Man" in the Teaching of Jesus', *ExpT* 60, 1948/49, 35.

[173]Thus conjecturally Bultmann, *Tradition*, 35 and Hauck, *Lukas*, 186. M. Goguel, op. cit. in note 172, 333 f. has pointed out correctly that the role of the Pharisees here contradicts so strongly the traditional picture of them in the Gospels that their mention could hardly be invented; but that Luke simply

saying with its contrast between Jesus' activity today and to-morrow and his being perfected on the third day shows that Jesus expected a violent end to his work. The appended saying 13.33 shows likewise that Jesus foresaw this to happen in Jerusalem. When he spoke at the same time of his imminent parousia, he certainly looked forward to be awakened from the death which would soon come upon him.[174] Therefore there can be no serious doubt that Jesus reckoned with a violent death to be followed by his resurrection, although we cannot of course know whether he entertained this expectation from the beginning of his ministry.[175]

If the predictions discussed here of the death and resurrection of Jesus afford therefore no authority for the assumption that Jesus expected his death and resurrection to be followed immediately by the dawn of the Kingdom of God and the parousia, neither can two further proofs brought forward for this assumption confirm this fact. Jesus is said to have been convinced that he must play the part of the Servant of God; and therefore to have fitted his death into the history of salvation and to have looked upon it as the decisive event for the coming of the Kingdom of God.[176] It

---

lets the Pharisees appear as the usual opponents of Jesus (Dibelius, *Tradition*, 163 note 1 (in German *Formgeschichte*, 163 note 1) is hardly probable. M. Black, *An Aramaic Approach to the Gospels and Acts*, 1946, 151 ff. wishes to establish the unity of Luke, 13.31–33 by reconstructing two parallel sets of couplets. This reconstruction is altogether possible, even if not certain, but it does not decide anything with regard to the meaning.

[174]Nikolainen, *Auferstehungsglaube*, 45 ff. emphasizes this, though without sufficient critical examination.

[175]C. J. Cadoux, *Mission*, 253 f. draws attention to the fact that of all the references to Jesus' death only Mark 2.20 is placed before the confession at Caesarea Philippi; but this is of course no certain proof that this is historically correct.—E. Schweizer, 'Eine hebraisierende Sonderquelle des Lukas?' *TZ* 6, 1950, 174, 183 would like to establish that Luke 9.44, the Lucan version of Mark's second prediction of the passion, because of its primitive form ('the Son of Man shall be delivered up into the hands of men'), represents a special tradition which goes back to Jesus himself. The reasons for this are that Luke already in 9.22 reproduces completely Mark's more detailed announcement of the passion and that in 24.7, also part of the special tradition, he refers back to 9.44. But quite apart from the assumption that Luke had before him a hebraising special tradition, it must be said that in 24.7 Luke refers back not only to 9.44 but also to 9.22; the short form of 9.44 can be understood just as well to be an intentional omission to avoid repetition as to be an earlier tradition. It is therefore not possible to prove by this road the great age of the primitive form of the announcement of the passion in Luke 9.44. J. Jeremias, *The Servant of God*, 102 (in German *TWNT* V, 712) also bases the great age of 9.44 only on the general way in which it is formulated.

[176]Cullmann, *Retour*, 26.

is true that today many consider it as certain that Jesus lived in the conviction that it was God's will for him to play the part of the Suffering Servant of God of Deutero-Isaiah. This assumption is often underpinned by the conjectural existence of a late-Jewish esoteric doctrine of the Suffering Servant of God and Messiah which Jesus is said to have accepted.[177] But the authorities for this conjecture of a late-Jewish secret doctrine of a suffering Messiah are altogether insufficient.[178] Others have therefore wished to ascribe to Jesus himself the combination of the ideas of the Suffering Servant and the Messiah and have seen in this the real key to Jesus' consciousness of himself.[179] But this thesis is controverted by the facts that no clear allusions at all to Isa. 53 can be found in Jesus' sayings, and that even the conception of the Servant of God does not appear in his mouth.[180] Nor do the eucharistic words constitute a link between Jesus' death and the atoning death of the Servant of God; and Mark 10.45 ('the Son of Man came not to be ministered unto, but to minister, and to give his life a ransom for many'), in which doubtless ideas of Isa. 53 are to be found, stands completely alone and cannot be explained with certainty.[181] That Jesus by taking on himself the role of the

[177]Thus J. Jeremias, 'Erlöser und Erlösung im Spätjudentum und Urchristentum', *Deutsche Theologie* 2, 1929 ,106 ff. and then frequently, recently: *The Servant of God*, 43 ff., 100 ff. (in German *TWNT* V, 676 ff., 710 ff.). For other supporters of this view cf. the bibliography of H. Riesenfeld, *Jésus transfiguré*, 1947, 314 ff., also Riesenfeld, op. cit. 81 ff.; Busch, *Eschatologie*, 90; W. Manson, *Jesus*, 110 ff., 171 ff.; Stauffer, *NT Theology*, 129 f. (in German 111 f.) and note 319; W. D. Davies, *Paul and Rabbinic Judaism*, 1948, 274 ff.

[178]See especially the arguments in H. H. Rowley, 'The Suffering Servant and the Davidic Messiah', *Oudtestamentische Studien* VIII, 1950, 100 ff.; also J. Héring, *La première épître de Saint Paul aux Corinthiens*, 1949, 21; P. Seidelin, 'Der Ebed Jahwe und die Messiasgestalt des Jesajatargum', *ZNW* 35, 1936, 194 ff.; E. Sjöberg, *Der Menschensohn im äthiopischen Henochbuch*, 1946, 116 ff.; O. Cullmann, *Gesù Servo di Dio*, 1948, 4 f.; K.-L. Schmidt, *Le problème du Christianisme primitif*, 1938, 45 f.; G. Wiencke, *Paulus über Jesu Tod*, 1939, 162 ff.; H. W. Wolff, *Jesaja 53 im Urchristentum*, ²1950, 53.

[179]W. L. Knox, *The Acts of the Apostles*, 1948, 72 f.; T. W. Manson, op. cit. in note 167, 1 f.; M. Buber, *Zwei Glaubensweisen*, 1950, 108 f.; C. J. Cadoux, *Mission*, 100 f.; E. G. Selwyn, *The First Epistle of Peter*, 1946, 93; Bowman, *Intention*, 144 ff.; H. H. Rowley, op. cit. in note 178, 133 f.; O. Cullmann, op. cit. in note 178, 5 ff. H. W. Wolff, op. cit. in note 178, 55 ff.; Taylor, *Mark*, 162.

[180]See especially C. T. Craig, 'The Identification of Jesus with the Suffering Servant', *Journal of Rel.* 24, 1944, 241 ff.; also R. Bultmann, TR, NF 9, 1937, 27 ff.; R. Bultmann, *TB* 20, 1941, 279; E. Lohmeyer, *Gottesknecht und Davidssohn*, 1945, 80.

[181]In what is probably the oldest version of the cup word, I Cor. 11.25, there is no reminiscence of Isa, 53; neither has J. Jeremias, 'Das Lösegeld für Viele', *Judaica* 3, 1947, 249 ff. been able to explain as regards Mark 10.45

Servant of God felt his death to be the redemptive event which would bring about the Kingdom of God is therefore unproven.

So there remains only one last argument for the assumption that Jesus thought his resurrection and parousia to be quite close together in time or contemporaneous; the saying to the malefactor: 'Today shalt thou be with me in Paradise' (Luke 23.43) is said to declare that Jesus 'connected his death with the parousia and not with the resurrection as an independent act'.[182] Now there can presumably be no doubt that Luke (23.39–43) was the first to differentiate between the two men crucified with Jesus (as opposed to Mark 15.32 par. Matt. 27.44) and that therefore this whole scene can scarcely rest on an old tradition.[183] But the conception contained in the saying of Luke 23.43, that the pardoned sinner will enter with Jesus immediately after his death into the place of glory,[184] is found in Jesus' thought also in the parable of the rich man and poor Lazarus (Luke 16.22 f.); but it does not mean here, any more than it does in late-Judaism or in Paul (Phil. 1.23 beside 3.20 f.), that the expectation of the final decision at the judgment of the world, in other words at the parousia, has been given up. For it is tacitly assumed that the intermediate state will give place to the final one only at the end of the world, even if a religious difference between the two periods will hardly have been noticed.[185] So even if Jesus, like some of his contemporaries, expected a preliminary parting at the death of the individual, it by no means follows from this that he thought of his death and the resurrection, which followed immediately upon it, as contemporary with the coming of the Son of Man in glory. Thus the fact that Jesus foresaw an interval between his death and resurrection

---

in what respect Jesus could describe his death as 'a ransom for many'; and H.W. Wolff, op. cit. in note 178, 61 f. simply waters λύτρον down to a summing up of the *kerygma* of the substitute in Isa. 53. Wolff's references to Luke 22.37 and Mark 9.12b are untenable for critical reasons.

[182]Michaelis, *Täufer*, 102; C. J. Cadoux, *Mission*, 294 f.

[183]See Hauck, *Lukas*, 284; Klostermann, *Lukas*, 225; Bultmann, *Tradition*, 337.

[184]There is no doubt in view of the parallel Jewish conception that 'paradise' designates the place of blessedness after death to which Jesus also will rise, see Volz, *Eschatologie*, 265; H. Bietenhard, *Die himmlische Welt im Urchristentum und Spätjudentum*, 1951, 171, 185. It is open to question whether the special reward of a martyr was in mind (thus Dibelius, *Tradition*, 203 [in German *Formgeschichte*, 204]) as the penitent thief could hardly, I suppose, be called a 'martyr'.

[185]Cf. Stauffer, *NT Theology* 211 (in German, 190); Nikolainen, *Auferstehungsglaube*, 28 ff.

immediately following it and the parousia expected during the lifetime of some of his contemporaries is in no way rendered doubtful by all the arguments I have discussed.

A number of additional texts confirm the fact that Jesus really reckoned with an interval between his resurrection and the parousia.[186] In Mark 2.18 ff. par. Matt. 9.14 ff.; Luke 5.33 ff. Jesus declares in answer to the reproachful question why his disciples do not fast like those of John: 'Can ye make the sons of the bride-chamber fast while the bridegroom is with them? As long as they have the bridegroom with them they cannot fast. But the days will come, when the bridegroom shall be taken away from them, and then will they fast in that day.' It is clear that here the impossibility of fasting in the present is contrasted with the necessity for the disciples to fast at a later time. This is usually interpreted as a contrast between the lifetime of Jesus and the time after his death; in that case the story declares that Christians must fast when Jesus is parted from them, whilst the disciples could not fast during Jesus' lifetime which is a period of joy. Then the question v. 19a would correspond with Jesus' situation, and v. (19b), 20 would represent an amplification from the point of view of the Church.[187] H. J. Ebeling has objected to this[188] on the ground that the Christian Church knew itself to be living in the period of salvation and therefore could not have added v. 20 to justify their practice of fasting as a sign of mourning which differed from that of Jesus; on the contrary this homogeneous passage 2.19, 20 is intended to declare that the Church cannot fast in the presence of its Master, but that she will fast when he shall have been removed from them at the time of the messianic woes; and since Jesus in Matt. 6.16 ff. recognizes fasting, the whole passage could not have originated with Jesus. But against this exegesis there is nothing to prove that the Church wished to base their present practice of not fasting on the alleged opinion of Jesus that it was only now that

---

[186]See for the following: Flew, *Church*, 30 ff.; Liechtenhan, *Mission*, 13 ff.; C. J. Cadoux, *Mission*, 299 ff.; O. Cullmann, *Peter: Disciple—Apostle—Martyr*, 1953, 200 f. (in German *Petrus, Jünger—Apostel—Märtyrer*, 1952, 224 f.).

[187]Thus recently e.g. Klostermann and Lohmeyer, ad. loc.; Bultmann, *Tradition*, 17 f.; J. Sundwall, 'Die Zusammensetzung des Markusevangeliums', *Acta Academiae Aboensis, Humaniora* IX, 1934, 16 f.; J. Jeremias, *TWNT* IV, 1096, 1098.

[188]H. J. Ebeling, 'Die Fastenfrage (Mark 2.18–22)'. *Theol. Stud. u. Krit.* 108, 1937/38, 387 ff. Branscomb, *Mark*, 53 f. also denies that the whole passage comes down from Jesus, because he did not speak of his death before the end of the Galilean period.

the disciples did not need to fast, but that they would have to do so again in the future. For if it is intended to justify the practice of not fasting, this can hardly be achieved convincingly by the promise of a period of fasting to come. Besides, the interpretation of ἀπαρθῇ ὁ νυμφίος (Mark 2.20) as the absence of the Messiah at the time of the messianic woes is completely arbitrary, as the conception is not found anywhere in late Judaism, still less in primitive Christianity.[189] So there remains no other possibility than to apply the contrast between Mark 2.19a and 2.20 in accordance with the customary exegesis to the time before and after the death of Jesus. Then it would naturally be simplest if one might trace the double saying as a whole back to Jesus;[190] for then it would be certain that Jesus meant ὁ νυμφίος to be himself and was speaking of his approaching death and the time thereafter. But it is most unlikely that Jesus, who gave no other directions for the behaviour of his disciples after his death (apart from the eucharistic saying in Mark 14.25 about to be discussed), should here have authorized in advance a practice of fasting for his disciples differing from that during his presence,[191] especially as the eucharistic saying considers the period of separation of the risen Lord from the disciples also in no way as one of mourning. The record has therefore certainly been amplified at the end by the conceptions of the Church; but it is open to question whether the excision of 2.(19b), 20 would restore the original state of the text which would lack a proper ending.[192] In any case the logion Mark 2.19a

[189] The passages cited by Ebeling from the *Testaments of the 12 Patriarchs*, which he has obviously taken from Strack-Billerbeck IV, 802 do not deal with an eschatological absence of the κύριος or of the πνεῦμα, but with the consequences of sin in the life of the individual! But neither in Mark 13.7 ff. and parallels any more than in II Thess. 2.2 ff. or in Revelation is to be found any indication that Christians will be separated from the exalted Lord before the end in any other way than in the present.

[190] Thus recently e.g. Hauck and Schniewind, *Markus*, ad loc.; A. E. Rawlinson, *Saint Mark*, 1925, ad loc.; Taylor, *Mark*, 210 ff.; A. Schweitzer, *The Mysticism of Paul the Apostle*, 1931, 114 f. (in German *Die Mystik des Apostel Paulus*, 1930, 115 f.); J. Behm, *TWNT* IV, 933; Bowman, *Intention*, 196 ff.; Bowman, *Maturity*, 129 f. (interprets the fasting of the disciples as the mourning of the Church over the removal of Jesus); M. Buber, *Zwei Glaubensweisen*, 1950, 105 (applies ἀπαρθῇ to the 'taking away'); probably also C. J. Cadoux, *Mission*, 190 f.

[191] Cf. J. Wellhausen *Das Evangelium Marci*, ²1909, 18 f.; and it will not do to transfer the predicted fasting of the disciples metaphorically to mourning (against Bowman, loc. cit. in note 190).—Lohmeyer, *Markus*, 59 also points to the further fact that in 2.20 the metaphor of the wedding is given up, as the end of a wedding is not marked by fasting.

[192] Thus rightly Dibelius, *Tradition*, 65 f. (in German *Formgeschichte*, 62 f.).

is old beyond a doubt. It has already been emphasized above that a purely proverbial meaning cannot be ascribed to the saying ('fasting is impossible during a wedding feast').[193] So then the text declares unequivocally that Jesus considers his presence to be a time of salvation in which the disciples' joy makes the custom of mourning impossible. But at the same time the designation of the period 'while the bridegroom is with them' points to an era when this eschatological joy will cease, and that of course cannot mean the parousia. Therefore this saying also refers on the one hand to the present as a time of eschatological completion, which is marked by the presence of the bridegroom, but on the other reckons with a longer or shorter period when Jesus will be separated from his disciples after his death.[194] Yet the resurrection is alluded to no more definitely than the parousia, although both are probably presumed with the word νυμφίος.

The fact that Jesus counted on an interval between his resurrection and the parousia follows also from Mark 14.25. It has already been pointed out that this eucharistic saying presupposes a certain interval between the death of Jesus and the coming of the Kingdom of God. For the prediction that Jesus will drink no more wine until he drinks it new in the Kingdom of God has a meaning in fact only if the Kingdom of God is not expected in the *most immediate* future and if the disciples are to come together for meals for some time without their departed Lord.[195] So the expectation of a considerable interval between resurrection and parousia is evident here, and this can probably be understood also from Mark 14.28. This saying is inserted into the pericope of the prediction of his desertion by the disicples ('However after I am raised up, I will go before you into Galilee'). It is repeated in Mark 16.7 by the angel at the grave with the addition that the disciples will see the risen one ('he goeth before you into Galilee; there shall ye see him, as he said unto you'). It is traditional to interpret this forward-looking saying as a prediction of Jesus' resurrection appearance in Galilee.[196] In this case it would be presumed that

[193]Note 123 on page 57.

[194]C. W. F. Smith, *Jesus*, 246 ff. objects to explaining 2.20 as a prediction of Jesus' death and describes it simply as part of the parable. But against this there is both the word ἀπαρθῇ which cannot describe the customary parting after a wedding festivity, and also the prediction of fasting which does not follow a wedding as a matter of course.

[195]See above pages 31 f. and my remarks in *Kirchenbegriff*, 36, 59 note 119.

[196]Cf. Klostermann and Schniewind, *Markus*, ad. loc.; J. Wellhausen, *Das Evangelium Marci*, ²1909, 119; A. Schlatter, *Markus der Evangelist für die*

there was to be no close connexion in time between the disciples'
experience of the resurrection appearances and the parousia. But
recently it has frequently been asserted that Mark 14.28; 16.7
predicts not resurrection appearances but the parousia in Galilee
in immediate connexion with the resurrection.[197] To support this
it is pointed out that in Mark 14.28 there is no mention of the
disciples seeing Jesus, so that his going to Galilee must have a
significance valid in itself; and that the appearances of a risen
person are so far from being a matter of course that they would
have to be specially mentioned, if they were intended here. And
Lohmeyer emphasizes further that also in Mark 16.7 the ἐκεῖ αὐτὸν
ὄψεσθε could not on the basis of primitive Christian usage indicate
any resurrection appearances, but only the parousia. But the
reference to the usage does not amount here in any way to a proof.
For προάγω occurs in the Synoptists both in the temporal sense of
'arriving earlier' (Matt. 21.31),[198] as well as in the spatial meaning
of 'going before' (Mark 10.32); and ὄψομαι is used by them just as
much for the experience of the parousia (Mark 13.26; 14.62) as for
the sight of the risen Lord (Matt. 28.10). It cannot therefore be
admitted that Mark 16.7 *must* indicate the parousia, and it is an
unwarranted assertion that the addition of the little sentence
ἐκεῖ αὐτὸν ὄψεσθε should turn the prediction in Mark 14.28
προάξω ὑμᾶς εἰς τὴν Γαλιλαίαν from a prediction of the joint experience of the parousia in Galilee into an announcement of the
resurrection experience. For in Mark 14.28 also the προάξω can
without difficulty be understood in a temporal sense and applied
to a renewed meeting of the disciples with Jesus in Galilee, so it
seems more appropriate to use προάξω in its temporal meaning.[199]
To omit in Mark 14.28 the indication that the risen Lord would
be seen in Galilee would be just as easy as to omit that the

Griechen, 1935, 259; E. Hirsch, *Die Auferstehungsgeschichten und der christliche
Glaube*, 1940, 14, 18; J. Finegan, *Die Überlieferung der Leidens- und Auferstehungsgeschichte Jesu*, 1940, 107; Taylor, *Mark*, 549, 608; C. J. Cadoux, *Mission*, 294
(doubts without reasons that 14.28 is historical).

[197] J. Weiss, *Das Urchristentum*, 1917, 12; Hauck, *Markus*, 194; E. Lohmeyer,
Galiläa und Jerusalem, 1936, 10 ff.; W. Michaelis, *Die Erscheinungen des Auferstan-
denen*, 1944, 62 ff.; R. H. Lightfoot, *Locality and Doctrine in the Gospels*, 1938, 63 ff.

[198] According to Jeremias, *Parables*, 101 note 54 (in German 104 note 2),
προάγει here has not a temporal but an exclusive meaning (rather than you),
but there is no authority for this meaning of προάγω.

[199] N. Huffmann, 'Emmaus among the Resurrection Narratives', *JBL*
64, 1945, 211 also draws attention to the fact that προάγω = 'to go before'
suits the risen Lord better than the Son of Man sitting in heaven.

parousia would take place immediately following on the resurrection if προάξω were interpreted with reference to the parousia; for both events were in no way included as a matter of course in the prediction of the resurrection. There is therefore no necessity at all to understand Mark 14.28 as a prediction of the parousia; to refer Mark 16.7 to this verse still remains the most probable interpretation. In that case Mark 16.7 shows not the expectation of a close connexion in time between the resurrection and the parousia, but on the contrary the hope that Jesus will appear after his resurrection to his disciples in Galilee; and this hope has of course a meaning only if such an appearance exhibits the heavenly *life lived* by him who was crucified, while his appearance in heavenly *glory* at the parousia must be considered as yet to come later. So Mark 14.28 confirms Jesus' reckoning on a longer or shorter interval between his resurrection and his parousia.

This fact is corroborated by several texts which become really intelligible only on this assumption. I have already pointed out that Luke 17.22 presupposes a time when Jesus will be separated from the disciples before the coming of the parousia.[200] Luke 18.7, 8a ('and shall not God avenge his elect which cry to him day and night, and he is long-suffering over them? I say unto you that he will avenge them speedily') also expects a time of continuous intercession for deliverance from unjust oppression,[201] and consequently a time when the disciples will be separated from Jesus before the final judgment promised to take place ere long. The texts in which Jesus tells his disciples that they will be persecuted (Luke 6.22 f.; Matt. 10.28, 38; Mark 8.34; 10.35 ff.) allude to the same situation, for they clearly envisage persecutions which will arise not only during Jesus' lifetime. The metaphor of the waiting servants which showed us the threatening proximity of the end can best be understood with the idea in mind of a period of waiting for Jesus after his disappearance from the sight of the disciples.[202] Then the puzzling text Matt. 23.38 f. = Luke 13.35 indicates the same fact. The saying in Matt. 23.37: 'O, Jerusalem, Jerusalem, which killeth the prophets, and stoneth them that are sent unto her, how often would I have gathered thy children together, even as a hen gathereth her chickens under her wings,

---

[200]See above page 29.
[201]Liechtenhan, *Mission*, 15; similarly C. J. Cadoux, *Mission*, 303. For the age of the text see above page 59.
[202]C. J. Cadoux, *Mission*, 311 f. See above pages 54 ff.

and ye would not!' is followed by the conclusion: 'Behold, your
house is left unto you desolate. For I say unto you, Ye shall not
see me henceforth, till ye shall say, Blessed is he that cometh in the
name of the Lord'. This text is today usually looked upon as the
original continuation of the preceding accusation in Matt 23.34–
36 concerning the killing and rejection by the Jews of the prophets
sent by God, although Luke (11.49–51; 13.34 f.) records the two
passages in different contexts. It is noted that the first passage,
Luke 11.49, is introduced by: 'therefore also said the wisdom of
God' and the conclusion is drawn that a Wisdom saying is put
here in Jesus' mouth; for Jesus could certainly not have said that
he had often wished to gather the children of Jerusalem; 'the
subject of this reflexion on history must be a supra-historical one,
namely wisdom'; Matt. 23.39 'ye shall not see me' must also, so it
is said, be understood with reference to the myth of Wisdom,
despised on earth and therefore returning to heaven.[203] But this
theory seems to me very open to question. Firstly there is no
sufficient reason to assume that Matt. 23.34–36 and 23.37–39
originally belonged together, as against Luke, since Luke is
certainly not in other cases given to tearing apart passages belonging together in his sources; besides the second passage is not
really a continuation of the first, but only a related idea added
because of its association.[204] Moreover it is altogether doubtful
whether the introduction of the σοφία τοῦ θεοῦ as a speaker in the
first passage in Luke 11.49 is original; for if in the parallel passage
in Matt. 23.34 Jesus appears as the sender of the prophets, wise
men and scribes (ἐγὼ ἀποστέλλω), this altogether unusual thought
can hardly be secondary, especially as one cannot see why
Matthew should change the σοφία who speaks in Luke into the
σοφοί sent by Jesus.[205] Finally the contents of Matt. 23.37–39 do
not at all oblige the words to be ascribed to a mythical being and
Jesus could very well use of himself the traditional picture of a

---

[203]Bultmann, *Tradition*, 120 f.; similarly Klostermann, *Matthäus*, 190 f.;
Hauck, *Lukas*, 186; A. Merx, *Das Evangelium Matthäus*, 1902, 338 f.; W.
Bousset, *Kyrios Christos*, ²1921, 51 note 3;Dibelius, *Tradition*, 245 (in German
Formgeschichte, 246); Meyer, *Prophet*, 48 f.; Grundmann, *Jesus*, 151. Against this
recently G. Schrenk, *Die Weissagung über Israel im Neuen Testament*, 1951, 66 note 11.
[204]Cf. T. W. Manson, *Sayings*, 102.
[205]Thus rightly E. Meyer, *Ursprung und Anfänge des Christentums* I, 1921,
234 note 2 and Reitzenstein, *ZNW* 26, 1927, 55 note 1.—W. D. Davies,
Paul and Rabbinic Judaism, 1948, 155 seeks in completely arbitrary fashion to
remove Wisdom as the subject of Luke 11.49 by conjecturing 'God in his wisdom said' (similarly C. J. Cadoux, *Mission*, 72 note 4, 192; Glasson, *Advent*, 99).

mother hen; besides there is no authority anywhere for connecting the wisdom myth with the expectation of the coming Messiah (Matt. 23.39). It is therefore extremely probable that in Matt. 23.37–39 we are dealing with an independent saying of Jesus from the oldest tradition,[206] and then there is no necessity for the assumption that 23.39 is a Christian addition to an originally Jewish text 23.37 f;[207] 23.39 must rather be considered as the original ending of 23.37 f. In that case it is stated concerning Jerusalem, which is refusing Jesus' message, that the temple is to be deprived of Jesus' presence,[208] and with this is connected the prophecy that Jesus will remain invisible to the Jews until they can greet him as the Messiah. There is a reliable tradition elsewhere also to which I shall have to return (see below pp. 99 ff.) that Jesus foretold the destruction of Jerusalem as an eschatological event (Mark 13.2 and par.). Beside this eschatological punishment for the Jews' unbelief is placed the present one: Jesus, destined to be the Messiah, will be taken away from mankind until the Messiah can be greeted with a benediction, for in this guise Jesus is then to appear in glory.[209] This prediction

[206]Thus also K. L. Schmidt, *Der Rahmen der Geschichte Jesu*, 1919, 272 f.; Schniewind, *Matthäus*, 230 f.; T. W. Manson, *Sayings*, 126 f.; Dodd, *Parables*, 62 f.; J. Jeremias, *TB* 20, 1941, 219; K. G. Goetz, *Das antichristliche und das christliche, geschichtliche Jesusbild von heute*, 1944, 101.

[207]Glasson, *Advent*, 100 ff. wishes to separate Matt. 23.39 = Luke 13.35 from the preceding verses because here God cannot be the speaker (see note 205), but Jesus himself; in Glasson's view Jesus is explaining that he is leaving Jerusalem till his return for the Passover, when the pilgrims are greeted with the cry: 'Blessed is he who cometh in the name of the Lord'. (Similarly, referring to the next Feast of Tabernacles, T. W. Manson, 'The Cleansing of the Temple', *Bull. of the John Rylands Library* 33, 1950/51, 279 note 1.) But such a commonplace statement would hardly have been introduced so solemnly ('ye shall not see me').

[208]Thus rightly Dodd and Jeremias, see note 206, also Liechtenhan, *Mission*, 16; G. Schrenk, *Die Weissagung über Israel im Neuen Testament*, 1951, 16, 65 f. To interpret οἶκος as the city of Jerusalem (thus e.g. Klostermann, *Matthäus*, ad loc.; C. J. Cadoux, *Mission*, 271; with hesitation O. Michel, *TWNT* V, 127) is less probable. ἀφίεται has undoubtedly a future meaning, as already in the majority of the Old Latin versions (*relinquetur demittetur*, see Jülicher, *Itala*, ad loc.) and probably also the Peshitta *mštbq*) as opposed to the Sinaitic Syriac (*š byq*), cf. also John 20.23 and Bl.-Debr. §323 with note.

[209]The ἀπ' ἄρτι in Matt. 23.39, missing in Luke 13.35, is undoubtedly an addition of Matthew (cf. H. J. Holtzmann, *Lehrbuch der Neutest. Theologie* I, ²1911, 388 note 3; W. Bieder, *Die Vorstellung von der Höllenfahrt Jesu Christi*, 1949, 55 note 153; differently e.g. K. Weiss, *Irrtumslosigkeit*, 170 ff.). To translate ἀπαρτί = 'certainly' (thus W. Michaelis in a letter referring to Bl.-Debr. §12.3 app.) is improbable.

corresponds exactly with the eucharistic saying in Mark 14.25; on both occasions Jesus counts on an absence which begins with his death and then ends with the parousia; and as this absence is considered in Matt 23.38 as a punishment, no close temporal connexion between the death and parousia of Jesus can be assumed, but a longish interval of time must be expected between his death and resurrection on the one hand and the parousia on the other. Thus this text also proves what seems to be established on many counts that Jesus expected a considerable period between his death and the parousia.

Yet one more passage could be quoted in support of this fact, but it is the subject of much debate.[210] W. Michaelis has argued[211] that the parable of the wicked husbandmen (Mark 12.1 ff. par. Matt. 21.33 ff.; Luke 20.9 ff.) presupposes that a historical development is expected between Jesus' death and the arrival of the Last Day, because according to 12.9 the vineyard is to be given to others after the tenants have killed the son; this is thought to refer to the time when the Church of Christ will be drawn from the Gentiles, and that this stands out even more clearly in Matt. 21.43. Now it is certainly not impossible that the parable is an allegorical interpretation of salvation-history originating in the early Church. Whilst many would like to deny that this parable, at least in its present form, was told by Jesus,[212] others maintain firmly that Jesus composed it in his last days,[213] or they try to reconstruct a possible original form of it.[214] C. H. Dodd, with the concurrence of Taylor, and J. Jeremias have gone beyond

[210]For the following cf. my paper 'Das Gleichnis von den bösen Weingärtnern' in *Aux sources de la tradition chrétienne, Mélanges M. Goguel,* 1950, 120 ff. There will be found a complete bibliography to which only C. W. F. Smith, *Jesus,* 184 ff. and Taylor, *Mark,* 472 ff. have to be added. I restrict myself here to the most important points and refer for details to the paper I have mentioned.

[211]Michaelis, *Verheissung,* 26 f.

[212]Klostermann and Lohmeyer, *Markus,* ad loc.; Bultmann, *Tradition,* 191; Jülicher, *Gleichnisreden* II, 406; C. Clemen, *Religionsgeschichtliche Erklärung des Neuen Testaments,* ²1924, 76 f.; J. Sundwall, *Die Zusammensetzung des Markusevangeliums* (see note 187), 73.

[213]Hauck and Schniewind, *Markus,* ad loc.; Schlatter, *Matthäus,* 629 ff.; Michaelis, *Sämann,* 212 ff.; E. Lohmeyer, *Zeitschr. f. Syst. Theol.,* 1941, 243 ff.; M. J. Lagrange, *Evangile selon saint Marc,* ³1920, 291; E. Meyer, *Ursprung und Anfänge des Christentums,* I, 1921, 166 ff.; M. Hermaniuk, *La parabole évangélique,* 1947, 47, 243; Taylor, *Mark,* 472 etc.

[214]Dodd, *Parables,* 124 ff.; B. T. D. Smith, *Parables,* 22 f., 59, 222 ff.; Liechtenhan, *Mission,* 36; Jeremias, *Parables,* 55 ff. (in German 54 ff.); C. W. F. Smith, *Jesus,* 184 ff.

this and denied that this is an allegory at all, and interpret the parable as a realistic description; the behaviour of the tenants is to be explained by the economic conditions in Palestine at that time, and the sending of the son after the forcible rejection of the slaves as a heightening of the literary effect. But the linguistic examination of the text shows that the wish to remove precisely these allegorical features was the only reason for the elimination of allegorical elements; and no indication can be found that in the case of the tenants we are here concerned with their behaviour towards a foreign landlord or with political motives at all. The introduction of the murder of the 'only' son cannot be understood in any way as a feature of a real parable. Therefore this parable can only be considered to be an allegorical representation of salvation-history until Jesus' coming. But there are two decisive reasons against attributing this allegorical description to Jesus. Firstly he could not be referring to himself by introducing the 'only' son into the parable, because Judaism did not know the messianic name 'Son of God'; and secondly the transference of the promise from the Jews who reject the son to the new people of God is here described as a punishment for the *murder* of the son, whilst in other cases Jesus lets this punishment follow on the rejection of his person without mentioning his death.[215] Therefore the parable in the form handed down to us cannot be traced back to Jesus and we neither know nor can we reconstruct another form. Consequently Mark 12.1 ff. cannot be used as a proof that Jesus expected an interval between his death and resurrection on the one hand and his parousia on the other. Nevertheless this fact is proved so conclusively by the other texts I have discussed that it is impossible from any point of view to accept the idea recently advocated in various forms that Jesus expected his resurrection and parousia to be closely connected in time.

8. POSTPONEMENT OF THE DATE ON WHICH THE KINGDOM OF GOD WILL COME?

It has been shown that Jesus expected the dawn of the Kingdom of God and therewith the parousia in the near future, which was to be limited by the lifetime of his contemporaries, but without

[215]Cf. Matt. 8.11 f.; 12.41 f.; 19.28; 21.43; 23.29 ff., 37 ff. and also A. Oepke, *ST* 2, 1948/50, 142 f.

defining the date any further. Yet did not Jesus after all postpone
the date quite clearly without regard to the lifetime of his generation by mentioning as a preliminary condition for its coming 'and
the gospel must first be preached unto all the nations' (Mark
13.10)?[216] This saying interrupts the continuity between Mark
13.9 and 13.11 and is lacking at this point in the parallels of
Matthew and Luke (though Matthew brings in a similar saying
at 24.14). So we certainly have here a detached saying which has
been interpolated secondarily into this passage.[217] Nevertheless
there can be no doubt that it belongs originally also to an eschatological context, since πρῶτον in the sense of 'first until' can be
applied only to the time before the *eschaton* (the amplified form in
Matt. 24.14 expressly interprets it thus).[218] This too is clear, that
δεῖ denotes the divine necessity, according to which this eschatological happening must take place, though the announcement
does not elaborate the way in which this divine necessity is
realized in history.[219] The saying therefore by no means expresses
a necessary decision that the whole of mankind must have heard
the gospel before the end can come; but it is stated unambiguously
that by then the preaching of the gospel must have penetrated to
all the people known at that time.[220] Now it is true that Jesus
announced explicitly that his mission was directed solely to the
Jews (Mark 7.27; Luke 19.9; Matt. 15.24 'I was not sent but unto

[216]Glasson, *Advent*, 146 ff. emphasizes expressly: 'It follows from all this
that if the ultimate aims of Jesus in his ministry and his death reached out
to the Gentiles it is difficult to maintain that he expected a speedy end to the
world'. Cf. also K. Weiss, *Irrtumslosigkeit*, 34 ff., 67 ff. ('The idea that the end
of the world and the judgment of the world is near . . . does not fit into
Jesus' universalism'); Meinertz, *Theologie* I, 64.

[217]See, recently, Taylor, *Mark*, 506 f. But there is no reason to consider the
saying 'as an addition to the original Mark' (against Hauck, *Markus*, 155 and
Sharman, *Son of Man*, 28 f.).

[218]There is no support in the text for applying Mark 13.10 to the time before the destruction of Jerusalem, since God is said to be able to punish mankind only if light has been offered to them (thus Feuillet, *R.B.* 55, 1948, 492 f.).
But why then must the *Gentiles* receive the preaching before the Jews can be
punished?

[219]See H. v. Campenhausen, *Die Idee des Martyriums in der alten Kirche*, 1936,
25; W. Grundmann, *TWNT* II, 23 f.; Liechtenhan, *Mission*, 32.

[220]In view of πάντα τὰ ἔθνη it is impossible to restrict the statement to the
announcement that 'the gospel is to be brought *to the Gentiles* at all', and
it is even more mistaken to give πρῶτον the meaning of 'above all' and
then to apply the message to the nations to the testimony before the authorities mentioned in 13.9; for πρῶτον never has this non-temporal meaning
in the synoptists (not even in Matt. 6.33), and the connexion with 13.9 is
undoubtedly secondary (against Michaelis, *Verheissung*, 19 f.).

the lost sheep of the house of Israel' is probably secondary in view of Matt. 10.6); but he did not turn away those Gentiles who were prepared to believe his message (Mark 7.24 ff.; Matt. 8.5 ff. = Luke 7.1 ff.; Luke 17.11 ff.); and he said equally clearly that the entry into the Kingdom of God stands open to those Gentiles who believe (Matt. 8.11 = Luke 13.29; Matt. 25.31 ff.). Jesus was therefore undoubtedly convinced that his message concerning the Kingdom of God was of decisive importance for the Gentiles also.[221] But his missionary instructions show quite a different picture. For here Jesus restricted the disciples' preaching unmistakably to the Jews (Matt. 10.5 f. 'Go not into the way of the Gentiles and enter not into any city of the Samaritans'; Matt. 10.23 'Ye shall not have gone through the cities of Israel, till the Son of Man be come').[222] And he expected that at the end of the days the Gentiles would stream in (Matt. 8.11 = Luke 13.29).[223] In view of these facts the assertion that before the end comes the message of the Kingdom of God must by divine necessity still be carried to all peoples can hardly be considered as one of Jesus' sayings, especially as the dispute in the early Church about the right to preach to the Gentiles could not be understood if there existed out of the mouth of Jesus an unequivocal command to do so.[224] B. Sundkler therefore states correctly with regard to Mark 13.10 'Il n'y a guère de doute que cette parole n'ait été formulée

[221]Cf. for this inclusive universalism of Jesus recently e.g. C. J. Cadoux, *Mission*, 153 ff.; C. W. F. Smith, *Jesus*, 139 ff.; Liechtenhan, *Mission*, 32 ff.; J. Munck, 'Israel and the Gentiles in the New Testament', *Studiorum Novi Testamenti Societas*, Bulletin I, 1950, 32, 37.

[222]In view of the early start of the mission to the Samaritans and the Gentiles, it is hard to make it credible that Matt. 10.5 was a creation of the Jewish Christians, who wished to restrict the mission of Jesus to the Jews in opposition to what actually happened (Grundmann, *Jesus*, 25; Leipoldt, *Jesus*, 200 f.; cf. also S. E. Johnson, 'Jesus and First Century Galilee', *In Memoriam E. Lohmeyer*, 1951, 81). But neither must one insinuate into the saying the meaning that the mission to the Samaritans and Gentiles was forbidden only *provisionally* and that Jesus expected a mission later on (Schniewind, *Matthäus*, 124; Michaelis, *Matthäus* II, 80; similarly Liechtenhan, *Mission*, 32).

[223]B. Sundkler, 'Jésus et les païens', *Arbeiten und Mitteilungen aus dem Neutest. Seminar zu Uppsala* VI, 1937 emphasizes that Jesus expected the happenings at the end of time to spread from Israel as the centre of the world over all the nations; see the concurrence of Dahl, *Volk Gottes*, 145; R. Bultmann, *Orient. Literaturztg.* 1939, 302 f.; Jeremias, 'The Gentile World in the thought of Jesus', *Studiorum Novi Testamenti Societas*, Bulletin III, 1952, 18 ff.

[224]See C. J. Cadoux, *Mission*, 142, 300 f.; Taylor, *Mark*, 507 f. (the assertion that Mark nevertheless 'truly represents the mind of Jesus (cf. 7, 27a) but does not give his *ipsissima verba*' sets aside the clear distinction between the goal of the gospel and the missionary commission.

sous l'activité missionaire de l'église'.[225] The objection has been raised to this inference that Jesus' range of vision could not have been more restricted than that of the Pharisees, that 'the preaching of the gospel to all the nations . . .' must have been 'a postulate of eschatology' for Jesus, because only thus could the nations be called *responsibly* into the Kingdom of God, and so for Jesus also 'the καιρός for preaching to the Gentiles is the interval between the resurrection and the parousia'.[226] But it is no sign of a restricted range of vision in Jesus that he does not concern himself with and arrange for winning the Gentiles, but leaves it to God's future; and what seems to us a postulate of eschatology need not on that account have seemed indispensable to Jesus. As this argument rests largely on postulates, it cannot upset the conclusion that Mark 13.10 is not traceable to Jesus. Therefore this saying also cannot call in question the result we have gained that Jesus expected the coming of the Kingdom of God within the generation of his hearers; yet at a distance of time, not defined more closely, from his impending death.

Nor can the objection be raised that Jesus nevertheless in his ethical directions by no means always reckoned with an early and sudden end, but assumed that the present world order would continue.[227] Still less can Mark 14.7 'ye have the poor always with you . . . but me ye have not always' or the gathering together of the new people of God by Jesus be adduced in order to prove that Jesus could not possibly have expected an imminent end.[228] For Jesus' ethics show what must be the disposition of those who are allowed to enter the Kingdom of God, but do not raise any question as to the length of time available for such

[225]In op. cit. in note 223, 11. Sundkler also emphasizes correctly that the saying appended to the pericope concerning Jesus' anointing by the woman 'Wheresoever the gospel shall be preached throughout the world, that also which this woman hath done shall be spoken of for a memorial of her', (Mark 14.9 par. Matt. 26.13) is also a secondary addition by the missionary Church (thus also with other arguments J. Jeremias *ZNW* 35, 1936, 76 f. and Liechtenhan, *Mission*, 31).

[226]Liechtenhan, *Mission*, 31 ff.; Bowman, *Maturity*, 186 ff.; A. Oepke, 'Jesus und der Gottesvolkgedanke', *Luthertum*, 1942, 48; A. Oepke, 'Der Herrnspruch über die Kirche Matt. 16.17-19 in der neuesten Forschung', *ST* 2, 1948/50, 146 f.; A. Oepke, *Das neue Gottesvolk*, 1950, 171 f.; G. Schrenk, *Die Weissagung über Israel im Neuen Testament*, 1951, 8, 15.

[227]Wilder, *Eschatology*, 41 f. referring to Otto, *The Kingdom of God*, 60 f. (in German *Reich Gottes*, 47 f.); also Glasson, *Advent*, 137 ff.; K. Weiss, *Irrtumslosigkeit*, 16 ff.; Meinertz, *Theologie* I, 63.

[228]Glasson, *Advent*, 137, 139 ff.

action. Mark 14.7 par. Matt. 26.11, which belongs quite unquestionably to the story of Jesus' anointing by a woman and is
subject to no historical considerations[229] does indeed count
clearly on a continuance of the world after Jesus' death, but gives
no kind of indication for how long. Further, Jesus' expectation
that the disciples will after his death continue to remain united in
the belief in his messiahship and will gather for a common meal,
gives no indication about the length of this interval between
resurrection and parousia.[230] On the contrary all these texts
confirm that Jesus did indeed count on a shorter or longer
period between his death and the parousia, but that he equally
certainly proclaimed the threatening approach of the Kingdom of
God within his generation.

[229]See for this J. Jeremias, 'Die Salbungsgeschichte Mc. 14.3–9', *ZNW*
35, 1936, 75 ff.
[230]The Jewish idea that repentance could hasten the coming of the Kingdom of God is certainly quite foreign to Jesus; Wilder, *Eschatology*, 84 f. can
quote no authorities for this assumption.

II

ESCHATOLOGICAL PROMISE, NOT APOCALYPTIC INSTRUCTION

1. RESURRECTION, WORLD RENEWAL, WORLD JUDGMENT

In view of this state of the facts which is confirmed on every side, the question concerning the essential meaning of this expectation now presents itself. By proclaiming the nearness in time of the Kingdom of God Jesus adopted the preaching of John the Baptist with regard to the immediately impending judgment and he also announced it himself. Futher, as we have seen, he spoke of the future appearance of the Son of Man 'in the glory of his father with the holy angels' (Mark 8.38), of the coming of the Kingdom of God with power (Mark 9.1), of the appearance of the Son of Man with the clouds of heaven (Mark 14.62), of the Son of Man sitting on the throne of his glory in judgment (Matt. 19.28). In all this Jesus accepted the conceptions of the late Jewish apocalyptic, and the question arises whether Jesus' eschatological message must not be simply fitted into this late Jewish apocalyptic, so that its real meaning would lie just in the revelation of the *imminent* eschatological catastrophes and happenings and in the summons connected with it to be ready for the judgment. M. Werner is the latest to put forward this view; according to him there exists no antithesis in principle or in essentials between Jesus and these apocalyptic writers as regards the nature of their *Weltanschauung*.[1] We must therefore inquire whether we can recognize in the traditional sayings of Jesus further particulars about his view of the expected eschatological events, and must examine what significance and what meaning the apocalyptic features have in his expectation.

It is of course obvious at once that we have an extensive apoca-

---

[1]Werner, *Dogma*, 41. See also F. Buri, *Die Bedeutung der neutestamentlichen Eschatologie für die neuere protestantische Theologie*, 1934, 37 and U. Neuenschwander, *Protestantische Dogmatik der Gegenwart und das Problem der biblischen Mythologie*, Diss. Bern, 1949, 168 ff.

lyptic text in the so-called 'synoptic apocalypse' (Mark 13 and par.); but as there is a very wide divergence about the historical arrangement of the document, we must first ask whether apart from this consecutive text apocalyptic features are to be found in addition to the passages already discussed. It is clear to begin with that Jesus speaks of or assumes the general resurrection as a preliminary condition of the judgment; the men of Nineveh and the queen of the south shall rise up at the judgment with the present generation (Matt. 12.41 f. = Luke 11.31 f.);[2] he who invites to a meal those who cannot repay it will receive the promise: 'thou shalt be recompensed in the resurrection of the just' (Luke 14.14). It can hardly be Jesus' intention to say here that the resurrection will concern only the just, but rather that it will bring a reward for them alone.[3] In his reply to the mocking question of the Sadducees about the relationship to her husbands of a dead woman Jesus derives the resurrection from the nature of God (Mark 12.18 ff. and par.).[4] Beyond this, the general resurrection is undoubtedly assumed when the judgment of races who died long ago, is mentioned (Luke 10.12 Sodom; Matt. 11.22 Tyre and Sidon).[5] Now it is significant that Jesus does not describe at all the process of the resurrection and only hints at the condition of the risen ones. Those who are rejected are said to be thrown in the γέεννα (Matt. 5.29 f.; Mark 9.45–47; Matt. 10.28; 23.33) which is sometimes spoken of as the hell of fire (Matt. 5.22; Mark 9.43 par. Matt. 18.8), sometimes presented as darkness and cold (weeping and gnashing of teeth Matt. 8.12 = Luke 13.28 and often thus in Matthew).[6] As regards the fate of

[2]See above pages 43 f. for this.
[3]Thus Klostermann, *Lukas*, 151; Nikolainen, *Auferstehungsglaube*, 41; differently Hauck, *Lukas*, 190; C. J. Cadoux, *Mission*, 226 f.; Taylor, *Mark*, 483 (appealing to Mark 12.25). Luke 20.35 also οἱ καταξιωθέντες τοῦ αἰῶνος ἐκείνου τυχεῖν καὶ τῆς ἀναστάσεως τῆς ἐκ νεκρῶν alters Mark 12.25 ὅταν ἐκ νεκρῶν ἀναστῶσιν to a similar ambiguous meaning, although Luke 20.37 as well as Mark 12.26 say ὅτι ἐγείρονται οἱ νεκροί and thereby undoubtedly mean the general resurrection of the dead.
[4]Glasson, *Advent*, 132 f. referring to Mark 12.26 f. gives it as Jesus' opinion that men 'go to whatever fate awaits them immediately after death', and thus takes out of Mark 12.18 ff. the expectation of the resurrection; but that is quite impossible in view of 12.25 ὅταν ἐκ νεκρῶν ἀναστῶσιν.
[5]Thus rightly H. Molitor, *Die Auferstehung der Christen und Nichtchristen nach dem Apostel Paulus*, 1933, 79 ff.
[6]See above pages 51 f. It is doubtful whether the quotation from Isa. 66.24 'where their worm dieth not and their fire is not quenched' in Mark 9.48 also belongs to the old tradition, because it 'had become a winged word in Judaism' and is missing in the parallel Matt. 5.29 f.; 18.8 (Lohmeyer, *Markus*, 196;

those commended at the judgment, only the statement 'the righteous shall shine forth as the sun in the kingdom of their father' (Matt. 13.43) is added to the conception of the heavenly feast, and the questionable age of Matt. 13.43 has already been pointed out.[7] Further descriptions of the just who are raised are completely lacking;[8] on the other hand Jesus declares in answer to the Sadducees' inquiry about the possibility of the resurrection 'When they shall rise from the dead they neither marry nor are given in marriage, but are as angels in heaven' (Mark 12.25 par. Matt. 22.30; Luke 20.35 f. is very much reshaped). This text is usually understood as suggesting the completely unearthly, transcendent way of life in the βασιλεία which is therefore beyond man's imagination.[9] It is true that M. Werner has objected to this that Jesus is only depicting here 'in complete agreement with apocalyptic eschatology the angel-like way of life of those chosen to share in the new age'.[10] Now it is doubtless correct that to describe the risen blessed ones as similar to angels comes from apocalyptic.[11] But there this description has only one purpose, to display plainly within the framework of an apocalyptic picture of the proceedings at the end of the world the supermundane glory of the just and the salvation awaiting them.[12] But Jesus places the statement of Mark 12.25 beside the rejection of the apocalyptic time-reckoning (Luke 17.20 f.) and the emphasis on the incalculable and sudden nature of the end (Mark 13.32, 35; Matt. 24.43 f.;

Strack-Billerbeck II, 19 f.; W. Michaelis, *Versöhnung des Alls*, 1950, 55 f.). But to strike out τὸ ἄσβεστον from τὸ πῦρ in Mark 9.43 and thereby to question an endless punishment (W. Michaelis, loc. cit.) is impermissible from the point of view of method.

[7]See page 52, note 105.
[8]Theissing, *Seligkeit*, 71 ff. also can cite as a portrayal of Jesus' view of the existence of the just at the end nothing more than 'spiritual' conceptions, such as sonship of God, fellowship with God, seeing God, etc.
[9]See e.g. Theissing, *Seligkeit*, 31 ff.; Nikolainen, *Auferstehungsglaube*, 36 f.
[10]Werner, *Dogma*, 41 f.
[11]See Volz, *Eschatologie*, 396 f., 400 f.
[12]Thus especially *Apoc. Baruch* 51.11 f. 'before them shall be spread the wide spaces of Paradise and they shall be shown the majestic beauty of the living beings who are nearest to the throne and of all the hosts of angels, But the glory will then be to the righteous as well as to the angels'. W. Baumgartner pointed out to me (in writing) that Jesus is here following a *definite* late Jewish representation of angels, the one according to which the angels are sexless (*Apoc. Enoch* 15.6 f.; b. Hagiga 16a); there was another view that the angels could consort with earthly women (*Apoc. Enoch* 6 f.; 15.3 f.; 106.6, 12; Slavonic *Enoch* 18.4 f.; *Jubilees* 4.22).

25.1 ff.; Luke 17.24);[13] and Jesus' rejection of a cosmic miracle as a means to awaken faith points in the same direction (Mark 8.12)[14] and so does most particularly the complete absence of any delineation of eschatological conditions.[15]

Now if we continue for the present to put aside Mark 13.1–27, this statement appears to be contradicted both by the conception of the renewal of the world (Mark 13.31 par. Matt. 24.35; Luke 21.33), and by the description of the judgment of the world (Matt. 25.31 ff.). The logion 'Heaven and earth shall pass away; but my words shall not pass away' (Mark 13.31) is an isolated detached saying with no original connexion with the sayings in 13.30 and 13.32 which have already been dealt with; and it is only attached to 13.30 through the catchword ($\pi\alpha\rho\acute{\epsilon}\lambda\theta\eta$—$\pi\alpha\rho\epsilon\lambda\epsilon\acute{\upsilon}\sigma\upsilon\tau\alpha\iota$).[16] The saying ascribes to the perishable sayings of Jesus an imperishable duration in contrast to the imminent passing away of the visible world. This estimation of Jesus' sayings corresponds in its essence altogether with Jesus' claim elsewhere that his decision represents the will of God absolutely (Matt. 5.21 ff.), so that there is no reason to consider this saying to have been formulated by the early Church.[17] Jesus expresses here the late Jewish view that the beginning of God's reign will be accompanied by the complete disappearance of the old world and the rise of a new one.[18] But on the one hand it is significant that this view has only once been expressed as a premise for the actual statement about the eternal

---

[13]Thus correctly M. Albertz, *Die Botschaft des Neuen Testaments* I, 1, 1947, 79 f.; cf. also E. F. Scott, *The Nature of the Early Church*, 1941, 33.

[14]M. Dibelius, 'Theologie des Neuen Testaments', *Heidelberger Skripten*, *Theol. Reihe* Heft 1, 1948, 14, drew attention to this.

[15]Wilder, *Eschatology*, 51, 56, 69 mentions that 'Jesus could envisage the future in non-dualistic, non-apocalyptic terms'. But that is correct only if it is always kept in mind that Jesus' prediction of the future refers to *the end of time*.

[16]J. Sundwall, 'Die Zusammensetzung des Markusevangeliums', *Acta Academiae Aboensis, Humaniora* IX, 2, 1934, 77; Taylor, *Mark*, 521.

[17]Against Bultmann, *Tradition*, 139; E. Fuchs, *Verkünd. und Forsch.*, 1947/48, 79 (it is untrue that Jesus' eschatological imperatives have no more meaning after the parousia, that therefore the early Church must be speaking here; Jesus did not utter imperatives only and in Matt. 7.24 = Luke 6.47; Mark 8.38 par. Luke 9.26 οἱ λόγοι μου denotes the entire message of Jesus, including his personal claim). There is also no reason to assume that the saying was remodelled to fit the Johannine sayings John 5.47; 6.63, 68; 14.10; 15.7; 17.8 (thus Taylor, *Mark*, 521), because Matt. 5.17; 7.24 also presuppose the eschatologically permanent significance of Jesus' sayings. But to extend οἱ λόγοι μου to 'my work' is also unsupported (against J. Jeremias, *ZNW* 38, 1939, 116).

[18]See Strack-Billerbeck III, 840 ff.

quality of Jesus' sayings and that, on the other hand, any more
detailed description of this new creation is completely lacking.[19]
So though it cannot indeed be denied that Jesus shared these
apocalyptic conceptions, yet it can also be asserted that he felt very
little interest in them.

But does not Matt. 25.31 ff. offer a representation of the world
judgment in apocalyptic colours? There can be no doubt that this
detailed description of it is intended to portray an expected actual
proceeding.[20] And it is equally clear that it 'is kept in general
within the pattern of Jewish apocalyptic'.[21] But the account
diverges from this pattern in that the Son of Man comes with
angels and sets himself upon the judgment seat, and especially
in that the good deeds done to the 'least of the brethren' of the
Son of Man are said to be done to the Son of Man himself. That
the Son of Man himself appears as judge with the angels is a conception met with also in other sayings of Jesus (Mark 8.38 and
par.).[22] Yet it is obscure whether the judgment is to comprise
Christians or all mankind, or even only the non-Christian nations,
and whether 'the least of the brethren' means all persons in distress or only members of the Christian community.[23] According
to the answers given to these questions the passage has been
frequently explained wholly, or at least in its present form, as a
community formation.[24] The examination of the terms ἀδελφός and

[19]Theissing, *Seligkeit*, 133 ff. can also only 'draw indirect conclusions about
the conditions of the renewed earth'. The conception of παλιγγενεσία found
in Matt. 19.28 in the sense of world renewal cannot be reproduced in Aramaic
and can hardly go back to Jesus (cf. Dalman, *Worte Jesu*, 145 and for the
whole saying page 47 above).

[20]There is no 'parable of the world judgment' (thus the title in the ninth
edition of the synopsis of the first three gospels by A. Huck, edited by H.
Lietzmann, 1936, 181; also Guy, *Last Things*, 35 and W. Manson, *Jesus*, 119
also speak of 'parable'). Against this rightly Th. Preiss, *Life in Christ*, 1954,
46 (in French *La vie en Christ*, 1951, 77).

[21]Klostermann, *Matthäus*, 204 with authorities.

[22]It can hardly be correct that the Son of Man in Mark 8.38 and par. (for
this see page 44 above) will appear only as a witness at the final judgment,
for to 'be ashamed' of the Son of Man coming with the angels must have a
decisive effect (against Jeremias, *Parables*, 143 [in German 146]). On the other
hand it is correct that Jesus nowhere else calls himself βασιλεύς (Jeremias, loc.
cit.); but Th. Preiss, op. cit. in note 20, 47 f. (in French 78 f.) conjectures
probably correctly that Jesus assigns to himself as the Son of Man the title of
'king' only at the parousia.

[23]See the survey of the history of the exegesis by W. Brandt, 'Die gering-
sten Brüder', *Jahrb. d. Theol. Schule Bethel* 8, 1937, 1 ff.

[24]According to some it is a matter of giving a Christian version to a description of the final judgment going back to Jesus, in which he has only

ἐλάχιστος leads to no decisive result. For ἀδελφός is found in Jesus' mouth in a figurative sense to denote a neighbour (Matt. 5.22 ff.; 7.3 ff.; 18.35) as well as Jesus' followers (Matt. 23.8); on the other hand Jesus speaks elsewhere of ἀδελφοί μου as in Matt. 25.40 only with reference to his followers (Mark 3.33 f. and par.). ἐλάχιστος is met with nowhere else at all in the synoptists to designate persons; μικρός is used figuratively once in the comparative of the man who knows himself to be small in the sight of God (Luke 9.40 ὁ μικρότερος ἐν πᾶσιν ὑμῖν ὑπάρχων = Matt. 18.4 ὅστις ταπεινώσει ἑαυτόν), but is met with otherwise only in a series of connected sayings which speak of the special honour done to these 'little ones' and of their being caused to stumble, an action which will not be left unpunished (Mark 9.42 = Matt. 18.6 = Luke 17.2; Matt. 10.42; 18.10, 14). It is hardly possible to recover the original wording of these sayings with complete certainty; Bultmann assumes that they were all concerned with children in the literal sense, and concludes that their origin was non-Christian;[25] by contrast O. Michel put forward the theory that 'these little ones' was a special name for the disciples, which reverses their designation in the sight of God, so that they are 'little' now, but are to be called 'great' in the age to come.[26] But the objection to referring these sayings to actual children is that there would in that case hardly be the need to warn against despising 'these little ones' (Matt. 18.10), and if this phrase originally meant the disciples of Jesus, he would surely have been unlikely to have said that only the sin of causing *them* to stumble was worthy of the worst punishment (Luke 17.2). The saying

---

secondarily become the world judge (Weinel, *Theologie*, 59; Grundmann, *Jesus*, 30; with hesitation Jeremias, *Parables*, 144 f. [in German 146]); others assume as its basis a Jewish apocalyptic description into which has been introduced Jesus' idea of the judgment according to the works of charity done to him unknowingly (thus or similarly A. Merx, *Das Evangelium Matthäus*, 1902, 365; Bultmann, *Tradition*, 130 f.; Klostermann, *Matthäus*, 204 f.; Wilder, *Eschatology*, 96); others again attribute the basis to the evangelist, but the 'ethical content of the passage' to Jesus' ideas (H. J. Holtzmann, *Lehrbuch der Neutestamentlichen Theol.* I, ²1911, 393 f.; Glasson, *Advent*, 129 f.) or consider the whole description Christian, because recipients and donors of the acts of charity are Christians (J. Wellhausen, *Das Evangelium Matthäi*, ²1914, 127, similarly Sharman, *Son of Man*, 56 ff.), whilst C. J. Cadoux, *Mission*, 321, 323 leaves open the origin of the text.

[25]Bultmann, *Tradition*, 152, 155, 158 f.
[26]O. Michel, ' "Diese Kleinen"—eine Jüngerbezeichnung Jesu', *Theol. Stud. u. Krit.* 108, 1937/38, 401 ff.; O. Michel. *TWNT* IV, 653 ff.

about giving to drink (Matt. 10.42) as well as that about the punishment of those 'who despise' these little ones (Mark 9.42 par. Matt. 18.10) can best be understood if Jesus by this altogether unusual expression meant none other than 'the poor' of the first beatitude (Matt. 5.3), the conception then has the same meaning as μικρότερος in Luke 9.48. If therefore we have no clear-cut name for the disciples, but only a designation of those to whom the Kingdom of God is promised, then the sayings of Jesus about 'these little ones' provide no compelling proof for the meaning of the superlative ἐλάχιστος in Matt. 25.40, 45. Now it is certain because of πάντα τὰ ἔθνη in 25.32 that all people will appear as the accused in the records of the judgment,[27] and in view of 25.34 ('inherit the kingdom prepared for you from the foundation of the world') and 25.37 ('the righteous shall answer') it can scarcely be thought that Christians would not be included in πάντα τὰ ἔθνη. So for this reason alone it is surely an improbable assumption that the judge of the world is asking about the behaviour of the heathen to the Christians. Besides, Matthew at any rate will hardly have forgotten the expectation expressed in 24.14 that before the end the gospel will have been preached to the whole world; so he will suppose that the question at the last judgment will be about the behaviour, not of non-Christians to the Christians, but of all those who have been reached by the gospel message towards all sufferers.[28] And as Jesus has also expressly emphasized the duty of helping *every* sufferer (Luke 10.30 ff.) it is the most probable assumption that 'my brethren' also does not indicate definite persons, as contrasted with all other persons, but means all persons who are one day to stand together before their κύριος (25.37, 44). In that case ἐλάχιστος is not a specifically religious designation, but describes, corresponding with the good deeds mentioned, those persons who are hungry, thirsty, naked, strangers, in prison, and therefore in need of help.[29] If this exegesis is correct, it is not the behaviour of men to the Christians which is here assumed as the standard for judgment, which would

[27]The idea has been intruded that this is only concerned with the judgment of the Gentiles, as a higher standard will be demanded of Jews and Christians (against W. A. Curtis, *Jesus Christ the Teacher*, 1943, 151 ff.).

[28]W. Brandt, op. cit. in note 23, 25, is correct in emphasizing this.

[29]Thus Schlatter, *Matthäus*, 726; Theissing, *Seligkeit*, 69 f.; Schniewind, *Matthäus*, 246 f.; W. Brandt, op. cit. in note 23, 26; W. Manson, *Jesus*, 119, Th. Preiss, op. cit. in note 20, 51 f. (in French 82 f.); G. Stählin TWNT V, 16; Jeremias, *Parables*, 145 (in German 146), probably also W. Michaelis, *Versöhnung des Alls*, 1950, 62.

lead to a date after Jesus for the origin of the text. Consequently there is also no reason for refusing to attribute this passage to Jesus on account of its apocalyptic colour or for simply denying its eschatological character.[30] For after all what distinguishes our passage is not only the standard for judgment, foreign to all Jewish tradition, but also the small part played by the setting as well as the nature and extent of the punishment or reward assigned. The significance of the description is clearly not just to throw light on eschatological proceedings,[31] but to teach what it is a matter of life and death for men to do in face of the impending judgment, and also to display the central significance of the person of Jesus when men's actions are examined at the last judgment. In that case Matt. 25.31 ff. is certainly not an indication that Jesus' eschatological message is concerned with apocalyptic instruction, but is on the contrary a proof that his proclamation of the imminence of the judgment and of the Kingdom of God does not derive its significance from apocalyptic revelation, however much Jesus reckoned with cosmic events, but that the real significance of the eschatological message must lie elsewhere.

2. THE ESCHATOLOGICAL DISCOURSE OF MARK 13

Now it is true that this inference seems to be contradicted by the most detailed eschatological passage of the synoptists, the so-called 'synoptic apocalypse' (Mark 13.1–27 and par.). Even today conclusions about this passage diverge widely. The average critical opinion assumes that the chapter is based on a Jewish apocalypse which was originally consecutive and was expanded by Christian additions;[32] others trace the whole chapter back to a

[30]Thus Duncan, *Jesus*, 196 ff. (the picture describes only the eternal principles of judgment) and Glasson, *Advent*, 130 ff. (a pictorial representation of judgment which runs through history; only the judgment of nations is concerned).

[31]Therefore nothing can be derived from Matt. 25.31 ff. either about the eternal election or rejection or about the nature of the reward or punishment of the righteous and the damned respectively. There is no proof at all (against W. Michaelis, *Versöhnung des Alls*, 1950, 56 ff.) that in fact in 25.46 κόλασις is meant to designate a purifying punishment and the adjacent αἰώνιος not the endlessness, but only the eschatological character of the chastisement.

[32]For the older representatives of this view see in H. J. Holtzmann, *Lehrbuch der Neutestamentliche Theol.* I, ²1911, 399 ff.; recently e.g. Bultmann, *Tradition*, 129 (13.7 f., 12, 14–22, 24–27 are an original Jewish text which was expanded by Christians in 13.5 f., 9–11, 13a, 23); B. T. D. Smith, *Parables*, 90

Jewish-Christian origin[33] or assume a more complicated previous history.[34] Contrasted with this is the view put forward by J. Schniewind that every single word of the discourse is stamped by the reality 'Jesus' and that in consequence of that fact 'the question of the "authenticity" becomes of secondary importance'.[35] F. Busch then attempted to show in a detailed examination[36] that the separation of Jesus' sayings from the tradition of the Church is 'an impossible venture'; only in the gospels taken as a whole lies 'the primary possibility of finding one's way about for all those who want to discover the actual history' (30 f.). Every verse in the gospel is said to find its unity in the *kerygma*, and therefore Mark 13 also contains 'the quintessence of the message of the Kingdom and the Messiah' (35); nor must inquiry about authenticity be made about the composition or the framework. Starting from this Busch then seeks to show in detail that Mark 13 is introduced as a 'Farewell discourse' of Jesus into the teaching concerning the suffering Messiah; 'Mark 13 is an explanation of Mark 8.34' (48). Therefore the chapter is not intended to describe

---

note 1; similarly Hauck, *Markus*, 153; Klostermann, *Markus*, 131 f.; J. Sundwall, 'Die Zusammensetzung des Markusevangeliums' (see note 16), 76 ff.; G. Hölscher, 'Der Ursprung der Apokalypse Markus 13', *TB* 12, 1933, 193 ff. (13.7 f., 12, 14–20, 24–27 a Jewish apocalypse which originated 'between the spring and autumn of A.D. 40' when the erection of a statue of Caligula in the temple was threatened); F. C. Grant, *The Earliest Gospel*, 1943, 62 (13.6–8, 14–20, 24–27 were enlarged before Mark to the form found in Mark); E. B. Redlich, *St. Mark's Gospel*, 1948, 29 f. 151; P. Feine–J. Behm, *Einleitung in das Neue Testament*, ⁹1950, 30; with hesitation C. J. Cadoux, *Mission*, 11 f., 273 f.

[33]E. Meyer, *Ursprünge und Anfang des Christentums*, I, 1921, 129 f.; Major, *Mission and Message*, 159 f.; Glasson, *Advent*, 76 ff., 185 ff.; Guy, *Last Things*, 58 f.; presumably also M. Albertz, *Die Botschaft des Neuen Testaments* I, 1, 1947, 180 f. (an apocalyptic broadsheet of twice seven sections).

[34]V. Taylor, 'The Apocalyptic Discourse of Mark 13', *ExpT* 60, 1948/49, 94 ff.; Taylor, *Mark*, 636 ff. assumes four sources (13.5–8, 9–13, 14–23, 24–27, 28–37), but of these, also according to Taylor, 13.5–8, 24–27 and 13.14–23 were already joined together before Mark.

[35]Schniewind, *Markus*, 157.—C. C. Torrey, *Documents of the Primitive Church*, 1941, 12 ff. maintains that the discourse is a unity which could have been spoken as a whole by Jesus in the situation described, with the exception of Mark 13.14a which was inserted in the year 40.

[36]Busch, *Eschatologie*. Michaelis, *Verheissung* 22 ff. has taken over the thesis of Busch in its essentials.—M. Barth, *Augenzeuge*, 1946, 125 ff. interprets Mark 13 as 'Jesus Christ's prediction of his passion and resurrection', yet 'this does not cast doubt on the exegesis of this chapter and its parallels as referring to the end of time'. But how anyone could understand this double meaning in Jesus' mouth, Barth does not explain!

the sequence in time of the final events, but to enjoin patience in the final tribulation, the termination of which through the parousia, though near, is unknown. In place of the eschatological drama of the apocalyptic in several acts, there appears the *one* last act; the inquiry about signs (13.4) is not answered because at the time of the tribulation in 13.14 ff. 'the evangelist will not have had his eye on any particular moment', and in the whole chapter only the time of desolation before the end and the happenings after the tribulation (13.24 ff.) are mentioned, and so in Mark 13 also the *kerygma* is only the *kerygma* of the crucified one. J. W. Bowman,[37] too, shows that in Mark 13 we have prophecy, not apocalyptic: Jesus constructs an 'anti-apocalypse' out of the Old Testament prophetic ideas: apart from 13.24–27 only the imminent destruction of Jerusalem and the signs pointing to it are mentioned. Jesus could speak as a prophet about the destruction of Jerusalem, whilst the end of the world would come one day without a sign. Now Busch is undoubtedly wrong when he says that the evangelist had no intention of describing a succession in time of eschatological happenings. For this intention follows quite unambiguously from ἀλλ' οὔπω τὸ τέλος (13.7),[38] ἀρχὴ ὠδίνων ταῦτα (13.8), πρῶτον δεῖ κηρυχθῆναι τὸ εὐαγγελίον (13.10), τότε . . . φευγέτωσαν (13.14), καὶ τότε ἐάν τις . . . εἴπῃ (31.21), μετὰ τὴν θλῖψιν ἐκείνην (13.24), καὶ τότε ὄψονται (13.26), καὶ τότε ἀποστελεῖ (13.27). Although Mark cannot in chapter 13 have forgotten his *kerygma* of the suffering Messiah, yet it is his intention here in the first place to impart a revelation about the eschatological events, their sequence, their meaning, their dangers. And therefore it is also

---

[37] Bowman, *Intention*, 55 ff.; Bowman, *Maturity*, 245 f.; cf. also already K. Weiss, *Irrtumslosigkeit*, 42 ff., 142 ff., who lets the prediction of the last judgment start in 13.21.—A. Feuillet goes even further in 'Le discours de Jésus sur la ruine du temple d'après Marc 13 et Luc 21.5–36', *RB* 55, 1948, 481 ff.; 56, 1949, 61 ff.; 'La synthèse eschatologique de Saint Matthieu (24–25)', *RB* 56, 1949, 340 ff.; 57, 1950, 63 ff.; according to him Mark 13.24–27 does not speak of the end of the world, but of the destruction of Jerusalem and the establishment of the new community connected with it! I will not enter into this monstrous exegesis here.—I was not able to consult A. Jones, 'Did Christ foretell the End of the World in Mark 13 ?', *Scripture* IV, 1951, 264 ff.

[38] In Luke 21.9 the delay of the parousia resulting from the prolongation of the time is strengthened by the alteration of ἀλλ' οὐκ εὐθέως τὸ τέλος. Similarly in Luke 21,12 the persecution is moved to a position *before* the signs by means of the πρὸ δὲ τούτων πάντων, and thereby a further postponement of the parousia is achieved. Matthew also has emphasized more strongly the sequence in time of the events (24.9 τότε, 24.10 καὶ τότε, 14.14 καὶ τότε ἥξει τὸ τέλος, 24.29 εὐθέως). On the other hand he shows no postponement of the parousia.

quite impossible to deny with Bowman the reference in Mark 13.5–23 to the final events; for the apocalyptic predictions of the earthquakes and famines as ἀρχὴ ὠδίνων (13.8), the announcements of family enmity and hatred before τέλος (13.12 f.), the description of the impending θλῖψις as one οἵα οὐ γέγονεν τοιαύτη ἀπ' ἀρχῆς κτίσεως . . . ἕως τοῦ νῦν καὶ οὐ γένηται (13.19) cannot be separated from οὔπω τὸ τέλος 13.7 and the cosmic catastrophe at the end of time 13.24 f. It is incontrovertible that Mark 13 as a whole is intended to be a prediction of the events immediately preceding the end and of the end itself.

It is not denied that within this discourse with its apocalyptic meaning Jewish apocalyptic material has been used to a considerable extent, and from this the inclusion of a Jewish or Jewish-Christian apocalypse has been inferred. But this assumption meets with the great difficulty that this alleged apocalyptic broadsheet must have been extremely short and colourless and would have had no actual bias that we can detect, since of course the typically Christian features were introduced into this 'apocalypse' later. Moreover there is no possibility of establishing an original *literary* sequence between the conjectured components of this apocalypse, so that the hypothesis of a *connected* apocalyptic basis for this chapter is hardly sufficiently well founded. On the contrary a strict analysis of the text reveals, as the previous discussion of 13.10, 28 f., 30, 31, 32, 33, 34–37 has already shown, that the whole discourse is constructed out of detached sayings or small groups of sayings of different origin,[39] so that to discover the original form of Jesus' message, the individual components must be disengaged and their origin determined. Therefore Busch's demand to abstain from separating Jesus' sayings from the tradition of the Church takes no account of the historical facts. So, if we omit 13.10, 28–37, sayings we have already discussed, there emerges from the analysis of Mark 13.1–37 the following picture: several texts clearly show the situation of the Christian community and predict that in the time before the coming of the *eschaton* the disciples will suffer persecution, will fall into danger through the pretensions of false messiahs, but are also to be supported by the Holy Ghost (13.6, 9, 11, 13, 21, 22 f.).

[39]Thus also Lohmeyer, *Markus*, 285 ff.; Dibelius, *Jesus*, 60 f. It is a further objection to assuming a 'little apocalypse' as a basis that Mark 13.15 f. is found in Luke 17.31 in a connexion presumably derived from Q and therefore a detached logion, and that Mark 13.6 can hardly have stood in the same source as 31.21.

That the traditional form of these texts may have been influenced by the experience of the Christian Church is clear (cf. especially 13.9). On the other hand the parallels in the rest of Jesus' traditional sayings show that Jesus reckoned on sufferings for his disciples (Luke 6.22; Matt. 10.28, 38; Mark 8.34; 10.35 ff.); and the danger of being led astray is also held up to the disciples elsewhere with a warning (Matt. 7.15; Luke 17.23). It is thus altogether possible that the texts in Mark 13.6, 9, 11, 13, 21–23 go back to Jesus' sayings, even though no details can be established with certainty.[40] In any case we are concerned here with predictions which do not deal with the actual eschatological happenings but refer to the whole period before the final events themselves.[41] Thus these sayings do not constitute an apocalyptic revelation properly so-called, and so their presence in the Jesus tradition cannot be invoked against the statement that Jesus' eschatological message does not derive its meaning from the apocalyptic description of eschatological proceedings.

In our analysis of Mark 13.1–37 we next find with regard to the temple the prediction 13.2: 'Seest thou these great buildings? There shall not be left here one stone upon another, which shall not be thrown down.' Mark unquestionably understood this destruction of the temple as a part of the final happenings, since

[40]W. Manson, 'The ΕΓΩ ΕΙΜΙ of the Messianic Presence in the New Testament', *JTS* 47, 1946, 137 ff. interprets the declaration ἐγώ εἰμι in Mark 13.6 as an expression of the fact that the parousia has come, so that we would have here a primitive Christian warning against the fanciful assertion that the end had come (as expressed in II Thess. 2.2). But this impersonal exegesis of the announcement ἐγώ εἰμι is hardly possible and so there is nothing against referring this warning back to Jesus (see the circumspect commentary of Taylor, *Mark*, 503 f. who conjectures with good reasons that ἐπὶ τῷ ὀνόματί μου 'is a "Christian" addition to a Jewish or Jewish-Christian source used in compiling the Apocalyptic Discourse', though he does not give sufficient grounds for tracing the saying back to such a source.—Barrett, *Spirit*, 130 ff. draws attention to the fact that, of all Jesus' sayings which promise the disciples divine assistance when accused (Mark 13.11; Matt. 10.19 f.; Luke 12.11 f.; 21.14 f.) in Luke 21.14 f. alone the Holy Ghost is not mentioned, and therefore considers the text with its strong Semitic flavour to be the oldest form. That is possible especially as the added ἐγώ in the first person often occurs in the sayings of Jesus (see K. L. Schmidt, *Le Problème du Christianisme primitif*, 1938, 35 ff.); in that case it is probable that this text also in its old form is to be traced back to Jesus.

[41]Dodd, *Parables*, 51 f. distinguishes the predictions which refer 'to forthcoming historical events' from those referring to 'events of a wholly supernatural order'. J. Jeremias, *TB* 20, 1941, 218, would prefer instead to distinguish between 'sayings dealing with events up to the parousia from those concerning the parousia and what follow it'.

the inquiry about their date (13.4) πότε ταῦτα ἔσται undoubtedly refers back to the destruction of the temple. The question whether this strictly eschatological interpretation reproduces the original meaning of the saying cannot be answered from its wording, since the hyperbole 'there shall not be left one stone upon another' might certainly also describe the razing of the city as a matter of history. There is on the other hand no need to regard the saying 13.2 as a *vaticinium ex eventu*, since, as has often been rightly emphasized, the temple was destroyed by fire.[42] Now Jesus foretold the destruction of the temple as an eschatological event elsewhere also (Matt. 23.38 = Luke 13.35, see above page 81); and in his trial his prediction of the destruction of the temple and of the building of a new messianic temple played a decisive rôle according to Mark 14.58 and parallels. As this accusation according to Mark 14.57 is said to have been brought by false witnesses and as moreover the account of the proceedings before the Sanhedrin has latterly on the whole been thought to be unhistorical, this saying about the temple is often taken out of Jesus' mouth and considered as an interpolation from Stephen's martyrdom.[43] But there is no doubt that this saying is firmly fixed within the oldest story of the Passion (cf. its repetition in Mark 15.29 and the use made of it in the Johannine version of the account of the cleansing of the temple John 2.19) and that it made difficulties for the earliest community, because the prediction was not fulfilled and was at variance with the attitude of the first congregation of Christians towards the temple (see the additions χειροποίητον and ἀχειροποίητον in Mark 14.58 and the radical reinterpretation in John, further the designation of the witnesses as false witnesses). If therefore it will scarcely be possible to reconstruct the original wording of the saying, and if the general misgivings about the report of the proceedings before the Sanhedrin are not justified,[44] it might after all be very probable that a saying of Jesus was handed down in which he predicted the destruction of the temple and its rebuilding after a short interval.[45]

[42]E.g. by Schniewind, *Markus*, 158; similarly Klostermann, *Markus*, 132; Lohmeyer, *Markus*, 268; Taylor, *Mark*, 501.

[43]Cf. H. Lietzmann, 'Der Prozess Jesu', *Sitzungsber. d. Berl. Akad., Phil.-hist. Kl.* 1931, 315 f.; J. Finegan, *Die Überlieferung der Leidens- und Auferstehungsgeschichte*, 1934, 72; Bultmann, *Tradition*, 126 f., 291.

[44]See above page 50.

[45]Thus also Hauck, Klostermann, Lohmeyer, Schniewind, *Markus*, on 14.58; Taylor, *Mark*, 566 f.; furthermore, Jeremias, *Weltvollender*, 39 f.;

That this saying can be understood only in a strictly eschatological sense as a prediction of the messianic temple is incontestable in view of the Old Testament and Jewish hope of the building of a new temple in the messianic age.[46] But then it follows that Mark 13.2 also must undoubtedly have a strictly eschatological meaning. And the theory that Jesus predicted the destruction of Jerusalem as a historical event because of the growing tension between the Jews and the Romans would not only take Mark 13.2 out of its connexion with Mark 14.58; Matt. 23.38, but would also ascribe to Jesus a prediction about the future course of earthly history without any parallel in the Jesus tradition.[47] Consequently Jesus did in fact think of the doom of the Jewish temple as connected

---

E. Lohmeyer, *Kultus und Evangelium*, 1942, 77 ff.; G. Bertram, *Die Leidensgeschichte und der Christuskult*, 1922, 56 f.; Dodd, *Parables*, 60 ff.; Flew, *Church*, 40 ff.; A. Oepke, 'Jesus und der Gottesvolkgedanke', *Luthertum* 1942, 47; Ph. Vielhauer, *Oikodome*, Diss. Heidelberg, 1939, 62 ff.; M. Simon, 'Retour du Christ et reconstruction du Temple dans la pensée chrétienne primitive', *Aux Sources de la Tradition chrétienne, Mélanges Goguel*, 1950, 249 f.; A. Oepke, *Das neue Gottesvolk*, 1950, 169.

[46]Whether this new building is thought only to be the coming upon the scene of the messianic community, or to be the rise of a heavenly temple as well, can hardly be settled. On the other hand it is impossible to apply the prediction to the formation of a new earthly community after the historical destruction of the temple (Otto, *The Kingdom of God*, 61 f. [in German *Reich Gottes*, 48 f.]; Glasson, *Advent*, 139 f.; Wilder, *Eschatology*, 51 note 26; O. Cullmann, *Peter*, 1953, 198 f. [in German *Petrus*, 1952, 222 f.]—Walter, *Kommen*, 85 ff. interprets it as the resurrection *and* the rise of the Church); for every Jew must have understood the prediction of a new temple building to be meant eschatologically, as a new temple building was expected from the messianic era (Jeremias, *Weltvollender*, 38 f.; Strack-Billerbeck IV, 2, 929 ff.; Lohmeyer, *Markus*, 327); and moreover Jesus could not make the rise of a new earthly community depend on the previous destruction of the temple at Jerusalem.

[47]Against Dodd, *Parables*, 60 ff., who assumes that Jesus foretold the doom of the temple 'as an impending event in history'. Dodd appeals to Matt. 23.34–36 as well in order to assert that Jesus also expected the punishment of the Jewish people, and all this in the very near future in immediate connexion with the crisis set in motion by his death. But Matt. 23.34–36 speaks of the punishment of the disobedient Jewish nation taking place in the very near future, within *history*, but does not connect this historical judgment with the death of Jesus. C. J. Cadoux, *Mission*, 275 f. also understands Mark 13.1 f. together with 13.7 f., 14–17, 19 f. as a prediction of the war between Jews and Romans and the historical destruction of Jerusalem and the temple (similarly Taylor, *Mark*, 500); and A. Feuillet, op. cit. in note 37, refers *the whole* of the prediction Mark 13.5–27 to the time up to the historical destruction of Jerusalem. There is this to be said against both these assumptions, that the interpretation of the apocalyptic texts of Mark 13.7–27 cannot be redirected to events occurring within history (see above pages 97 f. and below pages 102 f.).

with the dawn of the Kingdom of God. This makes it clear that he positively expected the entry of the Kingdom of God to be also an upheaval of cosmic proportions. But again any closer description of this upheaval is lacking and the eschatological destruction of the temple is only mentioned in order to express the depravity of the contemporary Jewish practices and the certainty of an eschatological worship of God according to God's will. Thus Mark 13.1, 2 does not contradict what has already been established, namely that the significance of Jesus' eschatological message cannot lie in the apocalyptic description of the future.

In our analysis of Mark 13.1–27 we have so far met on the one hand with texts which in their present form reflect the experience of the Christian Church (13.6, 9, 10, 11, 13, 21–23), and on the other the strictly eschatological saying of Jesus, 13.2, which fits as it stands into the picture drawn so far of Jesus' eschatological message and which is continued in 13.28–37. Besides these two kinds of texts we find in Mark 13 still another group of passages which bear a completely different character (13.7, 8, 12, 14–20, 24–27). It is these texts which are in the main ascribed to the Jewish or Jewish-Christian apocalypse alleged to have been used; they deal with earthly and cosmic signs foretelling the end of the world, giving instructions on how to behave in the last days and finally describe the cosmic catastrophe, the heavenly appearance of the Son of Man and the gathering of the elect at the end of time. The texts reveal at no point the particular circumstances of Jesus or of primitive Christianity, but reproduce throughout Jewish apocalyptic conceptions.[48] That would not by itself suffice to

[48]See the list of references in Lohmeyer, *Markus*, 271 ff. Lohmeyer also shows that the prediction 'when ye see the abomination of desolation standing where he ought not . . . ' (13.14) cannot be applied to the historical event of placing the statue of Caligula in the temple, but only to the appearance of the Antichrist (against G. Hölscher, *TB* 12, 1933, 197 ff.). C. H. Dodd, 'The Fall of Jerusalem and the "Abomination of Desolation" ', *Journal of Roman Studies*, 1947, 47 ff. considers Mark 13.14–20 as an independent secondary tradition beside Luke 21.20–24, and sees in Luke 21.20, 21b, 22, 23b, 24 as well as in Luke 19.42–44 a prediction of the Jewish war and the destruction of Jerusalem composed before the year 70; and the question whether this prediction goes back to Jesus Dodd leaves open. Now he has undoubtedly established that in Luke 21.20–24 a tradition independent of Mark has been incorporated and assimilated to Mark by means of Luke 21. 21a, 23a; and it might also be mentioned that the two predictions, Luke 19.42 ff. and 21.21 ff. make use of Old Testament conceptions and *need* not have been framed *ex eventu*. But firstly nothing proves that this prediction dates from a time long before the catastrophe and therefore from the time of Jesus, and secondly it is not proved that the two Lucan predictions are

prove that this group of texts does not go back to Jesus, since of course the whole stock from which Jesus derived his eschatological conceptions was naturally of Jewish origin. Nor is it very significant that these verses show an abundance of conceptions not found elsewhere in the synoptic sayings of Jesus;[49] for these could not be avoided if the thoughts here put forward were to be expressed. But these apocalyptic conceptions which do not occur elsewhere among Jesus' sayings happen to have one feature in common, namely that they have no parallels in all the rest of the tradition concerning the eschatological message of Jesus; this is true of the description of the catastrophe before and at the end of the world, as well as of the exhortation to find safety before the final catastrophe, of the lamentations over those who, when the end comes, will be physically encumbered and of the thought of gathering the elect from the four ends of the earth. In addition to this, the parenthesis ὁ ἀναγινώσκων νοείτω (13.14) proves, at least for this group of texts, that a literary tradition has been brought into use. Consequently these texts drop out of the otherwise reliable tradition of Jesus' sayings.[50] They also form an irreconcilable contrast with his refusal to search for apocalyptic enlightenment and for premonitions of the end (Mark 12.25; Luke 17.20 f., etc.; and see above page 90). We are not swayed by a theory of literary criticism nor by the wish to remove Jesus as far as possible from apocalyptic;[51] but, having established the peculiar character of these strictly apocalyptic texts from the point of view of the history of the tradition, and having considered the coherence of

---

primary with regard to Mark 13.14 ff. As Jesus foretold the destruction of Jerusalem as a strictly eschatological event, it is in any case impossible that these Lucan predictions go back to Jesus.

[49] ἀκοαὶ πολέμων, θροεῖσθαι, τὸ τέλος = the end of the world 13.7; σεισμοί, λιμοί, ὠδῖνες 13.8; ἐπανίστασθαι, θανατοῦν 13.12; βδέλυγμα τῆς ἐρημώσεως, Ἰουδαία 13.14; γαστήρ 13.17; χειμών 13.18; θλῖψις 13.19, 24; κολοβοῦν 13.20; ἥλιος, σελήνη, σκοτίζεσθαι 13.24; ἀστέρες, δυνάμεις = the stars 13.25.

[50] The prediction 'then shall they see the Son of Man coming in clouds with great power and glory' (Mark 13.26) naturally agrees with Jesus' expectation of the appearance on the last day of the Son of Man on the clouds of heaven (Mark 14.62; 8.38), but only because here as there the expectation is based on Dan. 7.13 f. But this in no way means that this apocalyptic hope must for Jesus have the same connexion with cosmic catastrophes, etc., as in Mark 13.26 (see Taylor, *Mark*, 519).

[51] With this intention Bowman, *Maturity*, 238 points to the fact that Jesus nowhere quotes apocalyptic literature and therefore betrays no knowledge of it. But this indisputable fact does not, of course, prove ignorance of the apocalyptic world of ideas.

Jesus' eschatological message as a whole, we are forced to assert
that these completely isolated components of the eschatological
discourse, Mark 13 and parallels, cannot belong to the oldest
Jesus tradition, but represent primitive Jewish-Christian traditional material which has been brought into use by Mark in
building up his eschatological discourse. Apart from this no other
texts of this nature have penetrated into the Jesus tradition. Since
these apocalyptic texts are to be removed from Jesus' eschatological message, it follows conclusively that this message stands in
complete contrast to the *Weltanschauung* of apocalyptic;[52]
therefore the significance of his proclamation that the Kingdom of
God is imminent cannot lie in the *fact* that the end of the world is
near, but must be looked for elsewhere.

[52]Against Werner, *Dogma*, 41, see above page 88. Correctly Bowman,
Intention, 52; Jesus' teaching is prophetic, eschatological, evangelistic, but
anti-apocalyptic, anti-pharisaic, anti-sadducean.

III

THE PRESENCE OF THE
KINGDOM OF GOD

1. JESUS' VICTORY OVER THE DEVILS

WE can now finally take up the decisive question already posed above as to what Jesus actually meant when he expected the imminent coming of the Kingdom of God. In discussing the texts which demonstrate this expectation, we were able again and again to establish the fact that Jesus saw this future eschatological consummation to be effective already in the present in that the *eschaton* showed itself effective in his own person. Consequently men are distinguished decisively by their acceptance or rejection of the Son of Man in action even now, yet expected to be fully effective only in the near future; thus the fundamental presupposition for the future eschatological judgment was created already in the present, in which Jesus was the determining factor (cf. Mark 2.19a; 8.38; Matt. 19.28; Luke 12.32; 17.20 f.; 24.26).[1] This conclusion is confirmed by other sayings of Jesus. In the Q version of Jesus' defence against the accusation of being allied with Beelzebub the sentence occurs in Matt. 12.28 = Luke 11.20: 'But if I by the Spirit (Luke: finger) of God cast out devils then is the Kingdom of God come upon you.' This is a detached saying[2] which cannot have belonged originally to the preceding saying in Matt. 12.27 and par., because otherwise the meaning of 12.28

---

[1] E. Fuchs, 'Christus das Ende der Geschichte', *EvT* 1948/49, 449 note 6 raises the objection that it is a hermeneutical mistake to force Jesus himself historically out of the New Testament, to isolate historically the witness of Jesus to himself; accordingly Fuchs will only allow Jesus to be sought in the New Testament as an object of the gospel message. But however correct it is to say that the New Testament speaks of Jesus only as the object of its message, it is wrong to let this historical Jesus be merged into the apostolic message as found in the New Testament, in other words to exclude the message of Jesus himself. In the *oldest* tradition of Jesus' message, to be ascertained by critical methods, we meet with the Jesus whose *historical* message alone confirms the correctness of the apostolic message. To set forth this oldest message is therefore not only a historical task, but one that is theologically indispensable, and no hermeneutic mistake.

[2] See Bultmann, *Tradition*, 11 f., 174.

would be that the Jewish exorcists would also prove by their actions that the Kingdom of God had come; and in Matt. 12.29 par. Mark 3.27 there follows the equally independent detached saying about the binding of the strong man. Matt. 12.28 has therefore been handed down without an original context. The protasis is completely unequivocal;[3] Jesus points to the exorcism of devils which he is effecting; that he is qualified for these deeds he traces back to God's direct commission and help. From the deeds which can be perceived Jesus deduces the fact not perceptible of itself: ἄρα ἔφθασεν ἐφ' ὑμᾶς ἡ βασιλεία τοῦ θεοῦ. φθάνειν is not found elsewhere in the gospels; yet its meaning in the rest of the New Testament is completely unambiguous. The old meaning 'to anticipate' is found only once more (I Thess. 4.15) whilst elsewhere the aorist means without exception 'has arrived, has reached' (Rom. 9.31; II Cor. 10.14; I Thess. 2.16; in Phil. 3.16 also this is the most likely meaning).[4] Therefore it is customary to translate Matt. 12.28 = Luke 11.20 also 'the Kingdom of God is come upon you'.[5] In face of this K. W. Clark has tried to show that φθάνειν always has the meaning 'to draw near, even to the point of contact, but the experience which draws near is still sequential'; in his view therefore ἔφθασεν is synonymous with ἤγγικεν and only conveys the fact that the Kingdom of God stands at the door.[6] Now it is true that φθάνειν certainly means 'to be on the point of reaching', but in the past tense it can equally well denote the entry of an event the *consequences* of which can already

---

[3]It can scarcely be decided with certainty whether ἐν πνεύματι or ἐν δακτύλῳ is the more original, but it is in fact inessential; yet in view of Luke's tendency to introduce the idea of the spirit into the text, the version 'with the finger of God' is probably the older (thus e.g. M. Goguel, *Jean Baptiste*, 1928, 195; M. Goguel, *RevHR* 132, 1947, 148 f.; W. Michaelis, *Reich Gottes und Geist Gottes nach dem Neuen Testament*, 1947, 15; F. J. Leenhardt, *Le Baptême chrétien*, 1944, 26; Barrett, *Spirit*, 63).

[4]The Vulgate renders it in all four cases with *prevenire*, the Peshitta with *'drk* (=*advenire*) in Rom. 9.31 (and wrongly also in I Thess. 4.15) or *mṭ'* = come.

[5]The Latin versions here diverge widely (*adpropiavit, appropinquavit, pervenit, praevenit, adceleravit*), see Jülicher, *Itala* on Matt. 12.28. The Old Syriac versions and the Peshitta render Matt. 12.28 and Luke 11.20 with *qrbt 'lykwn*.

[6]K. W. Clark, *JBL* 59, 1940, 374 ff. J. Weiss, *Reich Gottes*, 70 f. had already maintained that ἤγγικεν as well as ἔφθασεν were translation from the same word *mṭ'*; J. Y. Campbell, *ExpT* 48, 1936/37, 92 f. wished to translate: 'The Kingdom of God will be upon you immediately' and R. Liechtenhan, *Das Kommen des Reich Gottes nach dem Neuen Testament*, 1944, 6 translates: 'then is the Kingdom of God drawn near'.

be felt.[7] There can therefore be no question of φθάνειν ever being used as a real synonym for ἐγγίζειν and it is without doubt no accident that in Matt. 12.28 = Luke 11.20 as contrasted with Mark 1.15 etc. ἔφθασεν and not ἤγγικεν is used. It can therefore be said with certainty that Matt. 12.28 = Luke 11.20 must be translated 'the Kingdom of God has come upon you'.[8] It is therefore exegetically untenable to assimilate the prediction Matt. 12.28 simply to Jesus' proclamation about the proximity of the Kingdom of God, which is indeed likewise attested with complete certainty.[9] On the contrary in Matt. 12.28 also Jesus' conviction shows itself clearly that the future Kingdom of God had already

[7] See the authorities in Kümmel, *Kirchenbegriff*, 54 note 88; further examples in Liddell and Scott, 1927 under II, 2 and IV, 1.

[8] Thus correctly C. H. Dodd, *ExpT* 48, 1936/37, 138 ff. and Bl.-Debr., §101. The translation mentioned above in note 5 in some of the Latin and Syriac versions expressing 'come near' is therefore wrong. Dalman, *Worte Jesu*, 88 conjectures plausibly *mṭ'* as the Aramaic basis. This result cannot be evaded by accepting the translation 'to arrive', and then finding in it either 'a kind of anticipation of the Kingdom' or an inexact translation of the Aramaic (thus M. Goguel, *RevHR* 132, 1947, 137). The fact that in Greek less ambiguous expressions for 'being come' would have been more natural is no justification for the conjecture that the Aramaic expression at the back of it is intended to denote 'an intensification of the coming near, a borderline case of an approach which yet does not mean complete presence' (against Michaelis, *Matthäus II*, 153 f.). Least of all can the meaning of φθάνειν be claimed to be 'to come near' on the basis of modern Greek (thus Bultmann, *TLZ* 72, 1947, 272). For even if φτάνω in modern Greek means 'to arrive' (thus A. Thumb, *Handbuch der neugriechischen Volkssprache*, ²1910, 351), yet that does not enable the sense to be traced back to 'come near' in Hellenistic Greek; and if ἐγγίζειν in modern Greek has lost the temporal meaning altogether, this shows a diverging development of the meanings of ἐγγίζειν and φθάνειν from which the conclusion cannot be drawn that the two verbs were formerly synonymous.

[9] This is done by Michaelis, *Täufer*, 73 ff., when he claims that the meaning of ἔφθασεν in Matt. 12.28 must 'be determined by the homogeneity of Jesus' preaching of the Kingdom, as it is established by other passages', and therefore 'it is come upon you' *could* affirm nothing other than 'has come near'. Werner, *Dogma*, 50 f., has asserted in much the same way that the sense of the 'actually ambiguous' passage, Matt. 12.28, may only be interpreted 'with reference to the imminent expectation, clearly attested in our Lord's sayings, of the reign of God pictured as transcendent in the near future'. But linguistically Matt. 12.28 is not ambiguous in spite of the divergence of the old translations, and it is quite unjustified to use the assumption of the 'homogeneity' of Jesus' pronouncements as the starting point from which to reinterpret the language of a passage contrary to the regular and altogether suitable usage. When Jesus says that the Kingdom of God is come, that is by no means 'such a correction of the conception held by Jesus in common with his hearers that it could only be accepted if it were expressly (polemically) effected in Jesus' own words' (R. Bultmann, *TLZ* 72, 1947, 273). For even Judaism can allow for the possibility or the actual fact that the reign of God

begun in his activity.[10] It follows that the proclamation of the proximity of the Kingdom of God clearly derives its *special* meaning in Jesus' mouth through this unusual proclamation of the presence of the future eschatological consummation; and it follows likewise that it is the person of Jesus whose activities provoke the presence of the eschatological consummation and who therefore stands at the centre of his eschatological message.[11] Accordingly not apocalyptic instruction, but a mysterious yet unmistakable message from God who would operate in Jesus at the end of time would be the real meaning of Jesus' eschatological preaching.

This deduction is confirmed by the neighbouring saying in Matthew: 'No one can enter into the house of the strong man and spoil his goods except he first bind the strong man; and then he will spoil his house' (Mark 3.27 par. Matt. 12.29; Luke 11.21 f.). Here too we are concerned with a detached saying which is appended to the explanation about the attack on Jesus that he was in alliance with the devil (Mark 3.22–26 and par.).[12] The picture of

---

as king in the present is a reality (Volz, *Eschatologie*, 166 f.; cf. especially Siphre Deut 33, 2 §343, p. 398, 5 ff., ed. Horovitz-Finkelstein, where a divine 'appearance' for Egypt and the Lawgiving on Sinai is asserted).

[10]There are no grounds at all for designating this pronouncement as an 'utterance of "pneumatic" ecstasy', and therefore made on a special occasion (thus J. Weiss, *Reich Gottes*, 90; similarly also W. Bousset, *Jesus*, [4]1922, 36, and E. F. Scott, *The Nature of the Early Church*, 1941, 38 f.; Jesus is only expressing his lively sense of the reality of the Kingdom). It is wrong also that Matt. 12.28 means: 'It is not Jesus who "brings" the Kingdom, but the Kingdom brings him with itself (see Otto, *The Kingdom of God*, 103 [in German *Reich Gottes*, 80]); it is true that there is nowhere a question of a 'bringing' of the Kingdom by Jesus, there is certainly a question of God acting in Jesus, in whom the Kingdom becomes a reality.—Dibelius, *Jesus*, 66 concludes from the text only that signs of the coming Kingdom are already there; but surely this is a weakening of Jesus' statement which is consciously throwing overboard the eschatological teaching of the Jews.

[11]K. L. Schmidt, *Le Problème du Christianisme primitif*, 1938, 35 ff. has shown that the ἐγώ found also in Matt. 12.28 is frequent in the sayings of Jesus and has a distinctly messianic significance.

[12]Matt. 12.29 reproduces the setting of Mark; Luke offers in 11.21 f. a completely different setting (from Q?) in which the householder has become a lord of a castle who has to fight with a foe. That is unlikely to be original, but is an allegorizing transformation (against Otto, *The Kingdom of God*, 101 f. [in German *Reich Gottes*, 78], who wishes to infer without any justification from the Lucan setting that by the ἰσχυρότερος was originally meant God himself who had taken off the armour from 'the strong man', whilst in Mark-Matthew this action was only secondarily transferred to Jesus; thus also Klostermann, *Markus*, 37). C. W. F. Smith, *Jesus*, 245: Jesus is 'both agent and manifestation' of the Kingdom of God acting in the present, is correct.

the theft in the house of the strong man is doubtless intended
as a metaphor; Satan is the strong man, Jesus is the stronger one
who takes away from him those whom he dominates; the place
allotted to this saying in Mark is therefore certainly essentially
correct. It has been conjectured that Jesus is alluding in this metaphor to an Old Testament and Jewish turn of speech about a
robbery in the house of a strong man,[13] and this is altogether
possible; yet Jesus would then have been the first to apply the
metaphor to the fight against Satan as 'the strong man'. In any
case Jesus here also sees the fight against Satan taking place in his
acts of exorcism. But this fight has already been won, because
Satan must *be* bound if he can be robbed of the children whom he
has dominated. And as it is a definite Jewish expectation that in
the last day Satan will be bound,[14] this pronouncement too means
that the Kingdom of God has begun its operations. It is the
meaning of the mission of Jesus, when announcing the *approach*
of the Kingdom of God, to make this future at the same time
already now a present reality.

2. THE MESSIANIC ACTS OF JESUS

Some further texts point in the same direction. It is told in the
self-contained detached account in Matt. 11.2–6 = Luke 7.18–23
how John the Baptist sitting in prison and hearing of Jesus'
works, sent his disciples with the question whether he was 'he
that cometh'. In reply Jesus drew attention to what can be seen
and heard: 'The blind receive their sight, the lame walk, the lepers
are cleansed and the deaf hear, and the dead are raised up, and the
poor have good tidings preached to them. And blessed is he who
shall find none occasion of stumbling in me.'[15] It has been questioned whether the Baptist's inquiry is original, because he

[13]See Bultmann, *Tradition*, 103; W. Grundmann, *TWNT* III, 403 f.;
Barrett, *Spirit*, 62; W. Bieder, *Die Vorstellung von der Höllenfahrt Jesu Christi*,
1949, 35; Taylor, *Mark*, 241. There are no reasons for seeing the binding of
Satan accomplished in Jesus' temptation (against Jeremias, *Weltvollender*, 59;
Jeremias, *Parables*, 99 (in German 101); C. J. Cadoux, *Mission*, 65 f.).
[14]See the well-known passage in *Assumptio Mosis*, 10.1; '*et tunc parebit
regnum illius in omni creatura illius et tunc zabulus finem habebit*' and the
authorities quoted in W. Grundmann, *TWNT* III, 403 f.
[15]Luke's version agrees completely with that of Matthew as regards the
Baptist's question and Jesus' answer; in Luke the framework has been
dramatized secondarily by a description of Jesus' healing activity taking
place just at the time of this inquiry (see M. Dibelius, *Die urchristliche Überlieferung von Johannes dem Täufer*, 1911, 33).

expected an apocalyptic Messiah and never believed in Jesus'
messianic commission, so that he could not have asked this
question expressing doubt; and Jesus' saying in Matt. 11.5 f., it is
said, originally simply described the last days of bliss and was only
reshaped secondarily as an apologetic reply to the Baptist's
question.[16] Now Jesus' answer undoubtedly alludes to the
promises in Isaiah, and in particular the idea of the eschatological
good tidings to the poor is derived from there.[17] So Jesus is
certainly using here a traditional form to describe the last days of
bliss. But on the one hand the designation of the Messiah as 'he
who comes' was by no means a customary designation in the early
Church nor a current Jewish one, and a Christian formulation
would surely much more readily have employed current termino-
logy.[18] On the other hand the Baptist appears here in no way as a
witness to Christ, but as an uncertain questioner, which contradicts the tendency of the early Church to make him such a witness;

[16]Thus Bultmann, *Tradition*, 22; Klostermann, *Matthäus*, 95; M. Goguel,
Jean Baptiste, 1928, 63; A. Fridrichsen, *Le problème du miracle dans le Christianisme primitif*, 1925, 66 ff.; C. H. Kraeling, *John the Baptist*, 1951, 128 ff.
(considers the text to be a Christian solution of the contrast between the
messianic conception of the Baptist and the Christian conception of Jesus).—
The fanciful elimination of 11, 4–6 by Hirsch, 'Studie zu Matt. 11.2–26',
TZ 6, 1950, 241 ff. deserves no refutation.

[17]Isa. 29.18 f.; 35.5 f.; 61.1 (πνεῦμα κυρίου ἐπ' ἐμὲ οὗ εἵνεκεν ἔχρισέν
με. εὐαγγελίσασθαι πτωχοῖς ἀπέσταλκεν με, ἰάσασθαι τοὺς συντετριμμένους
τῇ καρδίᾳ, κηρῦξαι αἰχμαλώτοις ἄφεσιν καὶ τυφλοῖς ἀνάβλεψιν). See especially
for this Schniewind, *Matthäus*, 135 ff. But Jesus did not thereby apply the
suffering servant to himself (against Bowman, *Intention*, 147).

[18]The 'coming' of the Son of Man is spoken of in Dan. 7.13, the eschatological 'coming' of God is mentioned several times (Zech. 14.5; Mal. 3.1).
There is no authority for 'The Coming One' as a designation of the Messiah;
but its presence in late Jewish usage can be conjectured from observing how
S. of Sol. 2.8 *qol dodhi hinneh zeh ba*' was applied in the rabbinical tradition
both to God's eschatological coming (Siphre Deut 32.11 §314, p. 357, 2 f. ed.
Horovitz-Finkelstein; Tanchuma ed. Buber, Bemidbar §16, p. 7b; in German
in Strack-Billerbeck IV, 860) and also to the coming of the Messiah (*Pesiqta
de Rab Kahana* ed. Buber, par. Hachodesh, p. 47b; Rabbi Judan and Rab
Huna. Rabbi Judan in the name of Rabbi Elieser, the son of Rabbi Jose the
Galilean and Rab Huna in the name of Rabbi Elieser, the son of Jacob, say
'The voice of my beloved, behold, he cometh', that is the King Messiah; in
the hour when he comes, he says to Israel: 'In this moment you will be
redeemed'; then they say to him 'How can we be redeemed?' etc.; parallels
in *Midrash Shir hashshirim Sidra* 2 to S. of Sol. 2.8, ed. Warsaw, 1924, 30a).
Cf. Volz, *Eschatologie*, 177. There is as little reason to let the Baptist expect
only the 'Prophet of the last days' (Duncan, *Jesus*, 94 f.) or Elias (Schweitzer,
Quest, 372 f., in German *Leben Jesu*, X f., 419) as to deny that the concept
indicates a title and to regard it only as a paraphrase of the question 'wilt *thou*
come?' (Michaelis, *Matthäus* II, 114).

moreover the story even lacks an ending giving the reaction of the Baptist to Jesus' message. Above all, Jesus' answer is unusual owing to its veiled style, since the question about the Messiah is answered neither in the affirmative nor clearly in the negative either; but the attentive listener has the answer thrust towards him. So it is the most probable assumption that the story in its essentials represents an old reliable tradition.[19] According to this Jesus describes his own actions in traditional forms which speak of the salvation in the messianic last days; he points to the fact that the Old Testament promise of the glorious last days and of the eschatological messenger of joy is fulfilling itself even now. It is true that in spite of the visible happenings it is possible to overlook this fulfilment and not everyone is forced to notice it; for it happens in ambiguous fashion and men can therefore be deceived by the lowliness of the wonder-worker and may fail to be led to recognize in his acts the events predicted for the messianic end. So Jesus' reply to the Baptist's question claims that the acts and the message are to be regarded as a proof of the beginning of the Kingdom of God, and it sees this beginning taking place exclusively in Jesus and his activity. It is shown once more that the proclamation of the good news of the future coming of the Kingdom of God, which was Jesus' task, receives its particular and decisive character through the fact that the person of Jesus by his actions brings about already now what is expected from the eschatological future; thus the real meaning of the eschatological preaching lies just in this, that it points to the actual presence of him who will bring about salvation in the last days.[20] Again attention has been turned away from the How and When of God's eschatological coming to the present messenger of this eschatological consummation.

Moreover the presence of the messianic consummation of

---

[19]Thus also M. Dibelius, *Die urchristliche Überlieferung von Johannes dem Täufer.* 1911, 33 ff.; H. G. Marsh, *The Origin and Significance of New Testament Baptism,* 1941, 97 f.; W. Manson, *Jesus,* 38 f.; C. J. Cadoux, *Mission,* 57 f.

[20]Michaelis, *Täufer,* 75 f. disputes that the presence of the Kingdom of God is spoken of here; 'but Jesus is pointing to the fact that everyone must see in his full authority to heal that his consciousness of his mission, which links his person with the imminent end, is a gift of God.' But this unnatural exegesis completely overlooks πτωχοὶ εὐαγγελίζονται and passes over the fact that Jesus had been asked not whether he had the right to feel conscious of his mission, but concerning his eschatological office and that this inquiry is answered by pointing to the promised eschatological acts of salvation which he performed.

salvation in the acts *and* sayings of Jesus is revealed in the beatitude on the disciples in Matt. 13.16 (= Luke 10.23 f.): 'Blessed are your eyes, for they see, and your ears, for they hear. For verily I say unto you, that many prophets and righteous men desired to see the things which ye see and saw them not and to hear the things which ye hear and heard them not'. This logion has been handed down without a context and the beginning of its original wording can be won only by combining both versions.[21] It belongs to the series of beatitudes on those who are allowed to experience the time of salvation.[22] Now two things are significant in this beatitude: not only is there mention of ἰδεῖν (live to see) the events at the end of time, but also of hearing them, and this juxtaposition does not correspond to the Jewish parallels, but to Matt. 11.5 f.[23] This by itself indicates that it is not merely an eschatological form of words about salvation which has been taken over, but that a *definite* experience marked by hearing must also be thought of. And secondly this beatitude is not spoken of men of the eschatological future, but of men of the present time to whom it is given to see and to hear that which the devout men of the Old Testament longed for.[24] So here too the present is clearly designated as the time of eschatological fulfilment, and again it is the happenings manifested in Jesus' acts and words which bring about the 'presentness' of the future fulfilment.[25] Thus the promised eschatological happening gains its meaning in this case also from Jesus' acts of salvation which are taking place in the present. For these acts of Jesus depend on an authority which surpasses all that has gone before. That follows manifestly from

[21]It might perhaps have run as follows: 'Blessed your eyes which see what you see, and your ears which hear what you hear, for many prophets and righteous men . . .' Cf. Klostermann, *Matthäus*, 119; Bultmann, *Tradition*, 114; Michaelis, *Matthäus* II, 200 f.

[22]See the combination in G. Erdmann, *Die Vorgeschichte des Lukas- und Matthäusevangeliums und Vergils vierte Ekloge*, 1932, 45.

[23]I have already drawn attention to these facts in *Eschatologie*, 11 note 19. To the parallels mentioned there (*Ps. Sol.* 17.50 and *Pesiqta de Rab Kahana*, chap. 22 bis, p. 149a, ed. Buber: 'ashrey sha'ah shemmashiaḥ nibhra' . . . 'ashrey 'ayin shezzakh^ethah lirᵉ'otho.) there might be added *Orac. Sybill.* III, 371 f.; IV, 192.

[24]In Matthew and Luke those addressed in the beatitude are the disciples; but Bultmann, *Tradition*, 173 conjectures probably correctly that this application denotes a restriction.

[25]In face of the peculiarity due to the mention of hearing, it can hardly be correct that the saying 'does not express originally a direct application to the person of Jesus' (Bultmann, *Tradition*, 114; against this Flew, *Church*, 65). The application to the person is not expressed, but is unmistakably indicated.

Matt. 12.41 f. = Luke 11.31 f., where, contrasted with the wisdom of Solomon which filled the whole world and with the preaching of Jonah which converted the Gentiles, it is said of Jesus ἰδοὺ πλεῖον Σολομῶνος ('Ιωνᾶ) ὧδε. Although it is true that Jesus' superiority over all that happened earlier is not painted in messianic colours, yet this double saying also makes it clear that Jesus' acts have no parallels, and when it is associated with the sayings of Jesus just discussed here too Jesus evidently ascribes eschatological significance to his own activity.[26]

Finally I must mention at this point the difficult saying in Luke 10.18: 'I beheld Satan fallen as lightning from heaven'. The saying is presented by Luke as a reply to the statement of the seventy that the devils were subject to them. But in its wording it reveals no connexion with the question of exorcism, still less with that of the authority of the disciples for such action, so that we are probably concerned here with a detached saying. This saying is unusual in that Jesus here seems to report a vision which included the fall of Satan to the earth in the form of a phenomenon of light; in consequence it is often understood as a reliable report that Jesus experienced a vision.[27] As we hear of no other visionary sights or sounds (apart from the account of the baptism and the Q version of the temptation which cannot be used for biographical purposes),[28] other critics assume that we have here a figurative way of expressing what Jesus sees to be taking place in the work of himself and his disciples[29] or consider that it is not possible to

---

[26]See Schniewind, *Matthäus*, 158; Wilder, *Eschatology*, 150; Guy, *Last Things*, 46; Duncan, *Jesus*, 195 note 1. Mark 2.23–26 (the justification of the disciples plucking corn on the sabbath day by pointing to David's use of the shewbread) can hardly be used in this connexion against this (against Schniewind, *Markus*, 62; Wilder, *Eschatology*, 150); for here Jesus did not appeal to the special messianic rights of his disciples, but decides that the law of the sabbath may be broken for reasons of hunger in order to fulfil the real will of God for the laws of the sabbath (see *ZNW* 33, 1934, 121).

[27]J. Weiss, *Reich Gottes*, 93; Hauck, *Lukas*, 142; T. W. Manson, *Sayings*, 258; A. Frövig, *Das Sendungsbewusstsein Jesu und der Geist*, 1924, 93; A. Fridrichsen, *Le problème du miracle dans le christianisme primitif*, 1925, 96; A. J. B. Higgins, 'Jesus as Prophet', *ExpT* 57, 1945/46, 293; C. A. Webster, 'St. Luke 10.18', *ExpT* 57, 1945/46, 52 f.; K. L. Schmidt, 'Die Bildersprache in der Johannes-Apokalypse', *TZ* 3, 1947, 165 f.; Barrett, *Spirit*, 63 f.; H. Bietenhard, *Die himmlische Welt im Urchristentum und Spätjudentum*, 1951, 212.

[28]C. J. Cadoux, *Mission*, 66 considers that in Luke 10.17 Jesus refers back to the story of the temptation; this certainly gives no occasion for this idea.

[29]Rengstorf, *Lukas*, 138; A. Schlatter, *Das Evangelium des Lukas,* 1931, 279; F. Spitta, 'Der Satan als Blitz', *ZNW* 9, 1908, 162; M. Goguel, *La naissance du Christianisme*, 1946, 365 note 2; M. Goguel, *RevHR* 132

discover the original meaning of the saying.[30] Now of course we cannot say for certain whether the tradition has suppressed other accounts of Jesus' visionary experiences,[31] but even if it has not done so, there is no doubt of the possibility that Jesus had such experiences. And the wording of the saying with its comparison of Satan's fall in its swiftness and conspicuousness to a flash of lightning suggests a visionary experience more strongly than a figure of speech.[32] But even if it is hardly possible to give a certain answer to this question, there is no reason to doubt that this saying belongs to the oldest tradition, nor can there be any uncertainty about its meaning in the framework of Jewish conceptions;[33] the conquest of Satan by God, or by the Messiah expected in the last days, has already occurred; he is deprived of his power, his rule is broken. Now Jesus can have meant by this one thing only, that he has seen the defeat accomplished in the fight he is waging victoriously against the devils. So here too it is quite firmly established that the eschatological consummation, the Kingdom of God, has already become a present reality in the ministry of Jesus. And here too the message of the approaching Kingdom of God is actually illuminated by the knowledge that through Jesus' activities the future consummation is brought into the present.

This claim, that in his works the reality of the approaching Kingdom of God is already showing itself, Jesus expressed by

1947, 153 f. (admittedly doubts the authenticity of the saying); Bowman, *Intention*, 243 note 40; Bowman, *Maturity*, 244 f. (Jesus concludes from the success of the seventy that it concerns the Kingdom of God coming 'on the historical plane'!).

[30]Bultmann, *Tradition*, 174; M. Dibelius, *Die Botschaft von Jesus Christus*, 1935, 149. The interpretation of the verse ironically by M. van Rhijn (at the enthusiastic report of the disciples Jesus saw Satan falling from heaven) is correctly rejected by Jeremias, *Parables*, 98 note 44 (in German 101 note 4), as unwarranted.

[31]This was conjectured by H. Windisch, 'Jesus und der Geist nach der synoptischen Überlieferung', *Studies in Early Christianity, presented in Porter and Bacon*, 1928, 209 ff. On the other side Barrett, *Spirit*, 113 ff. pointed out that the 'pneumatic' features in the picture of Jesus are neither suppressed nor emphasized.

[32]The imperfect ἐθεώρουν need not conflict with this assumption, since it can describe a past continuous action (cf. Bl.-Debr., §327 with note and the parallels from Luke in J. Weiss, *Die Evangelien des Markus und Lukas*, [8]1892, 454). K. G. Kuhn in Michaelis, *TWNT* V 345 note 161 reminds us that there is only *one* past tense in Aramaic.

[33]See Strack-Billerbeck I, 167 f.

means more or less visible to the beholder in a series of actions in Jerusalem.[34] The account of Jesus' entry into Jerusalem (Mark 11.1–10 par. Matt. 21.1–9; Luke 19.28–38) is certainly difficult to interpret in detail; for the feature about the wondrous discovery of the animal he rode shows clearly that the story has been told as a 'legend', to describe 'an event of messianic significance'.[35] But this only proves that the beginning of this account has been given a legendary colouring, whilst the actual story of Jesus' entry appears on the contrary to be very primitive. To begin with, it is surely obvious that only Jesus' disciples and other Galilean pilgrims to the feast (cf. Mark 11.9a) take part in honouring Jesus, and this need therefore by no means have been particularly noticeable and in any case cannot have come to the ears of the Roman authorities. And then the cries of the crowd accompanying Jesus are neither messianic nor certainly eschatological. Mark 11.9a ('Hosanna, blessed is he that cometh in the name of the Lord') is a simple reproduction of Ps. 118.25a, 26 and therefore comes from the Hallel Psalms which were sung at a number of festivals and so were familiar to every Jew.[36] The introductory cry, *hoshiʿah naʾ* addressed in Ps. 118.25a to Yahve, is used in Mark without a definite application, but is there also no doubt addressed to God according to liturgical use; it can indeed be conjectured that the cry had become simply a formal festal cry, because *hoshaʿnaʾ* had acquired the derived meaning of the festal bouquet at the Feast of Tabernacles *and* of the songs sung at that time.[37] That this is a formula which need not express a *particular* petition is suggested also by the repetition ὡσαννὰ ἐν τοῖς ὑψίστοις which cannot be construed with certainty, so that its Aramaic wording remains open to question.[38] Now when to these formal cries is added: 'Blessed is he who comes in the name of the Lord' (Ps. 118.26), then the crowd accompanying Jesus can have meant by the cry ἐρχόμενος Jesus alone. But the customary cry for the festal pilgrims does not indicate any special dignity for Jesus; it is merely the fact that his companions come with him and strew

[34]It is wrong to bring in, as Guy does in *Last Things*, 47, Luke 14.21 ff. (the messianic feast as a present reality in Jesus' ministry), since the parable is doubtless describing the *eschatological* feast, whilst in the present it is only decided beforehand who will have a share in it.

[35]Dibelius, *Tradition*, 121 f. (in German *Formgeschichte*, 118 f.).

[36]Strack-Billerbeck I, 845.

[37]J. Elbogen, *Der jüdische Gottesdienst in seiner geschichtlichen Entwicklung*, ³1931, 219.

[38]Cf. Lohmeyer, *Markus*, 232; Schniewind, *Markus*, 139.

the way for him which shows that they want to pay him particular honour. Now from all this it follows clearly that in the mind of the disciples, or at any rate in that of the crowd, there can be no question of honour done to Jesus as to the Messiah. Nor can the following cry in Mark 11.10a 'Blessed is the kingdom that cometh, the kingdom of our father David' upset this opinion. For this cry does not bring Jesus as he enters into any connexion with the approaching Kingdom of God; at the most it might be supposed that the eschatological hope would be kindled by his entry.[39] But the cry, missing in Matthew and Luke, is in itself very remarkable (David is practically nowhere else called 'our father',[40] and there is nowhere at all any mention of the 'coming' of the kingdom of David). So this is plainly an un-Jewish way of speaking and Mark 11.10a is presumably a secondary construction.[41] There can therefore be hardly any doubt that Jesus' entry into Jerusalem had no messianic character in the minds of his companions.[42] But what Jesus himself wished to express by this action is a completely different question. The fact that the Christian tradition was at pains to display the messianic character of the happening (cf. already in Mark the legendary feature about finding the animal to ride on and then quite particularly the reshaping of Mark 11.9 in Matt. 21.9; Luke 19.38) proves that an event in the life of Jesus, which was at first sight unmessianic, underlies the transmitted legend.[43] But if Jesus only rode into Jerusalem on an ass amid the

[39]Thus A. Fridrichsen, *Le problème du miracle dans le christianisme primitif*, 1925, 44.

[40]Strack-Billerbeck II, 26.

[41]See Dalman, *Worte Jesu*, 181; Lohmeyer, *Markus*, 231 f.

[42]Schniewind, *Markus*, 139 f.; Bowman, *Intention*, 149 ff.; Otto, *The Kingdom of God*, 223 f. (in German *Reich Gottes*, 185 f.); Lohmeyer, *Markus*, 231; A. Fridrichsen, op. cit. in note 39, 44; Taylor, *Mark*, 452 ff. The conjecture that at least the disciples understand the event as messianic (Grundmann, *Jesus*, 152; M. Goguel, *La vie de Jésus*, 1932, 395; E. Meyer, *Ursprung und Anfänge des Christentums* I, 1921, 162 f.), has no support from the text, still less has the assumption that Jesus was honoured by the crowd as 'the prophet and Elias' (Schweitzer, *Quest*, 392, in German *Leben Jesu*, 440).—E. Werner, ' "Hosanna" in the Gospels', *JBL* 65, 1946, 97 ff. maintains that in Judaism at the time of Jesus Hosanna had a messianic meaning, that in this cry Jesus was addressed as Messiah. But even if the messianic interpretation of Ps. 118 were older than is actually attested, yet there is no indication at all that Hosanna in itself had a messianic ring and could have applied to Jesus in the mouth of the crowd.

[43]See M. Dibelius, *Tradition*, 122 (in German *Formgeschichte*, 119): 'The existence of this legend is most easily understood, if Jesus himself gave cause for it.'

reverential shouts of the crowd and if this fact was remembered as something remarkable, there can be no doubt that Jesus consciously associated himself with Zech. 9.9. For the verse: 'Behold thy king cometh unto thee; he is just and having victory; lowly, and riding upon an ass, upon a male ass, the foal of a she-ass'[44] was in early days applied by the rabbis to the Messiah[45] and so was probably known to Jesus with this meaning. But while the messianic exegesis of Zech. 9.9 by the rabbis probably did not seriously influence the active messianic expectation,[46] Jesus by a conscious act associates himself with the prediction and shows thereby that he wishes to be a Messiah without pomp, but yet just in this lowly action the eschatological consummation is already revealing itself.[47]

The cleansing of the temple by Jesus throws still more light (Mark 11.15–17 par. Matt. 21.12 f.; Luke 19.45 f.). It is true that here too it is not quite clear what happened. For how can Jesus, as a single individual, cleanse the great space of the 'Court of the Gentiles' of the sellers of the sacrifices and of the money-changers, in business there with the permission of the priesthood, without

[44]The translation of the Zürich Bible is corrected here by L. Köhler, *Kleine Lichter*, 1945, 52 ff.; the 'colt' of the synoptic account is taken from the Septuagint which has a wrong translation here, as Köhler has shown convincingly. So Jesus probably did not ride on a colt, which is really not practicable, but on a male ass.

[45]Strack-Billerbeck I, 842 ff.

[46]The theory that the Messiah would come riding on an ass to the *unworthy* Israelites (Sanh. 98a, in German in Strack-Billerbeck I, 843) is only an attempt to harmonize Zech. 9.9 with the expectation of a glorious Messiah (see G. F. Moore, *Judaism in the First Centuries of the Christian Era*, II, 1927, 334 f.) and not a popular conception. It may therefore not be concluded from Jesus' associating himself with Zech. 9.9 that he wished to accuse Israel of being unworthy (thus Grundmann, *Jesus*, 153).

[47]Thus e.g. C. J. Cadoux, *Mission*, 59; Lohmeyer, *Markus*, 232; Schniewind, *Markus*, 139; A. Oepke, *ST* 2, 1948/50, 137; M. Goguel, *La vie de Jésus*, 1932, 395; Bowman, *Intention*, 149 ff.; Bowman, *Maturity*, 68; Schweitzer, *Quest*, 391 f. (in German *Leben Jesu*, 440); Taylor, *Mark*, 452. Why 'the conjecture . . . that Jesus wished to dramatize the fulfilment of Zech. 9.9' should be absurd (Bultmann, *Tradition*, 281) is incomprehensible; and the doubt 'whether there is a basis of historical fact' (thus Ackermann, *Jesus*, 61) is unfounded. According to E. Pfennigsdorf, *Der Menschensohn*, 1948, 58, Jesus' messianic intention also is imported.—Jeremias, *Weltvollender*, 35 ff. wishes to prove the messianic character of the entry further also by the fact that a royal entry, followed by a cleansing of the temple, was a traditional symbol for the world crisis (thus also Jeremias, *Eucharistic Words*, 63 [in German 52]). But as the connexion in time between the entry and the cleansing is uncertain, this remains a mere conjecture, especially as the Jewish parallels for its connexion are uncertain (cf. Volz, *Eschatologie*, 217).

opposition or the intervention of the Jewish or Roman police?[48] And how can Jesus prevent the forecourt of the temple being used as a thoroughfare?[49] But even if Jesus' action should have had no such comprehensive effects as the synoptic account suggests, Jesus undoubtedly arrogates to himself a right which did not belong to him. It is hardly sufficient to see it as a prophetic action because according to Mark 11.17 Jesus appeals to the words of the prophets Isa. 56.7; Jer. 7.11.[50] For not only is there evidence since Ezekiel for associating the messianic era with the renewal of the temple,[51] but the expectation that the Gentiles will worship in Jerusalem refers also particularly to the messianic era;[52] and moreover Jesus' action in making a fundamental attack on the present form of worship far exceeds the authority claimed by a prophet. So Jesus by this act indubitably claims to realize already, now at this point, the eschatological hour as the eschatological saviour, and thus claims to perform a messianic action.[53]

[48]See E. Lohmeyer, 'Die Reinigung des Tempels', *TB* 20, 1941, 259. For the archaeological hypotheses cf. Lohmeyer, *Markus*, 235 ff.; and Strack-Billerbeck I, 763 ff., 850 ff.—T. W. Manson, 'The Cleansing of the Temple', *Bull. of the John Rylands Library* 33, 1950/51, 271 ff. advocates the view for which he offers very insufficient reasons that this incident occurred during the Feast of Tabernacles.

[49]See on this Strack-Billerbeck II, 27.—But it is fantastic to conclude from this that 'for several days (apparently three at least) he issued orders and these orders were obeyed (Mark 11.16)' (thus S. Kennard, *Jesus in the Temple*, Diss. Strasbourg, 1935, 3). There is also no reason to declare the cleansing of the temple to be unhistorical (against Ackermann, *Jesus*, 62).

[50]G. Schrenk, *TWNT* III, 243.

[51]Ibid. 238 f.

[52]Lohmeyer, *Markus*, 237 refers correctly to *Ps. Sol.* 17.30 f.

[53]Thus J. Klausner, *Jesus von Nazareth*, 1930, 432; Jeremias, *Weltvollender*, 43 (who cites as proof the discussion concerning his authority, Mark 11.27 ff., which however is uncertain); Schniewind, *Markus*, 142; Hauck, *Markus*, 135; Major, *Mission and Message*, 142; E. Meyer, *Ursprung und Anfänge des Christentums* I, 1921, 163; C. H. Dodd, *History and the Gospel*, 1938, 132; Taylor, *Mark*, 464; F. Braun, 'L'expulsion des vendeurs du temple', *RB* 38, 1929, 190 (emphasizes correctly that the people need not have understood the messianic significance of this action).—It is highly improbable that Jesus wished by this proceeding to turn Mal. 3.1 into action (Bowman, *Maturity*, 122 f.), especially as in it there is no mention of the *cleansing* of the temple. Still less did Jesus have the political purpose to rob of their powers the priesthood installed by Rome (thus S. Kennard, op. cit. in note 49, 3 ff.).—E. Lohmeyer, 'Die Reinigung des Tempels', *TB* 20, 1941, 257 ff.; E. Lohmeyer, *Kultus und Evangelium*, 1942, 44 ff. understands the cleansing of the temple to mean that Jesus cleansed the Court of the Gentiles in order thereby to make possible the Gentiles' eschatological adoration in the temple at Jerusalem. But this interpretation rests exclusively on the words πᾶσιν τοῖς ἔθνεσιν, which are taken into Mark 11.17 from Isa. 56.7, and overlooks the fact that Jesus'

If, as Jesus claimed, these two actions reveal the presence of the coming Kingdom of God in his works, then in conclusion Jesus' last supper also may be dealt with here. We have already seen that according to Mark 14.25 Jesus vowed in the presence of his disciples that he would no more drink wine until he drank it anew with them at the messianic feast.[54] But the disciples are now and henceforth to eat bread and drink wine 'until that day'. At the same time Jesus gives this eating and drinking in common a particular significance, as the words of interpretation show.[55] For the bread-word Mark 14.22 has no doubt preserved the oldest form; λάβετε· τοῦτό ἐστιν τὸ σῶμά μου.[56] Its meaning can only be determined with certainty if the Aramaic equivalent of σῶμα can be ascertained. J. Jeremias deduced from the supposition that 'σῶμα and αἷμα in Jesus' sayings represents a twin concept' that σῶμα—αἷμα must corespond here to an Aramaic *biśra'—dᵉmaʿ*.[57] But against this there is the fact that according to Jeremias' own argument σῶμα is only seldom found as the translation of *baśar* and that the pair σῶμα—αἷμα occurs elsewhere only in Heb. 13.11 where there is no doubt a particular occasion for it,[58] but quite

---

proceeding has in no way a clear reference to the Gentiles. So it remains essentially more probable that the action should be interpreted as a cleansing of the whole of the temple.

[54] See above page 31.

[55] We cannot enter here upon a discussion as to whether or not in Jesus' last supper we are concerned with the Passover meal. In spite of the detailed exposition of Jeremias, *Eucharistic Words*, 14–57 (in German 10–49) there are in my opinion weighty reasons against assuming a Passover meal (the absence of the Passover lamb in the Mark/Paul account, the impossibility of crucifying Jesus on the day of the Passover, the fact that the words of interpretation belong together and may not be separated by a meal-time, etc.), so that to understand the words of interpretation one must not start from the symbolism of the Passover rite. Thus also those scholars named in Jeremias, *Eucharistic Words*, 7–13 (in German 7–9), also W. Grundmann, *Die Gottes-kindschaft in der Geschichte Jesu*, 1938, 149; R. H. Lightfoot, *History and Interpretation in the Gospels*, 1934, 138 f.; M. Goguel, *L'Eglise primitive*, 1947, 346; C. T. Craig, *The Beginning of Christianity*, 1943, 126; Taylor, *Mark*, 664 ff.; K. G. Kuhn, 'Über den ursprünglichen Sinn des Abendmahls und sein Verhältnis zu den Gemeinschaftsmahlen der Sektenschrift', *EvTh* 1950/51, 515 ff. (contests the right to interpret the words in accordance with the circumstances of the Passover meal, but wishes to leave open the question whether or not Jesus' last meal was in fact a Passover meal).

[56] See list of references in Jeremias, *Eucharistic Words*, 99 ff. (in German 80 ff.).

[57] Jeremias, *Eucharistic Words*, 140 f. (in German 103 f.).

[58] Heb. 13.11 refers back to Lev. 16.27 where the blood of the animals of the sin-offering is contrasted with their bodies which are described in a paraphrase by detailing τὰ δέρματα αὐτῶν καὶ τὰ κρέα αὐτῶν καὶ τὴν κόπρον

especially that the altogether unusual parallelism σῶμα—αἷμα would hardly have been introduced in the place of the familiar one *biśra'—d⁴ma'* without a distinct reason. But as the supposition that Jesus must have used a familiar pair of concepts is unproven, *gupha'* which means 'body, self, I' may rather be assumed as the equivalent of σῶμα which is unusual beside αἷμα.[59] Jesus therefore distributes the bread which represents himself as he goes to his death. The disciples, by eating in common at the farewell meal the bread handed to them by the coming 'Son of Man', partake in advance of the messianic meal promised to them, experience in advance the consummation of the Kingdom of God. The cup-word also bears a similar meaning. Here indeed the question is hotly debated whether Mark or Paul give the oldest version of the word. But against the assumption maintained by Jeremias that here also Mark preserves the original wording,[60] there is the fact that the Marcan version is most easily explained by the law of liturgical assimilation and that Jesus as a Jew could hardly speak of the wine as his blood to be drunk. So Paul has probably preserved here the older form of the saying: 'This cup is the new covenant in my blood.'[61] According to this the disciples, whilst drinking the wine handed round by Jesus, obtain a share in the new eschatological covenant of God, made possible through

---

αὐτῶν; therefore σάρξ would fit very badly here. Besides there are good grounds for conjecturing in this place 'the influence of the account of the Last Supper' (see O. Michel, *Der Brief an die Hebräer*, ²1949, 344 note 2, and G. Bornkamm, *Das Anathema in der urchristlichen Abendmahlsliturgie*, 'Das Ende des Gesetzes', 1952, 139 note 19).

[59]G. Dalman, *Jesus-Jeschua*, 1922, 129 ff.; F. G. Kuhn, *TLZ* 75, 1950, 405 f.; J. Bonsirven, 'Hoc est corpus meum', *Biblica* 29, 1948, 205 ff. rejects *gwp'* in favour of *bśr'* because the *gwp'* 'was too uncertain in its meaning and not at all appropriate to indicate all that Jesus wished to put into "this is my body", namely his love as he went forward to suffer, his whole human and divine being which is to be the nourishment of those partaking of the communion'. But this objection is based on an impermissible over-interpretation of the conception of τὸ σῶμά μου and the suggestion is equally unconvincing that the use of σάρξ in John 6.51 ff. is only to be explained if Jesus had used *bśr'* in his bread-word.

[60]Jeremias, *Eucharistic Words*, 110 ff. (in German 83 ff.) and the scholars named there on page 115 note 1 (in German 86 note 1).

[61]Dibelius, *Tradition*, 207 (in German *Formgeschichte*, 208); H. Huber, *Das Herrenmahl*, Diss. Bern, 1929, 49 f.; J. Behm, *TWNT* III, 730 f.; M. Goguel, *L'Eglise primitive*, 1947, 345; Flew, *Church*, 99 f.; W. Marxsen, *Die Einsetzungsworte*, 1951 (according to the report in *TLZ* 77, 1952, 573); E. Schweizer, 'Das johanneische Zeugnis vom Herrenmahl', *Ev Th*, 1952/53, 342.

Jesus' death. That which the eschatological 'new covenant' foretold by Jeremiah will give some day, is for the disciples even now
a present gift, if they accept the cup offered them by Jesus, the
Son of Man to come, as he goes to his death and resurrection.
This demonstrates that Jesus in the 'twin symbol' of bread and
wine allows the disciples to share the messianic salvation in
present experience, and that the disciples by participation in this
meal come to know an eschatological communion rite which lets
them see the eschatological consummation in the present through
union with the departing Jesus.[62] The symbolic actions of Jesus
during his time in Jerusalem therefore confirm the statement that
Jesus perceived the coming consummation of salvation breaking
in on the present in his works.

3. THE END OF THE LAW AND THE PROPHETS

It is therefore a matter of course that Jesus expressed clearly for
once that with his entry the old aeon is at an end, because the
Kingdom of God is now appearing. I am referring to the much
discussed saying which speaks of the use of violence against the
Kingdom of God, reproduced by Matthew and Luke in different
versions and sequence: Matt. 11.12 f.: 'From the days of John the
Baptist until now the kingdom of heaven suffereth violence and
men of violence take it by force; for all the prophets and the law
prophesied until John', and Luke 16.16: 'The law and the prophets were until John; from that time the gospel of the kingdom
is preached and every man entereth violently into it'. The saying
stands in Matthew in the context of a series of sayings about John
the Baptist, in Luke in that of one about the law. Both contexts

[62]Cf. e.g. Wendland, *Eschatologie*, 188 ('anticipation of the messianic meal');
Lohmeyer, *Markus*, 304 ('the present hour and what happens in it belongs
thereby to the eschatological reality of God's reign'); E. Gaugler, *Das
Abendmahl im Neuen Testament*, 1943, 68 f. ('the gift of eschatological goods in
anticipation'); E. Schweizer, 'Das Abendmahl eine Vergegenwärtigung des
Todes Jesu oder ein eschatologisches Freudenmahl?', *TZ* 2, 1946, 92 ff.—
Schweitzer, *Quest*, 374 (in German *Leben Jesu*, XI f., 421) also wished to
interpret the miraculous feeding as an 'antitype of the messianic meal' (thus
also P. Nepper-Christensen, 'Wer hat die Kirche gestiftet?', *Symb. Biblicae
Upsalienses* 12, 1950, 32) and E. Lohmeyer, 'Das Abendmahl in der Urge-
meinde', *JBL* 56, 1937, 223 ff. would like to see in Jesus' meals with his
disciples in general a realization in the present of God's reign; according to
Jeremias, *Eucharistic Words*, 136 f. (in German 100) from the time of the
messianic confession at Caesarea Philippi 'every meal with Jesus was for his
own a symbol, an advance representation, indeed an anticipation of the meal
of consummation'. But none of this can be proved.

are plainly editorial, so that the saying was handed down originally without any context. Its difficulty lies not only in the debatable translation of βιάζεται, but also in the question which version and which sequence of both halves of the saying is actually original. So the original order of the two parts of the sentence cannot be established for certain. The starting point must be the statement about βιάζεσθαι. However this conception is understood, it is clear that Matthew offers an enigmatic and therefore a difficult statement, whilst Luke by introducing εὐαγγελίζεται and the middle voice form of βιάζεται produces an inoffensive and mitigating idea. Therefore Matthew has doubtless here preserved the more original version.[63] As for the other half of the sentence which connects the law and the prophets with John, the short and somewhat shocking form of Luke on the contrary, telling of the end of the law and the prophets, might have been toned down in Matthew.[64] This the original saying would have corresponded more or less to Luke 16.16a; Matt. 11.12, or in the reverse order.[65] When interpreting βιάζεται in Matt. 11.12 in addition to the linguistic instances, the parallelism of ἡ βασιλεία τῶν οὐρανῶν βιάζεται and βιασταὶ ἁρπάζουσιν αὐτήν must be especially considered. G. Schrenk has shown in a careful investigation[66] that the parallelism βιάζεται/ἁρπάζουσιν as well as the meaning of βιαστής require βιάζεται to be understood as denoting an act of violence in a bad sense. Therewith two interpretations which are always being brought forward drop out of account: 'The Kingdom of God forces its way through'[67] and 'the Kingdom of God is striven after with violence'.[68] So Matthew 11.12 must have the meaning:

[63]A comprehensive list of references in J. Weiss, *Reich Gottes*, 194; M. Dibelius, *Die urchristliche Überlieferung von Johannes dem Täufer*, 1911, 23 f.; M. Goguel, *Jean Baptiste*, 1928, 66 f.; G. Schreck, *TWNT* I, 611.

[64]Thus Goguel, loc. cit. in note 63.

[65]According to C. H. Kraeling, *John the Baptist*, 1951, 156 (cf. also Wilder, *Eschatology*, 149 note 5) Luke presupposes two periods (until John and from then on), Matthew on the other hand three (until John, from John until now, and from now on). But the second and third periods assumed by Matthew are for him also only *one* epoch.

[66]G. Schrenk, *TWNT* I, 608 ff.; cf. Michaelis, *Matthäus* II, 123.

[67]Thus Otto, *The Kingdom of Heaven*, 108 ff (in German *Reich Gottes*, 84 ff.); T. W. Manson, *Sayings*, 135; C. J. Cadoux, *Mission*, 130; Stonehouse, *Witness*, 247 f.; W. Manson, *Jesus*, 49; H. Clavier, *L'accès au royaume de Dieu*, 1944, 10 f.; Walter, *Kommen*, 13; Meinertz, *Theologie* I, 34; presumably also Schniewind, *Matthäus*, 140 f.

[68]Thus according to Schweitzer, *Quest*, 355 f. (in German *Leben Jesu*, 404) ('it is the host of penitents which are wringing it from God, so that it must come at the very next moment'), Werner, *Dogma*, 70 f.; similarly Leipoldt,

ince the appearance of the Baptist until the present moment the Kingdom of God is being violently assaulted and violent men wish to rob it. But this still leaves it obscure who is here thought of as the assailant and robber and who is to be robbed. The second question can be answered with certainty, since within the framework of Jesus' preaching there can be no thought of practising violence against God; the βιασταί must be attempting to rob men of the Kingdom of God.[69] On the other hand the first question can scarcely be answered confidently. Since the ministry of John is named as the point when the βιάζεσθαι began, a fight against the Kingdom of God must be meant; this fight seeks to injure the Kingdom of God which is being realized since Jesus' appearance. M. Dibelius[70] therefore wished to understand the text as meaning that during the interval between the ministry of John the Baptist and the present the Kingdom of God is handed over to the world rulers in the spiritual world; others think of the opposition to Jesus by his Jewish antagonists.[71] No argument can be brought forward to tip the scale between these two exegeses, nor can either be definitely refuted;[72] so the question must be left open. But the answer to it is not important with regard to what is decisive in our argument; for this at all events is clear: that Jesus considers his presence to be a time in which the Kingdom of God can already be attacked as being present. The ἕως ἄρτι can in this

---

esus, 119; A. T. Cadoux, *Theology*, 45, 54; P. Feine, *Theologie des Neuen Testaments*, [5]1931, 81; M. Buber, *Zwei Glaubensweisen*, 1950, 24 (in connexion with Luke 16.16b); C. T. Craig, *The Beginning of Christianity*, 1943, 81; E. Fennigsdorf, *Der Menschensohn*, 1948, 45.—Michaelis, *Verheissung*, 64 ff. has convincingly refuted Werner's objections to Schrenk's linguistic and exegetical arguments.

[69]Thus rightly G. Schrenk, *TWNT* I, 610; Schlatter, *Matthäus*, 368.

[70]M. Dibelius, op. cit. in note 63, 26 ff.; similarly Wilder, *Eschatology*, 84, 49, 181 f.

[71]Thus recently G. Schrenk, *TWNT* I, 610; Wendland, *Eschatologie*, 47 f.; Michaelis, *Verheissung*, 45; Michaelis, *Matthäus II*, 123; Schlatter, *Matthäus*, 368.

[72]Against Dibelius' exegesis M. Goguel, loc. cit. in note 63 has raised the objection that Jesus understood the power hostile to the Kingdom of God not in a collective sense, but as an individual, namely Satan; but however correct that may be in view of Mark 3.23 ff., yet Matt. 12.28 also clearly supposes that it is a *number* of devils against whom, as enemies of the Kingdom of God, Jesus fights; βιασταί *could* therefore very well refer to spiritual powers hostile to God.—A. Fridrichsen, 'Zu Matt. 11.11–15', *TZ* 2, 1946, 470 f. wishes to identify the βιασταί with the adherents of the Baptists who claim to possess the Kingdom of God; but in what way such a claim constitutes a 'robbery' remains completely unexplained.

connexion only be intended to express that the βιάζεσθαι and
ἁρπάζειν is merely a provisional happening which will come to an
end. All that we have found up till now to be Jesus' message confirms the interpretation that attack on the present activity of the
Kingdom of God can only mean hostile action against it as it
makes its appearance in Jesus, and that the limit of ἕως ἄρτι will
be the future dawn of the consummated Kingdom of God when
it appears ἐν δυνάμει. Moreover this exegesis is corroborated by
the other half of the saying, Luke 16.16a, according to which the
period of the old revelation of God came to an end with John the
Baptist. Consequently Jesus not only claimed to replace the Old
Testament revelation by the perfect revelation,[73] but he also proclaimed that thereby the eschatological consummation is already
in the present bringing the old aeon to an end. So this saying too
shows unequivocally that for Jesus the expected consummation of
salvation has become through his work a present reality and
derives its special significance from this realization. The fact that
for Jesus the Kingdom of God is a present reality is thereby
proved with as much certainty as the proclamation of its imminent
entry. It will not do to explain away this fact by pointing to the
alleged 'positive ambiguity' of some of the texts we have discussed.[74] Therefore the full meaning of the eschatological message
of Jesus can be grasped only by understanding that the preaching
both of the imminent future and of the presence of the Kingdom
of God must be taken seriously.

4. DOES JESUS KNOW OF AN EARTHLY EXISTENCE OF THE KINGDOM OF GOD AND OF ITS GROWTH?

Before we can finally determine the inner connexion between
the two sides of Jesus' eschatological message, we have yet to ask
whether the nature and extent of the presence of the Kingdom of
God in Jesus' message are in fact sufficiently described in the
exposition made so far. The question arises particularly because
the synoptists have preserved yet more pronouncements of Jesus
about the Kingdom of God, which are used again and again to
throw an essentially different light on Jesus' message concerning

[73]See my remarks in *ZNW* 33, 1934, 129 f.
[74]Thus Werner, *Dogma*, 50. U. Neuenschwander, *Protestantische Dogmatik
der Gegenwart und das Problem der biblischen Mythologie*, Diss. Bern, 1949, 170 f
stigmatizes without exegetical proofs as 'an attempt at apologetics' the view
brought forward here that Jesus proclaimed the presence of the reign of God

the presence of the Kingdom of God. I refer to the texts which
speak of the present attitude of men to the Kingdom of God and
to some of the parables about it.[75] The first group of texts offers
no difficulty. When the Kingdom of God is promised to those
who are like children (Mark 10.14 par. Matt. 19.14; Luke 18.16),
when Jesus tells the scribe who answered discreetly. 'Thou art not
far from the Kingdom of God' (Mark 12.34), when Jesus on the
contrary declares to the man who was ploughing and looked back
that he was not fit for the Kingdom of God (Luke 9.62), when
lastly the disciples of Jesus are commanded: 'Seek ye first the
Kingdom of God and his (i.e. God's) righteousness' (Matt. 6.33
= Luke 12.31), nothing is stated in these sayings, as has often
been pointed out, about the time when the Kingdom of God will

[75]There can be left out of account to start with some texts whose place in
the oldest tradition is doubtful: Luke 9.60b ('but go thou and publish abroad
the Kingdom of God') when compared with Matt. 8.22 is an addition by
Luke ('to preach the Kingdom of God' is used by Luke alone in Luke 4.43;
8.1; 9.2; 9.60; 16.16; Acts 28.23, 31); Matt. 5.19 cannot be original as it
contradicts Jesus' view of the commandments (cf. my arguments in *ZNW*
33, 1934, 128); Matt. 11.11b ('he that is but little in the Kingdom of Heaven
is greater than he') is a Christian limitation on Jesus' opinion of John the
Baptist in Matt. 11.11a (cf. M. Dibelius, *Die urchristliche Überlieferung von
Johannes dem Täufer*, 1911, 13 f.; E. Lohmeyer, *Das Urchristentum* I, 1932, 19
note 1); for Matt. 21.43 see page 53 note 111; Mark 4.11 ('unto you is given the
mystery of God, but unto them that are without all things are done in
parables'), in spite of the attempts to regard this saying as originally not concerned with the parable (thus in different ways Otto, *The Kingdom of God*, 91 f.
[in German *Reich Gottes*, 71 f.]; Jeremias, *Parables*, 11 ff. [in German 7 ff.];
C. Masson, *Les Paraboles de Marc* 4, 1945, 23 ff.; Flew, *Church*, 62 ff.; Taylor,
Mark, 255 ff.) can be considered only as an apologetic theory of parables of
the early Church (cf. Bultmann, *Tradition*, 351 note 1; Dodd, *Parables*, 13 f.;
H. J. Ebeling, *Das Messiasgeheimnis und die Botschaft des Markusevangelisten*,
1939, 179 ff.; F. Hauck, *TWNT* V, 754); Matt. 18.4 ('whosoever shall humble
himself as this little child, the same is the greatest in the kingdom of heaven)
is a secondary formation of Matthew (cf. Klostermann, *Matthäus*, 148).
Moreover it is certain that in the introductions to the parables in Matt. 18.
23 ff. (the unforgiving servant), 20.1 ff. (labourers in the vineyard), 22.2 ff.
(the marriage feast), the mention of the Kingdom of God is secondary (see
recently W. Michaelis, *Das hochzeitliche Kleid*, 1939, 159, 131, 26). Nor need
we consider the parables of the hid treasure and the costly pearl (Matt. 13.
44–46), because they only display the value of the Kingdom of God as a
warning, but make no statement about its character (cf. e.g. C. J. Cadoux,
Mission, 176 f.). Mark 14.38 'Watch and pray that ye enter not into temptation'
cannot be quoted as an authority for the eschatological presence of Satan's
final temptation (thus Taylor, *Mark*, 555), because πειρασμός is used here
without regard to time or strict reference to the last days, which is probably
the case also in Matt. 6.13 (cf. K. G. Kuhn, 'Πειρασμός—ἁμαρτία—σάρξ im
Neuen Testament und die damit zusammenhängenden Vorstellungen', *ZTK*
49, 1952, 220 ff.).

be in operation, but only about the behaviour necessary for those who wish to possess it. Since it is elsewhere perfectly clear that the entry into the Kingdom of God is for Jesus a future eschatological matter,[76] there is every reason to believe that all these sayings speak of those who are on the watch for the kingdom of God, and Mark 10.15 par. Matt. 18.3; Luke 18.17 'whosoever shall not receive the Kingdom of God as a little child, he shall in no wise enter therein' confirms this expressly.[77] It is therefore quite mistaken to extract from these texts again and again the idea of an actual Kingdom of God present in the life of Jesus' disciples.[78]

[76]See above pages 52 f.

[77]For the synonymous character of the expressions quoted cf. Windisch, ZNW 27, 1928, 166 ff.—The saying Mark 10.15 has been inserted only secondarily into the context of Mark 10.13 f., 16 (Lohmeyer, *Markus*, 202). The turn of speech 'to receive the Kingdom of God' is without any parallel in the gospels and can only be explained as an abbreviation for the phrase 'to receive the word of the Kingdom of God', for which there is no authority, or considered as a formulation of the language of the Church (thus Lohmeyer, *Markus*, 204 f.; J. Jeremias, *Hat die Urkirche Kindertaufe geübt?*, ²1949, 43 f.). Therefore Jeremias wishes to accept the version of Matt. 18.3 'except ye turn and become as little children . . .' as the more original one; but that is unlikely, because στραφῆτε is not a wrong translation for 'become again . . .' (as Jeremias says), but the Septuagint word for 'to be converted', cf. John 12.40 and Th. Zahn, *Das Evangelium des Matthäus ausgelegt*, 1903, 566 note 28. Mark 10.15a is therefore to be regarded, not as later than Matt. 18.3, but as influenced by the language of the Church, and it is not a proof that Jesus conceived the Kingdom of God to be present.—The saying Matt. 13.52: 'πᾶς γραμματεὺς μαθητευθεὶς τῇ βασιλείᾳ τῶν οὐρανῶν who bringeth forth out of his treasure things new and old' is of questionable age, because there are no parallels in the Jesus' tradition for the idea of a 'Christian scribe'; nor is the translation quite certain ('made a disciple for the Kingdom of Heaven' is more likely than 'made a disciple through the Kingdom of Heaven', cf. the Syriac translation *mtlmd lmlkwt* and H. Windisch, ZNW 27, 1928, 168; Bultmann, *Tradition*, 79; Michaelis, *Matthäus II*, 256.—C. H. Dodd, 'Matthew and Paul', *ExpT* 58, 1946/47, 297 note 1, wishes to follow the Peshitta in translating 'converted', but that is not certain even for the Peshitta nor vouched for in Jewish-Aramaic). But even if this should be a saying of Jesus, emphasis is only placed on the correct scriptural erudition, qualified by knowing about the Kingdom of God, but the Kingdom of God is not assumed to be a present power.

[78]Against Weinel, *Theologie*, 196 ('Sayings which recognize the Kingdom of God as a fellowship, e.g. Luke 9.62'); Wagenführer, *Kirchenbegriff*, 280 ('Those who stand in fellowship with Jesus are called children of God and—like Jesus himself—bearers of God's reign', referring to Matt. 5.3 ff.; Mark 10.14 f.); Leipoldt, *Jesus*, 119 ('Jesus therefore assumes that the Kingdom is a spiritual power' in view of Mark 12.34); A. T. Cadoux, *Theology*, 32, 51 ('the kingdom of heaven obviously means the way that God has worked in history and is working', alluding to Matt. 13.52; Mark 12.34 means that the scribe 'at least understood the demands of God's sovereignty'; Mark 10.15

There are essentially better grounds for a similar exegesis of those parables of the Kingdom which seem to speak of a present, unfolding reality (Mark 4.26 ff., 30 ff.; Matt. 13.24 ff., 47 ff.). Whilst scholars who maintain the real presence of the Kingdom of God in Jesus' teaching, and some others also in passing, quote one or other of the parables just named as authority for Jesus' conception of a growth of the Kingdom of God on earth, [79] Dodd has attempted to explain these parables in detail as 'Parables of Growth'. [80] With regard to these parables we must therefore ask whether they invalidate what we have ascertained up till now, namely that Jesus sees the coming Kingdom of God as present in his works alone, to the extent that for Jesus the Kingdom of God represents, independent of his person and his works, a power on

---

declares 'that the kingdom must be within the man as a condition of his being within the kingdom', etc.); Dodd, *Parables*, 47 (Mark 10.14 f. say 'that the coming of the kingdom is realized in experience'); Flew, *Church*, 25 (Matt. 21.31 shows 'the two classes of those who are in the new community of the new age'; thus evidently also Taylor, *Mark*, 115); F. Büchsel, *Theologie des Neuen Testaments*, 1935, 37 ('there are already now some to whom the kingdom of heaven belongs', Mark 10.14); P. Feine, *Theologie des Neuen Testaments*, ⁵1931, 79; Taylor, *Mark*, 423 f. ('the *present* Kingdom is received, the *future* Kingdom is entered', Mark 10.15; but Taylor would prefer the interpretation that the entry also is in the present. Cf. also 489 f. on Mark 12.34).

[79] Cf. of those named on page 16 note 3: Grundmann, *Jesus*, 42 f. ('The Kingdom of God begins here, now; it has its special sphere of activity in men's hearts'); Leipoldt, *Jesus*, 121 f. ('therefore the Kingdom develops'); Wagenführer, *Kirchenbegriff*, 277 ('hidden process of growth of God's kingdom'); A. T. Cadoux, *Theology*, 36 (the parable of the mustard seed describes Israel's growth, the parable of the seed which grows of its own accord 'God's action in the past as prefacing the present'); Glasson, *Advent*, 108 f. ('the seed growing secretly . . . illustrates the idea of growth and development'); A. Feuillet, *R.B.* 57, 1950, 87. Furthermore: Delling, *Zeitverständnis*, 124 f., 131 f. ('the Kingdom of God is something that grows'); M. Hermaniuk, *La Parabole Evangélique*, 1947, 273 f. ('the Kingdom of God appears in the Synoptists as a power of God which from now onwards renews the world in a continuous process'); Otto, *The Kingdom of God*, 113 ff. (in German *Reich Gottes*, 88 ff.) (the Kingdom of God is 'the secret miracle which . . . spreads itself victoriously, which *comes into existence* around and in men'; the parable of the mustard seed shows the kingdom 'as an eschatological *sphere of salvation* which . . . increases, spreads itself wonderfully'); Meyer, *Prophet*, 27 f. ('the Kingdom, embodied in the present only in a small fellowship, must grow organically'); Major, *Mission and Message*, 38; P. Feine, op. cit. in note 78, 79, 88 f.; W. Manson, *Jesus*, 47 f.; C. J. Cadoux, *Mission*, 113 f., 131, 196; Walter, *Kommen*, 54 ff.; Meinertz, *Theologie* I, 35 f.; Taylor, *Mark*, 115; E. Pfennigsdorf, *Der Menschensohn*, 1948, 48.

[80] Dodd, *Parables*, 175 ff.; likewise J. Knox, *Christ the Lord*, 1945, 23 ff., but cf. against this N. A. Dahl, 'The Parables of Growth', *ST* 5, 1951, 132 ff.

the earth. This question can be answered most easily in the parable of the seed growing secretly (Mark 4.26 ff.). The picture itself is completely plain and in its exegesis we have only to inquire which features are to be compared with the Kingdom of God,[81] that is to say, what the parable sets out to teach. One thing is clear; the sowing is mentioned as the starting point, but is not emphasized, so that the identity of the sower must not be sought. It is clear also that in the last verse there is an allusion to Joel 3.13 (ἐξαποστείλατε δρέπανα ὅτι παρέστηκεν τρύγητος) which proves the harvest to be a picture of the eschatological judgment.[82] As for the rest, on the one hand the stages of the growth of the seed are mentioned, on the other there is the fact that the husbandman has no share at all in its ripening, as this occurs αὐτομάτως and he does not understand this process at all. It is therefore very easy to see why a reference has been found in this parable to the secret growth of the Kingdom of God which began to germinate in Jesus.[83] Against this it is said that the modern idea of development is unknown in the New Testament[84] and that is certainly correct, but does not prove enough; the growth of the seed might nevertheless be emphasized.[85] It is important to notice that it is not the growth and ripening of the seed which is described as striking, but that the husbandman has no share in this growth, that the harvest comes without his assistance. So it is not the growth of the crop, but the certain arrival of the harvest which nothing can influence, that is the point of the parable.[86] If Jesus

[81]There are no grounds for striking out the introductory sentence, which is done by Weinel, *Theologie*, 52, 54; and Bultmann, *Tradition*, 186.

[82]The assumption that the whole or part of 4.29 has been added arises merely from denying that Jesus ever spoke in metaphors (against Jülicher, *Gleichnisreden* II, 545; J. Wellhausen, *Das Evangelium Marci*, ²1909, 34; B. T. D. Smith, *Parables*, 132). Against this G. Harder, 'Das Gleichnis von der selbstwachsenden Saat Mark 4.26–29', *Theologia viatorum, Jahrbuch der kirchl. Hochschule Berlin*, 1948/49, 51 ff.

[83]Thus also Jülicher, *Gleichnisreden*, II, 545; Klostermann, *Markus*, 43 f.; H. Clavier, *L'accès au royaume de Dieu*, 1944, 17. The assertion of Otto, *The Kingdom of God*, 113 (in German *Reich Gottes*, 88), that the parables in Mark 4.3–8 and 4.26–29 were originally one and the same is impossible from the point of view of style and contents, because the οὕτως in 4.26 refers to what follows and not to 4.3–8 which is alleged to precede it immediately.

[84]Gloege, *Reich Gottes*, 76 f.; Hauck, *Markus*, 58; Wendland, *Eschatologie*, 36; G. Harder, op. cit. in note 82, 68.

[85]'But after all, growth is growth; and in the case of all these parables, the process culminates in some sort of a climax of completeness' (C. J. Cadoux, *Mission*, 196); cf. Taylor, *Mark*, 266.

[86]P. Wernle, *Jesus*, 1916, 227; Schweitzer, *Quest*, 354 (in German *Leben Jesu*, 402 f.); J. Weiss, *Reich Gottes*, 84 f.; B. T. D. Smith, *Parables*, 130;

announces here that the Kingdom of God comes with certainty
and without human effort, after it has made a secret beginning in
the present, without its being possible to observe its growth and
development, or even necessary to conjecture them, then this
parable can hardly be considered as a summons to the preacher to
scatter the seed untroubled by the apparent present lack of success
and to leave all the rest to God;[87] for after all, the preacher has
not the least temptation to wish to hasten in any way the coming
of the Kingdom of God, so there is no need to deter him from
doing so.[88] Far less still can the parable be applied to the Kingdom of God as to a present fact, as to the harvest taking place in
the present, this hour of crisis (cf. Matt. 9.37 f.), and completing
God's work begun in the prophets.[89] For in that case the parable
would not only be a summons, this time to recognize the present
as the hour of fulfilment, but it would also contain the idea of a
development of the Kingdom of God from the time of the
prophets to that of Jesus, an idea which radically contradicts
Matt. 11.12 = Luke 16.16. Clearly the parable has rather a com-
forting meaning: the Kingdom of God comes surely without our
being able to hinder or to hasten it; the secrecy of its present
reality must not be allowed to endanger this certainty.

If therefore Mark 4.26 ff. does not support the idea that Jesus
thought of a Kingdom of God developing on earth, the question
arises even more definitely whether the parable of the mustard
seed (Mark 4.30–32 par. Matt. 13.31 f.; Luke 13.18 f.) is not to be
interpreted in this sense. The parable is handed down, as we
know, in two forms, as a narrative in Luke (probably from Q) and

---

C. W. F. Smith, *Jesus*, 81 ff.; R. Bultmann, *Theology of the New Testament*, 1952,
8 (in German I, 1948, 6 f.); C. Masson, *Les Parables de Marc* 4, 1945, 44; C. T.
Craig, *The Beginning of Christianity*, 1943, 88 f.; Branscomb, *Mark*, 83 f.;
Colwell, *Approach*, 67, 95; Jeremias, *Parables*, 91 f. (in German 94 f.); N. A.
Dahl, op. cit. in note 80; G. Harder, op. cit. in note 82, 61 ('It is God who is
deemed to be the sower and the reaper in the parable'; but the objection
raised by Harder, 69, to referring this parable to Jesus is completely unfounded). That Jesus himself is designated by the seed is an extremely unnatural and also an unproved assumption (against K. H. Rengstorf, *Die
Auferstehung Jesu*, 1952, 67 note 49).

[87]Thus Michaelis, *Sämann*, 54 ff.
[88]The parable most certainly does not teach by its allusion to the husbandman's co-operation with God and his firm reckoning on the harvest at a
definite time, 'that human agency had an indispensable part to play in securing
the triumph of God's cause' (C. J. Cadoux, *Mission*, 266).
[89]Thus Dodd, *Parables*, 176 ff.; Taylor, *Mark*, 266.

as description in Mark, while Matthew has combined the two.[90]
The Lucan form tells how a man has sowed a mustard seed in his
garden, how the seed grew and became a tree in whose branches
the birds lodge. In this version emphasis is therefore placed only
on the development of the tree which offers the birds shelter. Now
in the Old Testament a tree in whose branches birds can shelter
is a well-known symbol for an empire which affords protection to
many peoples (Dan. 4.12, 21θ; Ezek. 17.23; 31.6) and Luke 13.18
clearly alludes to these Old Testament passages (Mark 4.32 too);
so Dodd declared this form of the parable to be the original one
and wished to find in it the expression of the idea that now has
come the moment in the development of the Kingdom of God
when the blessings of the kingdom are accessible to all men: 'the
Kingdom of God is here, the birds are flocking to find shelter in
the shade of the tree'.[91] It is true that the Marcan version excludes
this view, for it emphasizes only the contrast between the very
small seed and the very great plant, and mentions the birds only
to illustrate the size of the tree.[92] But the view that the Marcan
version is the more original is supported both by the fact that in it
alone the choice just of the mustard seed is explained as being
proverbially the smallest grain (Matt. 17.20), and also because one
can understand the Q version to be a modification of the Marcan
one (emphasizing the development of the Kingdom of God into

[90]Thus e.g. Hauck, *Lukas*, 182.

[91]Dodd, *Parables*, 190 f.; likewise, Taylor, *Mark*, 269.—The Q version is
considered to be the more original also by Jülicher, *Gleichnisreden* II, 569 ff.;
B. T. D. Smith, *Parables*, 118; C. W. F. Smith, *Jesus*, 77; C. Masson, op. cit.
in note 86, 45 f.; T. E. F. Honey, 'Did Mark use Q?', *JBL* 62, 1943, 325 f.;
according to M. Black, 'The Problem of the Aramaic Element in the Gospels',
ET 59, 1947/48, 173, Q has faithfully preserved, except for the language, the
more original Aramaic version lying *behind* Mark.

[92]κατασκηνοῦν means 'to erect one's tent', 'to establish oneself' or 'to settle
down'. Consequently it can denote 'to live', which in the case of birds would refer to building nests (thus generally in Porphyrius, *De abstinentia* IV, 9 οὐδὲ ψυχὴ
ἐν μόνῳ ἀνθρώπῳ ἐπὶ γῆς κατεσκήνωσεν, of birds in particular Ps. 104 (103).12
ἐπ' αὐτὰ [sc. τὰ ὄρη] τὰ πετεινὰ τοῦ οὐρανοῦ κατασκηνώσει). But κατασκηνοῦν
can likewise mean quite generally 'to lie down, rest' (cf. Liddell and Scott, 912
and Bauer, *Wörterbuch*, [4]759; Bauer refers to a Christian tombstone, Liddell
and Scott to Ps. 16 (15).9 ἡ σάρξ μου κατασκηνώσει ἐπ' ἐλπίδι, which can
mean 'my flesh will rest in hope' just as well as the original text *bᵉ śari yishkon
labhetạh*, cf. the authorities for *shakhan* = 'to establish oneself' in Gesenius-
Buhl, *Hebräisches Handwörterbuch zum Alten Testament*, [17]1921, 827 under 1).
So one ought perhaps to translate Luke 13.19 κατεσκήνωσεν ἐν τοῖς κλάδοις
αὐτοῦ as 'they made their nests in its branches'; but Mark 4.32 ὥστε δύνασθαι
ὑπὸ τὴν σκιὰν αὐτοῦ τὰ πετεινὰ τοῦ οὐρανοῦ κατασκηνοῦν must certainly be
translated 'so that the birds of heaven can rest in its shade'.

a Church for all the nations), while the reverse modification could not be explained. If therefore the Marcan version must be accepted as the oldest form of the parable, some scholars find here too a description of how the Kingdom of God developed from a small start to a great finish.[93] But the emphasis is not laid on the gradual growing and unfolding of the seed step by step, but only on the contrast between the small beginning and the great ending.[94] Therefore this parable also must be intended to emphasize nothing but that the glorious finish is completely certain in spite of the humble start; there is no thought of a development from the one to the other. It must remain open to question whether Jesus wished to express at the same time, by bringing in the picture of the birds in the tree, the hope that the nations would enter into the perfected Kingdom of God;[95] this idea would, to say the least, be expressed only very obscurely by this metaphor. In any case this parable too is not intended to throw light on how the Kingdom of God comes to be, but to stir up faith in its certain coming.

But is not the parallel parable of the leaven (Matt. 13.33 = Luke 13.20 f.) to be judged differently? Here also the process is quite clear: the morsel of leaven which the woman mixes into the unusually large mass of meal affects the fermentation of all the dough. There is no emphasis on the small amount of the leaven and the large amount of meal concerned, but it is all on the unexpectedly great effect of the leaven.[96] This emphasis on the fermentation of the dough easily led to the notion that the parable

[93]Klostermann, *Markus*, 44; Jülicher, *Gleichnisreden*, II, 576 f.; Otto, *The Kingdom of God*, 123 f. (in German *Reich Gottes*, 97 f.); Weinel, *Theologie*, 196.

[94]Thus J. Weiss, *Reich Gottes*, 83; Hauck, *Markus*, 59; Schniewind, *Markus*, 78; Rengstorf, *Lukas*, 174; Michaelis, *Sämann*, 90 ff.; Schlatter, *Matthäus*, 442; C. Masson, op. cit. in note 86, 46; Jeremias, *Parables*, 89 f. (in German 92 f.); Colwell, *Approach*, 66; Branscomb, *Mark*, 85; R. Bultmann, op. cit. in note 86, 7 (doubts on insufficient grounds the original reference to the Kingdom of God); C. W. F. Smith, *Jesus*, 76 ff. (then strangely interprets the parable as meaning that the Kingdom of God must arouse attention in the world); N. A. Dahl, op. cit. in note 80, 148.

[95]Thus Schniewind and Rengstorf, loc. cit. in note 94; Taylor, *Mark*, 270; against this, Michaelis, *Sämann*, 93. Flew, *Church*, 27 f. wishes to infer from the metaphor of the birds that Jesus had the formation of a congregation in mind. But this interpretation is only possible if one fails to notice that the parable illustrates not the gradual addition of men to the congregation of Jesus, but only the inconceivably great *ending*, and for this purpose the birds are only mentioned to prove the greatness of this ending.

[96]Nor is there any emphasis on the *secret* action of the leaven (against Barrett, *Spirit*, 156).

was concerned with the inner penetration or transformation of
the world through the growing Kingdom of God.[97] But the
description clearly does not concentrate attention on the process
of fermentation, but on the fact that in spite of its insignificant
cause it has so great an effect. In addition to this, the parable of the
leaven is connected in the Q tradition with that of the mustard seed
and there is good reason to believe that this connexion is
original.[98] In that case it is the most probable assumption that
this parable too is only intended to display the contrast between
the small beginning and the great ending.[99] The all-embracing
Kingdom of God will come, even if the all too small beginnings
appear to gainsay it. Though this interpretation of the parable
remains uncertain owing to the brevity of the text, yet in no case
can the parable be used to justify the assumption that Jesus
announced a gradual penetration of the world by the forces of the
Kingdom of God.

There remains the question raised by the parable of the tares
(Matt. 13.24 ff.). Perhaps this parable deals with the growth or at
any rate with the presence on earth of the Kingdom of God? By
contrast with those discussed hitherto, it exhibits already in the
picture a number of striking features, and it has besides a detailed
interpretation (13.36 ff.) which explains its most important features
allegorically and describes the harvest in detail as the eschatological judgment. So the first question to be asked is whether this
interpretation belonged originally to the parable, in other words,
whether it reproduces the meaning of the parable truly.[100] Now it
is undoubtedly correct, as has often been emphasized, that this
interpretation does not give full allegorical value to *all* the ideas

[97] Jülicher, *Gleichnisreden* II, 578 ff.; Otto, *The Kingdom of God*, 125 (in
German *Reich Gottes*, 98 f.); H. Windisch, *TWNT* II, 907. Dodd,
Parables, 191 ff. wishes to detach this parable from that of the mustard seed
and to interpret it as meaning that Jesus' influence permeated from within the
dead lump of the religious Judaism of his time. C. W. F. Smith, *Jesus*, 72 f.
also disputes the reference of the parable to the future; it speaks of Jesus' own
presence as being the new factor in history, which none can escape.

[98] The assumption that this is not an original pair of parables (Bultmann,
Tradition, 186; Klostermann, *Matthäus*, 121 f.; Dodd, *Parables*, 191 f.) can be
supported only by insufficient and formal reasons (a new introduction, the
juxtaposition in Mark of the seed growing secretly and the mustard seed).

[99] Thus Hauck, *Lukas*, 183; Schniewind, *Matthäus*, 165; Michaelis, *Sämann*,
98 f.; Dibelius, *Jesus*, 56 f.; Bultmann, Colwell, Jeremias, loc. cit. in note 94;
N. A. Dahl, op. cit. in note 80, 149.

[100] Jülicher, *Gleichnisreden* II, 555 ff.; Schniewind, *Matthäus*, 167; Michaelis,
Sämann, 66 ff.; Michaelis, *Matthäus* II, 236 ff. support the view that the parables and the interpretation belonged together originally.

in the parable; nor is it permissible to maintain *a priori* that Jesus did not compose any allegories, and that for this reason the interpretation, and even the parable which has always been connected with it, could not have originated with Jesus.[101] It is also correct that by the strange introduction of the enemy who sowed the tares and the remarkable question of the servants the parable positively invites an allegorical explanation.[102] The interpretation 13.36 ff. is striking also because the conversation between the householder and his servants (13.27–29), so important in the parable, is omitted altogether. Moreover the expression ἡ συντέλεια τοῦ αἰῶνος is a Jewish idea found in the New Testament in Matthew only and I have already referred to the doubt whether Jesus ever used the term αἰών.[103] Jesus speaks of the angels of the Son of Man and generally of the βασιλεία of the Son of Man only in Matthew and Luke in texts that are clearly secondary (Matt. 16.28 compared with Mark 9.1 and Luke 9.27; Matt. 20.21 with Mark 10.37; Matt. 16.27 with Mark 8.38 and Luke 9.26; Luke 22.29 f.; Matt. 24 31 with Mark 13.27).[104] Further the interpretation is altogether lacking in consistency, since in 13.36–39 the parable is treated as an allegory, and then suddenly in 13.40–43 its last feature, the harvest (13.30), is considered merely as a description and *compared* to the procedure at the last judgment. Moreover the interpretation shows, as Jeremias has proved convincingly,[105] 'a simply unique collection of the linguistic characteristics of the evangelist Matthew'. But above all the interpretation obviously misses the real gist of the parable. For the parable lays all the emphasis on the fact that the tares must not be separated from the wheat before the harvest and mentions only in the conclusion that this separation will take place soon enough at the harvest. But the interpretation emphasized exclusively the fate of the good and the bad at the last judgment and omits completely the admonition to undertake no separation before this eschatological time. So there can be no doubt that the interpretation is a secondary

[101]Against Jülicher, *Gleichnisreden* II, 555 ff.; T. W. Manson, *Sayings,* 193.
[102]H. J. Schoeps, *Theologie und Geschichte des Judenchristentums,* 1949, 120 note 1; on 127 note 1 he has succumbed to this temptation and suggests Paul as the ἐχθρός in 13.25.
[103]See page 49 note 98.
[104]But the reign of Christ is not thereby given a prior place in time as an earlier stage, before the consummation of the reign of God (against C. H. Dodd, 'Matthew and Paul', *ExpT* 58, 1946/47, 294).
[105]Jeremias, *Parables,* 64 ff. (in German 63 ff.).

addition formulated by Matthew which does not belong to the original parable.[106]

In the parable itself two features are striking. Firstly the tares growing among the wheat strike the servants as something not natural and the householder can explain the presence of the tares only by the activity of 'the enemy'; and secondly the servants suppose that they can pull out the tares, but the householder regards such a proceeding as unnatural. On account of these features the parable has been understood as an allegory, or at least it has been assumed that allegorical features have penetrated into it from the application, so that an original form without these features must be postulated for Jesus.[107] Now it cannot be denied that the shaping of the details of this parable is explained by the intended application; but it must be emphasized just as strongly that the individual features can be understood as part of the description of an actual occurrence.[108] To sow tares is certainly not usual; but it is clearly presumed that the tares are growing up in such an unusual quantity that no natural explanation of their presence is possible. And that an enemy should do something unnatural out of hate is a human experience all the world over.[109] The servants' question whether they should weed out the tares requires no explanation, for as G. Dalman has pointed out,[110] it is usual to weed the cornfields in the spring, and tares, especially darnel which is the meaning of ζιζάνια is pulled out carefully. If this happens too late, there is the risk of pulling up the corn with it; so the parable clearly supposes that the excessive presence of the darnel was discovered too late and although the zealous servants still want to weed, the householder prefers to wait to

---

[106]Thus J. Weiss, *Reich Gottes*, 40 f.; Klostermann, *Matthäus*, 123; Bultmann, *Tradition*, 202 f.; B. T. D. Smith, *Parables*, 198 f.; Dodd, *Parables*, 183 f.; Jeremias, *Parables*, 67 (in German 66); C. W. F. Smith, *Jesus*, 88; R. Liechtenhan, 'Das Gleichnis vom Unkraut unter dem Weizen', *Kirchenbl. f. d. ref. Schweiz*, 1943, 147 f.; R. Liechtenhan, *Mission*, 23 f.; F. Hauck, *TWNT* V, 752 f.

[107]Thus e.g. B. T. D. Smith, *Parables*, 197; Jülicher, *Gleichnisreden*, II, 555 ff.; M. Dibelius, *Die Botschaft von Jesus Christus*, 1935, 143.

[108]This is emphasized by Dodd, *Parables*, 184 f.; Michaelis, *Sämann*, 72; R. Liechtenhan, *Kirchenbl.* (see note 106), 147, 166 f. Bultmann, *Tradition*, 191 also considers it a 'pure parable'.

[109]B. T. D. Smith, *Parables*, 197 note 1 refers to H. Schmidt und P. Kahle, *Volkserzählungen aus Palästina*, 1918, 31, where a story is told of a man who sowed the seed of rushes in his neighbour's garden, spoiling it for years (the story is also in G. Dalman, *Arbeit und Sitte in Palästina* II, 1932, 308 f.).

[110]G. Dalman, op. cit. in note 109, 248 f., 323 ff. and fig. 56, 73.

avoid the risk to the corn. There is no other evidence for binding weeds in bundles, but there is some for burning them after the harvest. So it is plain that for the sake of the application the parable presents striking features, but by no means impossible ones. Thus there is no reason to doubt the authenticity of the parable as far as the story is concerned. We must then ask what is its purpose. It is obviously intended to emphasize that the separation of the good from the bad is impossible before the final judgment, that it must on the contrary be left to God at the last judgment. Now according to the introduction ὡμοιώθη ἡ βασιλεία τῶν οὐρανῶν ἀνθρώπῳ σπείραντι κτλ the Kingdom of God is to be compared with this idea; but since the connecting links in the introductions to parables are well known to be vague, it is not clear what comparison is intended. If the whole proceedings described are applied to the Kingdom of God, the exegesis is suggested that its coming will not be prevented by the presence of sinners, 'the coming of the Kingdom is itself a process of sifting, a judgment'.[111] Now it is significant that Dodd then feels himself obliged to deny that the judgment is presented as a new event in the future. But the emphasis is not on the growth of the Kingdom of God in the present, but on the separation taking place at the judgment, at the coming of the Kingdom of God, that therefore nothing may be separated before then. So it only tells that there are now some who are destined for the Kingdom of God and some who are to be excluded from it.[112] But is not the warning to refrain from making a separation now between these persons an affair of the early Church, which Jesus could not have given?[113] Against this assumption many scholars have correctly emphasized that Jesus was well aware of Satan's resistance to the Kingdom of God which was at work in anticipation in his person (Matt. 11.12), and that the disciples would be bound to endeavour to separate clearly already now the true adherents of Jesus from those people not to be tolerated round him (Mark 9.38 ff.; Luke

---

[111]Dodd, *Parables*, 185. According to Stonehouse, *Witness*, 238 the parable teaches that before the end of the world the Kingdom of God contains good and bad. Somewhat differently H. Clavier, *L'accès au royaume de Dieu*, 1944, 18.

[112]Thus also Wendland, *Reich Gottes*, 34 f.; Michaelis, *Sämann*, 73.

[113]Thus A. Fridrichsen, *Le problème du miracle dans le Christianisme primitif*, 1925, 108 f.—C. W. F. Smith, *Jesus*, 87 f.; J. Weiss–W. Bousset, *Die Schriften des Neuen Testaments neu übersetzt und für die Gegenwart erklärt* I, ³1917, 322; B. W. Bacon, *Studies in Matthew*, 1930, 97 assume as well that Matt. 13. 24 ff. is a development of Mark 4.26–29.

9.52 ff.).[114] Therefore Jesus can well be thought to have told this parable which shows that in his view a separation is taking place in the present, the result of which will only be brought to light by the coming judgment. The disciples are to know about this eschatological significance of the present, but they are not to make this separation themselves, because 'with their restricted sight they are unfit to administer justice'.[115] So this parable also certainly does not speak of the present growth and existence of the Kingdom of God, but shows that the present possesses a definite eschatological character on account of the breaking in of the coming Kingdom through Jesus in the present.

It only remains to ask whether the parable of the dragnet (Matt. 13.47 ff.) does not presuppose the present existence of the Kingdom of God. For it tells how in fishing all kinds of fish are caught, but that, when they are sorted on the shore, the useless ones are thrown away; in the appended interpretation this sorting is taken as a picture of the separation of the bad from the righteous, and the evil fate of the bad is especially described. Now this interpretation 13.49 f. approximates strikingly to the secondary interpretation of the parable of the tares 13.40–42 (13.50 agrees word for word with 13.42; 13.49 like 13.41 describes the angels at work sorting at the last judgment, the wording of 13.49a is identical with that of 13.40b; in both places the expression peculiar to Matthew συντέλεια τοῦ αἰῶνος occurs). The interpretation 13.49 f. emphasizes only the separation at the end, thus passing over (as in 13.36 ff.) the story in 13.47, 48b. So it has often been considered that the interpretation in 13.49 f. is a secondary addition of Matthew, and that the original parable does not speak of the separation at the last judgment, but of the state of the Kingdom of God in the present; all men receive the summons now, but they are separated according to their response to it.[116] But the objection to this assumption is that 13.48 already

114Cf. Michaelis, *Sämann*, 74 f.; B. T. D. Smith, *Parables*, 198; Schniewind, *Matthäus*, 164; Schlatter, *Matthäus*, 349; R. Liechtenhan, *Kirchenbl.* (see note 106) 168; Jeremias, *Parables*, 155 f. (in German 157 f.); J. Jeremias, 'Der Gedanke des "Heiligen Restes" im Spätjudentum und in der Verkündigung Jesu', *ZNW* 42, 1949, 192.—E. Wilhelms, 'Der fremde Exorzist, Eine Studie über Mark 9.38 ff.', *ST* 3, 1950/51, 162 ff. emphasizes correctly the great age of Mark, 9.38 ff.
115Schlatter, *Matthäus*, 442; somewhat differently N. A. Dahl, op. cit. in note 80, 152.
116Thus or similarly Jülicher, *Gleichnisreden* II, 565 ff.; Dodd, *Parables*, 187 ff.; B. T. D. Smith, *Parables*, 201; Otto, *The Kingdom of God*, 126 ff. (in

clearly introduces the separation which will take place at the end, so that the interpretation of 13.49 f. seems altogether relevant, even if its formulation must undoubtedly be ascribed to Matthew.[117] But though the interpretation emphasizes only the separation when the end appears, does not the parable nevertheless presuppose the Kingdom of God to be a present power in which good and bad will remain together until the final separation?[118] This impression is given only because the awkward introduction of the parable connects the idea of the Kingdom of God grammatically with its opening word, the net. Actually it is not the net, but the procedure of fishing which is compared with the Kingdom of God. There can therefore be no doubt that Jesus intends this parable to speak in the first place of the fact that when the end comes an inexorable separation will take place which the bad cannot escape; the entry of the Kingdom does not mean that God will then take no notice of men's behaviour in the present. But if so, why is there any mention at all of the fishes ἐκ παντὸς γένους which the net gathers? It might be assumed that this feature of the parable belongs only to the vivid description in the story and requires no further explanation; but against this it can be said that the idea by itself of the inexorable separation at the end could have been set forth much more impressively by other pictures. It is probably more correct to assume that emphasis is to be laid on Jesus' summons to *all* men, not in the sense that this is an impressive order to the disciples to offer the gospel to all mankind,[119] but that the gospel is represented as the message addressed as a matter of course to all men. So it is just in view of the universal purpose of the gospel that the seriousness of the decision it demands must be set forth by pointing to the separation

---

German *Reich Gottes*, 99 f.) (Otto strikes out 13.48 as well and applies the parable to men 'of every kind', not to good and bad; but it is arbitrary to cut out 13.48 and ἐκ παντὸς γένους refers not to men, but to the fishes); T. W. Manson, *Sayings,* 197; C. W. F. Smith, *Jesus,* 102; Jeremias, *Parables,* 67 (in German 67).

[117]See the list of linguistic peculiarities in Jeremias loc. cit.

[118]See e.g. Schniewind, *Matthäus*, 168: 'the picture belongs together with that of the fishers of men; men are caught, are gripped by God; but which of them can be used, will appear only at the last judgment. The thought of the Church coming into being suggests itself. Both good and bad are mixed up in it'; Stonehouse, *Witness*, 238.

[119]Jesus certainly does not justify his summons to *all* mankind in this parable. (See C. W. F. Smith, *Jesus*, 103.)

at the last judgment.[120] So the parable does not warn against premature separation, like that of the tares, but admonishes the hearers. There is no mention whatever of the Kingdom of God being present.

The discussion of these parables concludes the examination of all the passages which might possibly be brought forward, because of their clear reference to the eschatological event, in order to determine the temporal meaning of Jesus' eschatological message. Recent research has not indeed confined itself to those passages which speak indisputably of the future or the presence of the Kingdom of God and the Messiah. Against the background of Jesus' whole message and in a variety of forms the theory has been maintained that the foundation of the messianic community necessarily belongs to the present messianic activity of Jesus, that the circle of the twelve was to form the original foundation of this new community and that it made its appearance according to Jesus' will at the latest at the last meal with his disciples.[121] Some scholars were of the opinion that this message of Jesus, that the eschatological consummation was present in the new community gathered round the earthly Jesus, could not be derived from the sources or contradicted the authenticated

[120]Thus Schlatter, *Matthäus*, 447 f.; Wendland, *Eschatologie*, 36; Jeremias, *Parables*, 156 f. (in German 159 f.); N. A. Dahl, op. cit. in note 80, 150 f.— Michaelis, *Sämann*, 122 f.; Michaelis, *Matthäus* II, 253 interprets the catch of fish also as 'the gathering of mankind to the last judgment', that is to say, he applies the *whole* parable to the last judgment. But although it would thereby be explained homogeneously, it is unlikely that the simile of fishing is to be applied to the gathering of mankind for the last judgment, as Michaelis suggests, because in that case ἐκ παντὸς γένους would have little meaning; on the contrary the *sum total* of those embraced by the last judgment would somehow have to be indicated by the picture.

[121]The thesis, demonstrated by F. Kattenbusch, 'Der Quellort der Kirchenidee', *Festgabe für A. von Harnack*, 1921, 143 ff. and carried further by K. L. Schmidt, 'Die Kirche des Urchristentums', *Festgabe für A. Deissmann*, 1927, 258 ff. and the article ἐκκλησία, *TWNT* III, 522 ff. was adopted by A. Juncker, 'Neuere Forschungen zum urchristlichen Kirchenproblem', *N. Kirchl. Zeitschr.* 40, 1929, 126 ff., 180 ff.; G. Gloege, *Reich Gottes*; W. Bieder, *Ekklesia und Polis im Neuen Testament und in der alten Kirche*, Diss. Basel, 1941; F. J. Leenhardt, *Etudes sur l'église dans le Nouveau Testament*, 1940; L. Goppelt, *Typos*, 1939, 127 ff.; Wendland, *Eschatologie*, 146 ff.; H. Windisch, 'Urchristentum', *Th. Rdsch.* N.F. 5, 1933, 248 ff. Similar opinions are held by Flew, *Church*, 17 ff.; Stauffer, *NT Theology*, 30 f. (in German 15 f.); Liechtenhan, *Mission*, 7 ff.; J. Knox, *The Man Christ Jesus*, 1942, 41; T. W. Manson, 'The New Testament Basis of the Doctrine of the Church', *Journ. of Eccles. History* 1, 1950, 1 ff.; Jeremias, *Eucharistic Words*, 139 (in German 102); Glasson, *Advent*, 139 ff.; Bowman, *Intention*, 193 ff.; Bowman, *Maturity*, 305 f.; Duncan, *Jesus*, 223 ff.; Stonehouse, *Witness*, 235 ff.; P. Nepper-Christensen,

account of his eschatological message; so they assumed that
Jesus expected that there would come into being in the time after
his death and resurrection a community which anticipated the
eschatological consummation.[122] I have endeavoured to show
elsewhere[123] that the sources do not yield sufficient facts on which
to base this theory that Jesus saw in the circle of disciples gathered
round him a closed *congregation* or indeed knew that in this congregation the operation of the Kingdom of God had begun, that
therefore Matt. 16.18 f. (Thou art Peter and upon this rock I will
build my church; and the gates of Hades shall not prevail against
it. I will give unto thee the keys of the kingdom of heaven and
whatsoever thou shalt bind on earth shall be bound in heaven;
and whatsoever thou shalt loose on earth shall be loosed in heaven)
cannot be considered to belong to the oldest Jesus tradition. The
objections to these arguments by A. Oepke and others[124] have not
been able to weaken the objections brought against the authenticity of Matt. 16.18 f. nor could they shake the assertion that
Jesus did not wish to collect a 'congregation' around him in his
lifetime nor even wish to gather the 'remnant';[125] so there can be

---

'Wer hat die Kirche gestiftet?', *Symb. Bibl. Upsalienses* 12, 1950, 23 ff.;
similarly also N. A. Dahl, op. cit. in note 80, 115 ff. Naturally Roman Catholic
research traces the origin of the Church back to Jesus and declares Matt. 16.
18 f. to be an authentic saying of his; cf. recently e.g. K. Buchhein, *Das
messianische Reich*, 1948, Walter, *Kommen*, 41 ff., and Meinertz, *Theologie* I, 69 ff.

[122]L. Brun, 'Der kirchliche Einheitsgedanke im Urchristentum', *Ztsch. f.
Syst. Theol.* 14, 1937, 86 ff.; Wendland, *Eschatologie*, 175 f.; O. Cullmann,
Königsherrschaft Christi und Kirche im Neuen Testament, 1941, 19 ff.; O. Cullmann,
Peter, 1953, 158 ff. (in German *Petrus*, 1952, 176 ff.); Werner, *Dogma*, 637;
Michaelis, *Täufer*, 105 ff.; Michaelis, *Verheissung*, 27 f.; Michaelis, *Matthäus*
II, 340 ff.; A Oepke, 'Jesus und Gottesvolkgedanke', *Luthertum*, 1942, 33 ff.;
A. Oepke, 'Der Herrenspruch über die Kirche (Matt. 16.17–19) in der
neuesten Forschung' *ST* 2, 1948/50, 110 ff.; A. Oepke, *Das neue Gottesvolk
in Schrifttum, Schauspiel, bildender Kunst und Weltgestaltung*, 1950, 166 ff.

[123]Kümmel, *Kirchenbegriff*, 27 ff.; cf. also R. Bultmann, 'Die Frage nach der
Echtheit von Matt. 16.17–19', *TB* 20, 1941, 265 ff.; M. Goguel, 'Jésus et
l'Eglise', *RHPR*, 1933, 197 ff.; H. Strathmann, 'Die Stellung des Petrus in
der Urkirche, Zur Frühgeschichte des Wortes an Petrus Matt. 16.17–19',
Ztschr. f. Syst. Theol. 20, 1943, 223 ff.; E. F. Scott, *The Nature of the Early
Church*, 1941, 25 ff.; C. J. Cadoux, *Mission*, 306 ff.; Barrett, *Spirit*, 135 ff.

[124]A. Oepke, *ST* (see note 122); P. Nepper-Christensen, loc. cit. in note
121; O. Cullmann, *TZ*. 1, 1945, 147; O. Cullmann, *Christ and Time*, 1951,
71 note 3, 149 f. (in German *Christus und die Zeit*, 1946, 62 note 3, 131 f.);
Liechtenhan, *Mission*, 7 ff.

[125]For this last point cf. especially A. Oepke, *ST* (see note 122), 113, 140;
A. Oepke, *Das neue Gottesvolk* (see note 122), 165; J. Jeremias, *ZNW* 42,
1949, 191 ff.

no question of the presence of the Kingdom of God in the
'congregation' during his lifetime. There are also weighty objections still to be made to the assumption that Jesus expected a
closed community to arise after his death and that he saw in this
the people of God of the last days; but this matter needs renewed
discussion. However, even though I must not discuss it here in
detail,[126] there can be no doubt that Jesus nowhere said or intim-
ated that the presence of the coming Kingdom of God would
show itself during the interval between his death and the parousia
in the fellowship of his disciples. Jesus saw the Kingdom of God
to be present before the parousia, which he thought to be imminent, only in his own person and his works;[127] he knew no other
realization of the eschatological consummation.

[126]I intend to clarify this question further, especially by examining Oepke's
useful studies in the *ST* cited in my note 122.

[127]Cf. H.–D. Wendland, *Geschichtsanschauung und Geschichtsbewusstsein im
Neuen Testament*, 1938, 75; F. Büchsel, *Jesus*, 47: 'The presence of the Kingdom of heaven depends upon the activity of Jesus.'

IV

THE MEANING OF JESUS' ESCHATOLOGICAL MESSAGE

Now at last the concluding and decisive question can be posed: what meaning is there in the fact that Jesus placed side by side the conceptions that the Kingdom of God was expected soon, that its coming was expected within his generation, and that the expected Kingdom of God was present; and that in addition to this he even emphasized that the hour of its coming is unknown? In the course of the previous discussion it has already become clear that the very numerous pronouncements of Jesus about the future of the Kingdom of God and the equally indisputable ones about the presence of the *eschaton* demolish the arguments for those descriptions of Jesus' message according to which Jesus announced either only eschatological occurrences in the future or only a present time of eschatological fulfilment.[1] It is therefore completely certain that Jesus' eschatological message cannot be regarded simply as a particular form of Jewish apocalyptic, and also that it does not detach itself completely from the expectations for the future of the contemporary Jewish eschatology by reason of its interpretation concerned only with the present. So if there is every reason to believe that the imminent coming and the present efficacy of the Kingdom of God are announced side by side in Jesus' message, we must ask whether this juxtaposition is due to historical accident or whether it expresses precisely the particular quality of Jesus' eschatology. It has been supposed at times that the imminent expectation should be considered as a later stage in the development of Jesus' thought,[2] but in that case it would be indeed surprising if this later stage had permeated so thoroughly the whole tradition of Jesus' sayings. Others have expressed the contrary view that in Jesus' consciousness the date of the end was

[1]For the representatives of both views see notes 2 and 3 on page 16.
[2]According to P. Wernle, *Jesus*, 1916, 237 f. Jesus did not at the same moment reckon with the small beginnings of the Kingdom of God in the present and the swift catastrophe of the world, but 'the so-called belief in a catastrophe was rather the conception of his last weeks'.

in course of time postponed more and more[3] and this must
naturally have brought with it a stronger emphasis on the decisive
role of the present. But against these different assumptions of a
development in Jesus' eschatological thinking, there is on the one
hand the argument that the detached sayings in the synoptic
tradition afford no suitable material for determining such developments, so that they could at most be put forward hypothetically
and *could* never be proved. On the other hand more or less convincing reasons can be produced for assuming both a gradual
weakening and also a gradual strengthening of Jesus' imminent
expectations, so that the two arguments cancel each other out. But
above all, not only are the pronouncements about the future and
the present found in isolated detached sayings which could only
be placed in order of development by guess-work, but it emerged
from the discussion of Mark 8.38; Matt. 19.28; Luke 12.32 that
Jesus connects the present, being *by its very nature* an eschatologically *fulfilled* present, with the expected future, because the
encounter with the man Jesus in the present demands a decision
which will be the determining factor for the eschatological
verdict of Jesus when he comes as the Son of Man. For all these
reasons it is impossible to assume that the juxtaposition of pronouncements about the nearness, the remoteness and the presence
of the Kingdom of God in Jesus' message is explained by the fact
that, though in the tradition these conceptions were placed *side*

---

[3] J. Weiss, *Reich Gottes*, 100 f. assumes that Jesus to begin with believed 'in
an early glorious victory of God's cause', but that under the pressure of sad
experiences the date was postponed. C. J. Cadoux, *Mission*, 18, 183 ff., 252 ff.
also wishes to prove that Jesus at first expected his preaching of the Kingdom
of God to be successful, but later recognized the necessity for his suffering
and then emphasized his parousia; but Cadoux does not conclude from this
that the date of the Kingdom of God is postponed. M. Goguel, *Rev HR*
106, 1932, 387 f., 396, sees a development from the expectation of a very
early coming of the Son of Man (Matt. 10.23) through the view that some
would experience the coming of the Kingdom of God (Mark 9.1) to the dis-
claimer that he knew its date (Mark 13.32); H. Windisch, *Die Katholischen
Briefe*, [2]1930, 101 seems to see this development taking place only beyond
Jesus' life.—R. M. Grant, 'The Coming of the Kingdom', *JBL* 67, 1948,
297 ff. assumes that Jesus first expected that the Kingdom of God might
come at any moment, but that he then recognized in Jerusalem that God
alone knew the hour (Mark 13.32); and Meyer, *Prophet*, 128 assumes that
Jesus' 'hope for an early coming of the last days grew faint'.—Taylor, *Mark*,
386 maintains that Jesus originally expected the swift dawn of the Kingdom
of God (Mark 9.1) and only later on (according to Mark 6.13) that the Son of
Man must suffer.—Against these views A. Schlatter, *Die Geschichte des
Christus*, 1921, 153 and Delling, *Zeitverständnis*, 130 note 1.

by side, yet in Jesus' thinking they belonged to periods following one *after* the other in time.

Since therefore it must be accepted that these different pronouncements of Jesus concerning the time of the *eschaton* were spoken during the same period, an attempt has recently been made to overcome the difficulty by seeking to eliminate the conception of time itself from Jesus' eschatological message, as being inadequate to express his meaning. On these lines some have tried to show that the nearness and remoteness in time of the parousia seems to be a matter of complete indifference to Jesus, and so to us also, because in view of the completed achievement of Jesus 'the length of the period between this completion and the so-called last things is rendered indifferent'.[4] But again and again in the course of the exegetical discussion of Jesus' announcements concerning the future there has appeared the undeniable fact that for him the prediction of the future entry of the eschatological consummation had such an actual 'futurist' meaning that an answer could be given about the *interval* of time within which this entry is to take place, even though Jesus has consciously avoided a more precise description of the future eschatological events, as in apocalyptic. Completely to eliminate the conception of time contradicts unequivocally all the facts established by exegesis. Therefore as a rule the conception of time has not been removed thoroughly from Jesus' thinking as a matter of principle, but an

---

[4]Delling, *Zeitverständnis*, 103; cf. also 102 ('nearness or remoteness in time is a matter of indifference'), 120 ('the word eschatology . . . should not be used any more for Jesus' expectation of the future'), 123 ('even though the ἤγγικεν in fact points to begin with to the imminent entry of the coming events, yet it becomes clear from the contexts how small an emphasis is thereby placed on a time-limit'); C. W. F. Smith, *Jesus*, 283 (for Jesus the Kingdom of God was at hand. 'We suspect that to him it was not a question of farness or nearness in time, but of the spiritual and immediate presence of a God who might at any moment disclose his activity in the field of history'); Sharman, *Son of Man*, 135 ff. ('The Kingdom of God, as conceived by Jesus, would seem to be as timeless as the co-existence of God as Norm and Man as Loyalist toward that Norm—something belonging within the Past—Present—Future'); Bowman, *Maturity*, 255 ('the best proof of our Lord's prophetic —i.e. non-temporal standpoint relative to the end of the age and his own advent as Son of Man is to be derived from his clear intention to found the . . . church'; cf. also 61: 'the category of "time" was of no interest to him', that is, *qua* prophet).—C. C. McCown, 'In History or Beyond History', *Harv. Theol. Rev.* 38, 1945, 151 ff. recognizes historically Jesus' 'futurist' eschatology, but disputes that history receives its meaning either from eschatology or from a perfect world beyond history; the meaning of history would be 'within history' alone; the word 'eschatology' should disappear as quickly as possible from theological usage.

attempt has been made to explain away the expectation of the future in favour of a message simply concerning the present, because the Kingdom of God has to do with things, not in time, but beyond time.[5] Behind this effort either to eliminate Jesus' predictions of the future by exegesis[6] or to interpret them by establishing the real meaning of what is *really* intended by the contemporary language,[7] there lies the deeper concern to bring out the thoughts of Jesus in their permanent significance for the faithful of today. This is seen particularly clearly in Dodd, Bultmann and Wilder. Dodd, in the appendix to his book about the development of the apostolic preaching,[8] has described how

[5] Cf. Wendland, *Eschatologie*, 34 ('The future means "the coming-to-us of God" . . . the present is the time of decision, qualified by the "coming-to-us of God" '), 45 f. ('The Reign cannot be described by the conception of "the end of time" alone, because it is equally beyond time and eternal. Because of its eternal character beyond time the Reign becomes near and present'), 51 ('we must start from the Reign as concerned with the end of time, but must grasp equally the inner polarity of the idea of the Reign as being concerned with the end of time and beyond time and therefore must find the presence of the Reign grounded in fact and in principle'); Gloege, *Reich Gottes*, 109 ('In the realm of the New Testament present and future meet each other perfectly in the conception of the Kingdom'), cf. also 66 ff.; Bultmann, *Jesus*, 49 ('The future of the Kingdom of God is not . . . something which comes once in the course of time . . . This future is . . . a genuine future, not a somewhere and a somewhen, but that which advances towards a man, which confronts him with a decision'), 53 ('the expectation of the end of the world imminent in time belongs also to mythology, . . . expression and conviction that man must make a decision in the present itself'); Bultmann, *Urchristentum*, 102 ('The knowledge that the attitude of man towards God decides his destiny and that his time for decision has been granted a respite is clothed in the conception that the world's hour of decision has come'); A. E. J. Rawlinson, *Christ in the Gospels*, 1944, 51 (The language of our Lord with regard to the immediacy of the coming of the Kingdom of God with power within the lifetime of that generation expresses the truth that human life always stands in immediate relation to its consummation in eternity); Wilder, *Eschatology*, 182 ('The apocalyptic event in the future is essentially of the character of myth, and the interim thus created is formal and conceptual rather than real'); E. Fuchs, 'Christus das Ende der Geschichte', *EvTh* 8, 1948/49, 450 note 10 ('The New Testament knows . . . the nearness and remoteness of a "time" which no longer "has any extension" . . . This time has absolutely nothing to do with circular or linear'); Meinertz, *Theologie*, I 37 ('That the Kingdom of God is time-less, or rather *beyond time*, is essential in order to solve the tension between the present existence and the future consummation, much more to make it fruitful').

[6] Thus C. H. Dodd, *Parables*, but also the majority of the scholars named on page 16 note 3.

[7] Thus Wendland, Bultmann, Wilder, Fuchs, see note 5.

[8] C. H. Dodd, *The Apostolic Preaching and its Developments*, 1936, Appendix: Eschatology and History, 193 ff. See the account of its contents by W. Gutbrod, *TR*, NF 12, 1940, 79 ff. and my discussion in *TR*, NF 14, 1942, 93 ff.

according to the message of the New Testament man once 'was confronted *within history* with the eternal God in his kingdom, power and glory, and that in a final and absolute sense' (238). Since therefore the New Testament knows only 'realized eschatology', the Jewish eschatological imagery can only be applied in a *symbolic* sense to this historical reality. To speak of the parousia of Christ is therefore only a form for expressing the fact that *this* history bears a supra-historical character; and it would be meaningless to speak of a future parousia, since 'the time-scale is irrelevant to that which has never received embodiment in the form of time and space, and therefore has no existence in the temporal order' (203). So Dodd repudiates the 'futurist' eschatology because the conception of time has no meaning in view of events which belong to eternity. On the other hand Bultmann in his essay on 'Neues Testament und Mythologie'[9] put forward the challenge to 'demythologize' the message of the New Testament; according to him we have finished with the mythical world picture, but the critical destruction of the New Testament mythology must not lead to the suspension of the New Testament *kerygma* altogether; such a demythologization only carries out the intention of the New Testament and discloses the truth of the *kerygma* to the men of today who do not think in mythological terms. This means when applied to the question of the 'futurist' eschatology that 'the mythological eschatology is untenable for the simple reason that the parousia never took place as the New Testament expected, but that the history of the world ran on' (5; in German 18) and 'the age of salvation has already dawned for the believer; the life of the future has become a present reality' (20; in German 31). The cross 'is an eschatological event in and beyond time, for as far as its meaning—that is its meaning for faith—is concerned, it is an ever-present reality (36; in German 46). Finally Wilder in his chapter on 'Historical and Transcendental Elements in Jesus' view of the Future' in the course of his inquiry into the motives and driving forces of Jesus' ethics,[10] wished to prove that the eschatological conception of God's reign does not exclude, but interprets the future of human society in

[9]First published in 'Offenbarung und Heilsgeschehen', *Beitrag zur EvTh* 7, 1941, 27 ff., reprinted in H. W. Bartsch, *Kerygma and Myth*, 1953, 5 ff. (in German, *Kerygma und Mythos*, 1948, 15 ff.) (which is quoted here).

[10]Wilder, *Eschatology*, 53 ff. (its essential features are also reprinted in the essay 'The Eschatology of Jesus in Recent Criticism and Interpretation', *Journal of Religion*, 28, 1948, 177 ff.).

this world. The present as the time of fulfilment in its full significance 'could only be conveyed by eschatological language' (57). Jesus' eschatology with its emphasis on the coming of the Kingdom of God and of the judgment must be regarded 'as symbolic of the historical crisis of his time and its outcome' (60). His predictions of the future had to do with the last things, 'but it was directed to the present moment and to the actual scene and was lived out in the concrete process of history, and it bore on that concrete process in its future aspects' (70). The conceptions of the coming reign of God, of the judgment, of the supernatural rewards were for Jesus forms of expression for the future which cannot be imagined, but is certain and is fixed by God. 'Yet this temporal imminence of God is but a function of his spiritual imminence, and it is this latter which really determines conduct' (161).

It is clear that these scholars are by different paths pursuing the same goal, namely to get rid of the expectation of an eschatological future consummation as being inapplicable for modern man and his moral problems, and yet to preserve as authoritative for him the essential content of the message of the New Testament, that is to say of Jesus. But Dodd is treading a path barred by methodology when he interprets the eschatological conceptions of the future as purely symbolic ('symbolic character of the "apocalyptic" sayings') (105) or gets rid of the predictions of the future altogether by means of an exegetical re-interpretation. Against this it must be emphasized that this 'symbolic' character of Jesus' eschatological predictions of the future cannot exist in reality; for the fact that in some texts Jesus restricts the imminent coming of the Kingdom of God to the period of the generation of his contemporaries proves beyond a doubt that for Jesus the future as an actual happening *in time* was something essential.[11] This shows that for Jesus the category of time, and consequently speech about God's action in a *definite* future and in the *definite* presence of Jesus is not irrelevant, but absolutely indispensable.

[11]Flew, *Church*, 32 note 1 also emphasizes against Dodd that the statements about the future coming of the Son of Man must not be interpreted Platonically, but Hebraically. C. J. Cadoux, *Mission*, 296 note 3 concludes 'that, in face of the evidence, this elimination of futurist eschatology from the teaching of Jesus must undoubtedly be regarded as erroneous'. C. T. Craig, 'Realized Eschatology', *JBL* 56, 1937, 22 f. is correct in claiming that Jesus ought to have told his hearers clearly if, in contrast to Palestinian Judaism, he wished to advocate an eschatology in which the eternal world does not follow *in time*.

This is true firstly because the indisputable juxtaposition of statements about the present and the future in Jesus' message makes it plain that Jesus understood *his* presence to be in a quite definite, but by no means traditional relationship to the eschatological future, and so to be a *particular* period in God's history of salvation advancing swiftly towards the end. But it is above all true because Jesus sees God's action towards men being accomplished purely and simply in the context of history proceeding from the creation to the redemption in the last days, and that means within real and unrepeatable time.[12] Now Bultmann and Wilder acknowledge fully that Jesus, like the whole of the New Testament, meant the eschatological prediction to be understood as something real in the future and that Jesus considered his own appearance to be an event in time.[13] But the value of this exegetical judgment is at once taken away when Bultmann interprets the 'futurist' eschatology as nothing but a part of the mythological picture of the world from which we must free the New Testament, and when Wilder understands the eschatological statement as pure myth which reproduces a conception, not a reality.[14] Therefore the mythological statement concerning the future actually means for Bultmann that man is confronted with a

[12]"The New Testament understands time as the sphere of the divine activity. Therefore all the New Testament statements about the works of God are determined by a time-coefficient and cannot be interpreted legitimately or classified appropriately without this coefficient' (Stauffer, *Die Theologie des Neuen Testaments*, 59; cf. Eng. trs., 75). O. Cullmann, *Christ and Time* (see n. 124, p. 139), described the biblical conception of time correctly as linear and naïvely in a straight line (esp. 51 ff., in German 41 ff.). When E. Fuchs, loc. cit. in note 5, maintains against this that the New Testament knows of a time which no longer extends itself nor enters into history, a time in which man 'himself finally wins or loses, so that at one with it he wins or loses himself', he reduces New Testament time and therewith also temporal eschatology to anthropology and simply denies the facts of the situation, namely that Jesus' preaching about the Kingdom of God, imminent and now already in operation, is speaking not about any kind of time, but about a time which is once for all and therefore *definite*.

[13]Cf. Bultmann's review of Cullmann's *Christus und die Zeit* in TLZ 73, 1948, 665: 'Since in fact eternity is represented or imagined in New Testament thought as continuous time, the author can rightly designate Christ as the centre of the line of time'. But then he continues: 'but not as the centre of history nor of the history of salvation'! Cf. also Wilder, *Eschatology*, 161: 'It is true that Jesus taught that the new era is to have its all-important manifestation in a supernatural way: advent of the Son of Man, Judgment and the miraculously instituted Kingdom', but Wilder then adds: 'these conceptions stand to Jesus . . . as *representations* . . . of the unprophesiable, unimaginable but certain, God-determined future'.

[14]Wilder, *Eschatology*, 182; see that quotation above in note 5.

decision in the 'now' and for Wilder that the imminence of the coming of the Kingdom of God in the future is only a form for expressing the spiritual proximity of God, which is to determine the attitude of men. Now the question of the correctness and the limits of the demythologization of the New Testament cannot be set out here in its full extent;[15] but this much must be said with regard to the problem of the 'futurist' eschatology in Jesus' message: Since the New Testament announces as its central message an act of God at a definite moment in history to be a final redemptive act, the mythological form of the conception cannot simply be detached from this central message; for it would mean that the New Testament message itself is abrogated if a timeless message concerning the present as the time of decision or concerning the spiritual nearness of God replaces the preaching of the eschatological future and the determination of the present by that future. For this would result in a complete disintegration of Jesus' message that man through Jesus' appearance in the present is placed in a definite situation in the *history* of salvation advancing towards the end, and the figure and activity of Jesus would lose their fundamental character as the *historical* activity of the *God* who wishes to lead his kingdom upwards. Therefore it is impossible to eliminate the concepts of time and with it the 'futurist' eschatology from the eschatological message of Jesus (and from the New Testament altogether);[16] so we still have to answer the question

[15]See my essays: 'Mythische Rede und Heilsgeschehen im Neuen Testament', *Conjectanea Neotestamentica* 11, 1948, 109 ff. and 'Mythos im Neuen Testament', *TZ* 6, 1950, 321 ff. The most important part of the discussion is collected in *Kerygma und Mythos* I, 1948; II, 1952, ed. by H. W. Bartsch (the first of the above named essays is reprinted in II, 153 ff.). Further literature is listed in *Kerygma und Mythos* II, 209 ff.; to this must be added: F. Buri, 'Theologie und Philosophie', *Th. Z.* 8, 1952, 116 ff.; R. Schnackenburg, *Münchener TZ* 2, 1951, 345 ff.; E. Fuchs, 'Frontwechsel um Bultmann?', *TLZ* 77, 1952, 11 ff.; G. Gloege, *Mythologie und Luthertum, Das Problem der Entmythologisierung im Lichte lutherischer Theologie*, 1952; K. Barth, *Rudolf Bultmann, Ein Versuch ihn zu verstehen*, 1952; H. Traub, *Anmerkungen und Fragen zur neutestamentlichen Hermeneutik und zum Problem der Entmythologisierung*, 1952.

[16]F. Holmström, *Das eschatologische Denken der Gegenwart*, 1936, 247 f. has emphasized correctly against Bultmann that eschatology is here 'detached dialectically from its secure anchorage in historical time', because 'here "the last things" do not mean the last events "at the end" in the temporal sense, but the absolute connexions in a metaphysical or "existential" sense'. Cullmann, *Retour*, 14 also attacks the conversion of eschatology into the idea of 'being confronted with a decision'; Cullmann, *Hoffnung*, 29; *Christ and Time* (see n. 124, p. 139), 53 (in German 45). Buri, *Die Bedeutung der neutestamentlichen Eschatologie für die neuere protestantische Theologie*, 1934, 28 also emphasizes 'that

concerning the theological meaning in Jesus' mouth of this preaching of the *coming* Kingdom of God together with the statements about the presence of this eschatological consummation.

But one more preliminary question must first receive a reply. Jesus does not only proclaim in quite general terms the future coming of the Kingdom of God, but also its *imminence*. What is more: on the one hand he emphasized this so concretely that he limited it to the lifetime of his hearers' generation; yet on the other hand he only expected a *part* of them to live to experience this eschatological event; so he did not wish to limit its proximity too closely.[17] It is perfectly clear that this prediction of Jesus was not realized and it is therefore impossible to assert that Jesus was not mistaken about this.[18] On the contrary it must be unreservedly admitted that Jesus' eschatological message remained confined at least in this respect to a form conditioned by time, which proved untenable owing to developments after the beginning of Christianity.[19] Now the significance of what has just been established must certainly not be overrated. For the number of texts which place a definite limit to the imminent expectation (Matt. 10.23; Mark 9.1; 13.30) is extraordinarily small and it is correct to conclude from this fact that this idea did not receive much emphasis in Jesus' message.[20] These few texts which speak of a definite limit to the imminence of the Kingdom of God are contrasted with a large number which represent the time when

---

the category of time is indispensable for New Testament eschatology'. Flew, *Church*, 31 points out that the time factor is essential in the Jewish world-view which Jesus shared; and P. S. Minear, *Eyes of Faith*, 1946, 107 f. shows that the Hellenistic contrast between time and eternity does not appear in the Bible. H. Schlier, 'Über das Hauptanliegen des 1. Briefes an die Korinther', *EvTh* 8, 1948/49, 463 f. also objects to eliminating concrete eschatology. Th. Preiss, 'The vision of history in the New Testament', *Life in Christ*, 1954, 66 (in French *Le Vie en Christ* 1951, 95) stresses that we must not demythologize the conception of time in the New Testament, especially with regard to the end of history.

[17]See C. J. Cadoux, *Mission*, 299 f.

[18]Thus Michaelis, *Verheissung*, 59 from the assumption that at most Mark 9.1 allows the date of the Last Day to be indicated more precisely; furthermore K. Weiss, *Irrtumslosigkeit, passim*; Bowman, *Maturity*, 247; M. Barth, *Augenzeuge*, V.

[19]Thus e.g. F. Büchsel, *Jesus*, 1947, 53 f.; Bultmann, *Urchristentum*, 102; C. J. Cadoux, *Mission*, 343; J. Héring, *Le royaume de Dieu at sa venue*, 1937, 49.

[20]M. Dibelius, *DLZ* 66/68, 1947, 12 conjectured that Jesus proclaimed that the dawn of the Kingdom is indeed imminent, 'but rejected emphatically every kind of chase after an apocalyptic *terminus ad quem*'; three texts which

the Kingdom of God will come to be threateningly near, but yet unknown, or even emphasize expressly that the time must remain completely unknown (Mark 13.32) so that even Jesus could not know it. Now there is no doubt a contradiction between the prediction of a concrete date for the coming of the Kingdom of God and the emphatic statement that this date could not be known. Since neither of these two contradictory statements can be removed by critical methods, we can only ask whether this contradiction can be explained or must be left as it is. It is not much use pointing to the fact that in view of Jesus' declaration that not even the Son knew the hour (Mark 13.32) his pronouncements about the date within this generation appear to be provisional, and 'did not spring from Jesus' unlimited and unconditionally valid knowledge',[21] for what is correctly established by this is after all only that Jesus neither could nor wished to give an exact account about the date of the end, but not the fact that besides this there is also an inexact, yet clearly defined statement about it. Any attempt to find psychological or biographical grounds for the existence of this concrete pronouncement by referring these sayings to definite intentions to teach the disciples or by placing them in a definite period of Jesus' activity, would rest merely on unfounded conjectures without any support from the sources. The contrast might perhaps be reconciled by pointing out that the pronouncements concerning the oppressively imminent, yet still unknown date of the end could easily be fitted into the more precise estimate of the arrival of the end during the lifetime of Jesus' generation: within the bounds set by this more precise estimate Jesus emphasizes that the exact date is unknown.[22] But such a conjecture would not only be impossible to prove, but it would also try to know more than we can know. Yet on the one hand reference can rightly be made to the fact that 'to link tension and expansion in the expectation of the end is peculiar to the whole of biblical

---

nevertheless speak of fixed dates must therefore be considered as secondary intrusions of apocalyptic ideas, not as sayings of Jesus. But against this assumption it may be said that only in the earliest period of the formation of the tradition could such a limitation of the final date have been attributed to Jesus secondarily, and that there are no sufficient grounds for this assumption.

[21]Michaelis, *Verheissung*, 45, cf. also 29.
[22]Thus J. Weiss, *Reich Gottes*, 104.

eschatology and is grounded in pastoral care',[23] and on the other hand it must be frankly confessed that we do not know how to strike a balance between these two series of assertions;[24] yet this only means that we can gain no clear insight into one aspect of the *forms in which Jesus conceived* his eschatological message.

But in reality the solution of this problem is of very subordinate importance because the question of the appointed date of the Kingdom of God was for Jesus in no way a vital concern. This conclusion, to which attention has frequently been drawn recently,[25] follows unequivocally not only from Luke 17.20 f., but also from the fact that Jesus again and again proclaimed in the most varied fashion the urgent imminence of the end, but at the same time stressed that its date was unknown (Mark 13.32, 34 ff.; Matt. 24.42 ff.; etc.). Besides this, as was already established above,[26] Jesus' message concerning the future was not intended to be an apocalyptic revelation, but a prophetic message concerning the imminent Kingdom of God, so that the apocalyptic interest in the date and the premonitory signs is necessarily lacking in Jesus. So we can at last put the question as to what Jesus actually wished to say when he proclaimed the imminent Kingdom of God and combined with it the witness to its presence. Now the prediction of the imminent coming of the Kingdom of God was not fulfilled; moreover Jesus wished to make no apocalyptic prediction of the future and the most striking element in his eschatological message is the existence of the pronouncements concerning the present beside those about the future. Consequently it has recently been thought that the true meaning of Jesus' eschatological message lies in this message of salvation fulfilling itself in his person, so that, beside this, the statements about the future which undoubtedly exist lose their significance

---

[23]A. Oepke, *ST* 2, 1948/50, 145; cf. also Meinertz, *Theologie* I, 58 (who indeed speaks incorrectly of the 'timeless words of the prophets').

[24]It is striking that this problem is very seldom dealt with in the literature. Apart from the theses named in the notes 140 on page 64 and 18 and 21 on pages 149 f., I can only refer to P. Feine, *Theologie des Neuen Testaments*, [5]1931, 78. who like A. Oepke (see note 23) finds the solution of the difficulty in the 'peculiarity of biblical prophecy' which sees the full realization of what is to come at one time palpably near, at another in distant periods and spaces; but yet that still does not explain why Jesus clothed the message of the *imminence* of the Kingdom of God occasionally in a form giving relative precision to the appointed day.

[25]Cf. Michaelis, *Verheissung*, 25; Cullmann, *Hoffnung*, 37; Bultmann, *Urchristentum*, 102; Colwell, *Approach*, 101.

[26]See chapter II.

and become unimportant.[27] But although it is quite correct that
the true meaning does not lie in the message that the Kingdom of
God is *near*, yet we must also clearly hold fast to the fact that in
the centre of Jesus' message there stood the announcement of the
imminent *future* coming of the Kingdom of God; this follows
both from the large number of Jesus' sayings which lay stress on
this fact, and also from the circumstance that the disciples were
sent out with *this* news and in view of *this* news were urged to
hurry (Matt. 10.7, 23). Now Jesus certainly did not speak of the
future coming of the Kingdom of God in order to predict
apocalyptic drama, but in order to make it clear to men that they
are living *now* in the last days, that now the consummation of
salvation cannot be long delayed. The message of the imminent
coming of the Kingdom of God is therefore intended to confront
men with the end of history as it advances towards the goal set by
God;[28] the expectation of the *future* eschatological action of God
cannot be detached from the eschatological message of Jesus,
because only in this form could expression be given then and
now to the certainty that God's will for our salvation is working
towards complete realization, that God's Kingdom will appear in
full reality.[29] The imminent expectation is therefore not merely a
necessary contemporary form in which to express the certainty
that the Kingdom of God is beginning even now, but Jesus uses
the imagery of his time to describe the *nearness* of the Kingdom of
God in order to clothe *in living words* the certainty of God's
redemptive action directed towards the consummation. If therefore
the *imminent* expectation, being a necessarily contemporary form of
expression, can certainly be detached from Jesus' message, the *future*

---

[27] J. Jeremias, *TB* 20, 1941, 222: 'The *imminent expectation* of the
parousia and of the eschatology is not anything which might have an independent existence within the framework of Jesus' message, but it is in the
last resort nothing but the expression of the certainty that with Jesus'
ministry *hic et nunc* the hour of fulfilment . . . has dawned.' Cf. also Cullmann, *Retour*, 27: 'So the essential element in the proximity of the Kingdom
is not the final date, but rather the certainty that the expiatory achievement of
Christ on the cross constitutes a decisive stage in the approach of the Kingdom of God.'

[28] 'The chief interest which eschatology . . . has to preserve is the news in
the gospel of God's summons during a limited period of grace' (F. Holmström, *Das eschatologische Denken der Gegenwart*, 1936, 416).

[29] P. S. Minear, *Eyes of Faith*, 1946, 228 f. emphasizes that the reference to
the nearness of the future aeon corresponds to the conviction that the tension
between the two aeons must be brought to an end by the swift intervention
of God.

expectation is essential and indispensable, because in this form alone can the nature of God's redemptive action *in history* be held fast.[30]

Jesus does not *describe* the coming of God in the future; he speaks of the Kingdom of God as 'joy' (Matt. 25.21, 23), 'glory' (Mark 10.37), 'life' (Mark 9.43, 45, 47; 10.17), 'light'(Luke 16.8).[31] The theological meaning of these picture-words could only be brought out by examining in detail Jesus' message about God the judge and father.[32] Yet such an examination against the background of the contemporary Jewish beliefs in God shows one thing beyond all doubt: had Jesus announced only God's future eschatological action, then his eschatological preaching, however much it contrasted with apocalyptic and diverged from the Jewish conception of law, would have remained in essential agreement with the late Jewish expectation of salvation; and this looked for no salvation in the present and so the preaching about the future could find expression *only* in hope.[33] Now it is just here that there lies what is peculiar in Jesus' message about God, and this peculiarity is rooted in his eschatological preaching. For we have seen that Jesus linked the present in a quite peculiar way to the future by speaking of his return as judge and by making the attitude of men to the earthly Jesus the criterion for the verdict of Jesus, the eschatological judge. This in itself turns Jesus' presence into a *real* eschatological present, instead of its being merely a period for awaiting the eschatological consummation. Jesus gives its full meaning to this eschatological character of the present primarily through the numerous statements in which he declares the coming Kingdom of God to be realizing itself already in his person, his actions, his message. For these statements about the present are no chance remarks, but provide the key to the meaning of Jesus' preaching about the future: he who will bring in the Kingdom of God in the future has appeared in the present in Jesus himself, and in him the powers of the coming aeon are already at work; therefore Jesus can proclaim the approaching

[30]See also Dibelius, *Jesus*, 125: Whoever recognizes in the person of him who proclaims the gospel 'the authentic mark that God is real, . . . sees at the same time that this reality does not yet exist in time and space; but he knows also that it does exist, that—no matter in what manifestations—it must come at some time—otherwise God would not be the Lord of the world and of history'.

[31]Cf. for this Theissing, *Seligkeit*, 76 f.

[32]Cf. my essay: 'Die Gottesverkündigung Jesu und der Gottesgedanke des Spätjudentum', *Judaica* 1, 1945, 40 ff.

[33]Cf. also H. Preisker, *Neutestamentliche Zeitgeschichte*, 1937, 273.

Kingdom of God with *unique* authority and can send out a summons for decision concerning this βασιλεία; for this reason also an acceptance of this preaching of Jesus about the kingdom means hoping not merely for the future, but hoping with an assurance based on the experience of God's redemptive action in the present; therefore adherence to the man Jesus means adherence to the coming Kingdom of God at work in advance already in the present. Hence the message that the Kingdom of God is present in Jesus' activity in no way reduces the value of his pronouncements about the future, but makes them all the more truly convincing and inevitable. For Jesus' disciple can have a sure hope that the end of the world is coming, that the last hour which points to the end is dawning, not because Jesus has proclaimed the *nearness* of the end; but God's purpose for the world will most certainly be accomplished because Jesus could proclaim the paradoxical message, contrary to every Jewish conception, that the future Kingdom of God is already at work in the present.[34]

Now at last it can be fully and finally understood why Jesus speaks of future eschatological events and makes use of several conceptions of apocalyptic, but nevertheless does not offer apocalyptic teaching, but an eschatological message: the intrinsic meaning of the eschatological event he proclaims does not lie in the end of the world as such, but in the fact that the approaching eschatological consummation will allow the Kingdom of *that* God to become a reality who has already in the present allowed his redemptive purpose to be realized in Jesus.[35] It is by what Jesus teaches and does, by his loving desire to help as well as by his message of divine forgiveness and purpose, above all by his going to the cross and his certainty of the resurrection, that the meaning of the words 'the Kingdom of *God* is at hand' can be understood (cf. Matt. 11.4 ff.; 12.28; 13.16 f.; Mark 2.5 ff.; Luke 17.25; I Cor. 11.25). Only by the whole of Jesus' message about God taken together, and by the interpretation of the meaning he attached to

---

[34]Cullmann, *Retour*, 26 says that the essential meaning of Jesus' message about the *nearness* of the Kingdom of God lies in this 'that in fact with Christ the kingdom has approached . . . that we have entered with him into the last period of this present world' (similarly Cullmann, *Hoffnung*, 32). But this statement is only valid if it is deduced not from the message about the *nearness* of the Kingdom of God, but from that of its *presence*.

[35]'Jesus in his characteristic words about the Kingdom of God reasons from present events and experiences to the coming of that Kingdom, not vice versa. His gospel of the End rests on the certainty of the power of God which is with him in the present' (W. Manson, *Jesus*, 50).

his person can the intrinsic meaning of his eschatological message be fully understood. For, as we have seen, its meaning does not lie in revealing apocalyptic secrets nor in giving the present a significance arising from a divine reality beyond time, but it lies just in this, that in Jesus the Kingdom of God came into being and in him it will be consummated. The promise of Jesus receives its peculiar and reliable character through its fulfilment in him himself; therefore it can confidently be asserted that his eschatological message provides the framework within which he conceived that God's final redemptive action in the present *and* in the future could be known. Promise and fulfilment are therefore inseparably united for Jesus and depend on each other; for the promise is made sure by the fulfilment that has already taken place in Jesus, and the fulfilment, being provisional and concealed, loses its quality as a σκάνδαλον only through the knowledge of the promise yet to come. Just as it will not do to see the meaning of Jesus' message about the advent of the Kingdom of God in the proclamation of imminent apocalyptic events which then after all did not take place, so his eschatological message cannot be restricted to giving an 'eschatological' significance to the present. On the contrary the inseparable union of hope and present experience demonstrate the fact that the true meaning of Jesus' eschatological message is to be found in its reference to God's action in Jesus himself, that the essential content of Jesus' preaching about the Kingdom of God is the news of the divine authority of Jesus, who has appeared on earth and is awaited in the last days as the one who effects the divine purpose of mercy. So for the believer the question is not whether he will accept the correctness of an apocalyptic prediction or of an interpretation referring to the present of that which relates to the beyond, but whether he will respond to the divine mission of *that* Jesus who could promise us the reign of God, because it was already being fulfilled in him. The Christian can assent to this question with complete confidence only because he knows of God's action in raising the one who was crucified and in founding his Church through the gift of the Spirit which lies beyond the earthly activity of Jesus. But the Christian knows also that the possibility of such a faith is bound up with the reality of the Jesus in whom God brought his salvation to fulfilment in history and through whom God authoritatively promised his approaching consummation of history.

SUPPLEMENTARY BIBLIOGRAPHY

GENERAL

G. R. BEASLEY-MURRAY   *Jesus and the Future. An Examination of the Criticism of the Eschatological Discourse, Mark 13, with special reference to the Little Apocalypse theory*, 1954.

E. DINKLER   'Early Christianity', *The Idea of History in the Ancient Near East*, 1955, 171 ff.

T. W. MANSON   *The Servant-Messiah. A Study of the Public Ministry of Jesus*, 1953.

W. MICHAELIS   'Kennen die Synoptiker eine Verzögerung der Parusie?', *Synoptische Studien A. Wikenhauser dargebracht*, 1954, 107 ff.

W. MICHAELIS   *Die Gleichnisse Jesu. Eine Einführung*, 1956.

E. PERCY   *Die Botschaft Jesu. Eine traditionskritische und exegetische Untersuchung*. Lunds Universitets Årsskrift, N.F. Avd, 1, Bd. 49, Nr. 5, 1953.

E. SCHWEIZER   'Erniedrigung und Erhöhung bei Jesus und seinen Nachfolgern', *Abhandlungen zur Theologie des Alten und Neuen Testaments*, 28, 1955.

E. SJÖBERG   *Der verborgene Menschensohn in den Evangelien*. Skrifter utg. av Kungl. Humanistiska Vetenskapssamfundet i Lund 1955.

ON INDIVIDUAL PASSAGES

C. K. BARRETT   'Paul and the "Pillar" Apostles', *Studia Paulina in honorem J. de Zwaan*, 1953, 11 f. (on pp. 100 f.).

W. BAUER   'The "Colt" of Palm Sunday', *JBL* 72, 1953, 220 ff. (on pp. 116 f.).

K. BEYSCHLAG   *Die Bergpredigt und Franz von Assisi*, 1955, 44 (on p. 44).

R. BOHREN   *Das Problem der Kirchenzucht im Neuen Testament*, 1952, 30 ff. (on pp. 100 f.).

H. V. CAMPENHAUSEN   *Kirchliches Amt und geistliche Vollmacht in den ersten drei Jahrhunderten*, 1953, 140 ff. (on pp. 138 f.).

W. D. DAVIES   ' "Knowledge" in the Dead Sea Scrolls and Matt. 11.25–30', *Harvard Theological Review*, 1953, 113 ff. (on pp. 40 f.).

G. DELLING   *Der Gottesdienst im Neuen Testament*, 1952, 30 ff. (on pp. 100 f.).

M. DIBELIUS   'Gethsemane', *Botschaft und Geschichte* I, 1953, 263 (on pp. 125 f.).

E. DINKLER   'Jesu Wort vom Kreuztragen', *Neutestamentliche Studien für R. Bultmann*, 1954, 110 ff. (on p. 79).

C. F. EVANS   'I will go before you into Galilee', *JTS* 5, 1954, 3 ff. (on pp. 77 ff.).

W. R. HUTTON   'The Kingdom of God has Come', *ExpT* 64, 1952–53, 89 ff. (on pp. 22 ff.).

W. G. KÜMMEL   'Jesus und die Anfänge der Kirche', *Stud. Theol.* 7, 1954, 1 ff. (on pp. 138 ff.; additional literature given there).

O. KUSS   'Bemerken zum Fragenkreis: Jesus und die Kirche im Neuen Testament', *Theologische Quartalsschrift*, 1955, 28 ff. (on pp. 138 ff.).

M. MEINERTZ   'Die Tragweite des Gleichnisses von den 10 Jungfrauen', *Synoptische Studien A. Wikenhauser dargebracht*, 1954, 94 ff. (on pp. 56 ff.).

W. MICHAELIS   'Zelt und Hütte im biblischen Denken', *EvTh* 1954, 47 (on pp. 130 f.).

C. F. D. MOULE   'From Defendant to Judge—and Deliverer: An Inquiry into the use and limitations of the theme of Vindication in the New Testament', *Studiorum Novi Testamenti Societas*, Bulletin III, 1952, 40 ff. (on pp. 72 f.).

K. TH. SCHÄFER   ' ". . . und dann werden sie fasten, an jenem Tage" (Mark 2.20 and par.)', *Synoptische Studien A. Wikenhauser dargebracht*, 1954, 124 ff. (on p. 75).

P. SEIDELIN   'Das Jonaszeichen', *ST* 5, 1952, 119 ff. (on p. 68).

V. TAYLOR   'The Origin of the Markan Passion-Sayings', *New Testament Studies* 1, 1954–55, 159 ff. (on pp. 67 f.).

A. VÖGTLE   'Der Spruch vom Jonaszeichen', *Synoptische Studien A. Wikenhauser dargebracht*, 1954, 230 ff. (on p. 68).

INDEX OF NAMES

INDEX OF NEW TESTAMENT REFERENCES